TERRITORIES & TRAJECTORIES

· · · · ·

TERRITORIES & TRAJECTORIES

Cultures in Circulation

Edited by Diana Sorensen · Introduction by Homi Bhabha

DUKE UNIVERSITY PRESS DURHAM AND LONDON 2018

© 2018 Duke University Press. *All rights reserved.*
Printed in the United States of America on acid-free paper ∞
Text designed by Courtney Leigh Baker and cover designed
by Matt Tauch. Typeset in Garamond Premier Pro
and DIN by Westchester.

Library of Congress Cataloging-in-Publication Data
Names: Sorensen, Diana, editor.
Title: Territories and trajectories : cultures in circulation / edited by
Diana Sorensen ; introduction by Homi Bhabha.
Description: Durham : Duke University Press, 2018. |
Includes bibliographical references and index.
Identifiers: LCCN 2017058059 (print) | LCCN 2018001544 (ebook)
ISBN 9780822371564 (ebook)
ISBN 9780822359234 (hardcover : alk. paper)
ISBN 9780822370260 (pbk. : alk. paper)
Subjects: LCSH: Culture diffusion. | Culture—Philosophy. |
Cultural policy. | Arts and society.
Classification: LCC GN365 (ebook) | LCC GN365 .T47 2018 (print) |
DDC 306—dc23
LC record available at https://lccn.loc.gov/2017058059

Cover art: Reena Saini Kallat, *Woven Chronicle*, 2015. Circuit boards,
speakers, electrical wires and fittings. Courtesy of the artist.

Contents

Acknowledgments · vii

Introduction: On Disciplines and Destinations · 1
HOMI K. BHABHA

Editor's Introduction: Alternative Geographic Mappings for the Twenty-First Century · 13
DIANA SORENSEN

PART I
Travel and Transmission

1. The Diplomacy of Exoticism: Brazilian Accounts of the Global South · 35
ROSARIO HUBERT

2. Hearing Geography in Motion: Processes of the Musical Imagination in Diaspora · 47
KAY KAUFMAN SHELEMAY

3. A Chinese Fan in Sri Lanka and the Transport of Writing · 68
XIAOFEI TIAN

PART II
Portable Materialities and Crossings

...

4. The Portability of Art: Prolegomena
to Art and Architecture on the Move · 91
ALINA PAYNE

5. Genealogies of Whitewash: "Muhammedan Churches,"
Reformation Polemics, and the Aesthetics of Modernism · 110
FINBARR BARRY FLOOD

6. Mobility and Material Culture: A Case Study · 151
DIANA SORENSEN

PART III
Worlding, Rights, and Regimes of Representation

...

7. World Literature and the Health Humanities:
Translingual Encounters with Brain Disorders · 163
KAREN THORNBER

8. In But Not of Europe? The Precarious Rights of Roma
in the European Union · 185
JACQUELINE BHABHA

9. From World History to World Art:
Reflections on New Geographies of Feminist Art · 201
SHU-MEI SHIH

PART IV
Crosscurrents and Displacements

...

10. Technologies of Uncertainty in the Search for Flight MH370 · 223
LINDSAY BREMNER

Contributors · 257   Index · 261

Acknowledgments

This book originated in a Radcliffe Exploratory Seminar: we are indebted to the Radcliffe Institute for Advanced Study and its efficient, supportive staff for all they did to make this seminar a productive and far-reaching discussion. All along, Homi Bhabha's friendship and intellectual generosity contributed in important ways to the collective effort and to my own. In fact, he gave us the gift of our title and of the most generous interlocution. The contributors have been exciting, engaged partners in our enterprise, and I thank them all for their participation. Doctor Sarah Zeiser at Harvard University has been a magnificent assistant in every effort to put this volume together. I remain deeply grateful to her for her goodwill, intelligence, and competence: I cannot imagine this book without her scholarly disposition, and impeccable attention to detail.

Introduction

On Disciplines and Destinations

HOMI K. BHABHA

A remark by Ernst Bloch apropos of *The Arcades Project*: "History displays its Scotland Yard badge?" It was in the context of a conversation in which I was describing how this work—comparable, in method, to the process of splitting the atom—liberates the enormous energies of history that are bound up in the "once upon a time" of classical historiography. The history that showed things "as they really were" was the strongest narcotic of the century. —WALTER BENJAMIN

I

Diana Sorensen invites her contributors to elaborate a mode of cultural criticism grounded in a "new geographical consciousness" composed of multicentered circuits, ex-centric itineraries, and contingent configurations of time, sign, and sensibility. A significant impediment to the pedagogy of mobility, Sorensen argues, is the large and leaden footprint of the nation-state as it leaves a lasting imprint on the organization of knowledge. There are sound historical and economic reasons that "nation-based" institutions exist—national universities, national museums, national archives—even as they frequently project a composite image of cultural heritage, territorial integrity, and civic identity. National institutions occupy what Benedict Anderson aptly called (after Walter Benjamin) a temporality peculiar to the nation-space: "homogenous empty time."[1] The effect of this national temporality on orders of knowledge is to create curricular pedagogies that are, for the most part, as Sorensen writes, "taking distance from older notions of stability and containment derived from the nation-state" (13).

The nation-state's geographical imaginary is not inert, of course. National spaces have well-defined and copiously configured movements of social transformation and cultural mobility. The movement of people from the country to the city, for instance, traces the emergence of the commercial spirit, the establishment of urban growth, and the development of a civic consciousness. Coastal regions are restless thresholds of trade, cultural exchange, and the porosity of peoples and things. And inner cities are turbulent spaces of migration waves, with inflows of first-generation migrants and outflows of succeeding generations that reform the domestic demography. Geopolitical mobility is as much an incipient aspect of the restlessness internal to the nation-form as an indication of the circuitous and contingent networks of globalization.

In what sense, then, does a nation-centered discourse create an immobile curricular perspective? The nation's dominion over disciplinary domains is established by prioritizing linguistic authenticity, affirming cultural supremacy, and making claims to historical continuity and political progress. These shared discourses of national legitimation are articulated in affective structures of belonging that feel invariably "local" despite their hybrid, international, or intercultural genealogies. Stephen Greenblatt speaks saliently of this very experience in arguing that "one of the characteristic powers of culture is its ability to hide the mobility that is its enabling condition."[2] To imagine a pedagogy that departs from the normalization—one could even call it the *nationalization*— of knowledge, I want to return to the restless mobility of peoples *within* the nation to which I have just alluded. Although patriotic, nationalist discourse promotes an iconic ideal of "the people," *e pluribus unum*, conceived in a social space of consent and consensus, the territoriality of the nation as a place of belonging is an unsettled, anxious *habitus*. Migrants, the unemployed, the poor, and the homeless—among other marginalized communities—search restlessly for a "homeland" within the hegemony of the nation. Theirs is a mobility that moves from one rented home to another, from one job to another, from one part of the country to another, and from one border or frontier to another. The claims for a post-national—or transnational—geography of mobility must be seen in a complex and necessary relation to social mobilities internal to the structure of nation-states and geopolitical regions.

In making this argument I am reminded of Edward Said's essay "History, Literature, and Geography" (1995), which reaches out from the "multiply-centered" geographic consciousness of the late twentieth century to connect with Raymond Williams's reflections on the "difficult mobility" between the country and the city. The world we live in, Said writes, is "a world . . . mixed up, varied, complicated by the new difficult mobility of migrations, the new independent states, the newly emergent and burgeoning cultures."[3] Said's account did not prepare me for Williams's explicit reference to internal mobility within the nation as a form of migrant consciousness. In his discussion of Thomas Hardy's *The Return of the Native*, Williams writes of the ambivalent relations between "the migrant and his former group . . . caught up in the general crisis of the relations between education and class, relations which in practice are between intelligence and fellow feeling." The homeland to which the internal migrant belongs is a border country of uneasy transitions and liminal self-identifications. Deeply embedded in Williams's rich dialectic of the country and the city is a conflict of values—proximate yet polarizing—that reveal migration to be a borderline condition for both culture and consciousness. "But the real Hardy country, we soon come to see," Williams writes, "is that border country so many of us have been living in: between custom and education, between work and ideas, between love of place and an experience of change."[4]

Williams's use of the metaphor of migration to articulate the tipping point of historical transition in Hardy's Wessex compels our attention today. We are pressured to learn to live—and to think—in terms of the border country of aporetic conflations in which the sovereignty of the nation may be diminished by the dominance of neoliberal encroachments of global markets and postnational governance, and yet the exigent pressures of everyday economic and ethical life are still firmly located in the search for security and community that is profoundly connected to the symbolic and material necessities of national belonging. When such an ambivalent and contradictory condition is mapped onto the extensive scales and rapid technological movements of global transnational geographies—both physical and virtual—it is only too easy to lose sight of the everyday violence and endurance experienced by those for whom finding a "homeland" is a restless struggle to occupy the sifting grounds of living on borderlines *within* the nation. To perceive this melancholic mobility of the un-homed with any clarity, one has to resort to a smaller scale of representation that magnifies the detail of displacement and dispossession. In *After the Last Sky*, Said adopts a scalar diminution that strangely enlarges the quotidian Palestinian quest for a harried homeland. He writes:

> Palestine is a *small place*. It is also incredibly crowded with the traces and claims of peoples. Its legacy is not just one of conquest and resettlement, but also of reexcavations and reinterpretations of history. . . . Cover a map of Palestine with the legends, insignia, icons, and routes of all the peoples

who have lived there, and you will have no space left for terrain.... And the more recent the people, the more exclusive their claim, and the more vigorous the pushing out and suppressing of all others. In addition, each claim invents its deflections, shoving matches, and dislocations.⁵

The concept of the "border country" sets the tone for what it means to be restlessly unhomed *within* the nation or the region, and it is from this perspective of the anxiety of accommodation that I want to approach the curricular conditions of cultural mobility. The pedagogical return to a "home discipline" is, in the process, estranged and enhanced; and the grounds of curricular knowledge are extended in an interdisciplinary and extraterritorial direction. Jacqueline Bhabha's essay on the European Roma makes a moving case for acknowledging the conditions of "constitutive displacement" as the basis for the political and ethical "right to have rights." The long history of social mobility, and the inherited traditions of cultural translation, define the life world of Roma peoples, and it could be argued that their very existence instantiates, *avant la lettre*, the values of free movement, legal protection and equitable access to social welfare that provides the constitutional framework of the European Union. Yet the political and legal bias toward "demonstrable residential permanence" deprives the majority of the Roma population of the benefits of European citizenship (194). The Roma live in that border country where the customary and communitarian genealogies of "belonging"—constitutive displacement—are violated by the sedentary strictures of legal personhood that are discriminatory both in principle and in practice. In taking up the Roma case, Bhabha's essay interrogates the foundational assumptions of the Universal Declaration of Human Rights that ground legal identity in the permanence of place. Her intervention is an illustration of the important role of activism associated with the disciplinary domain of human rights studies—an activism that demonstrates the need to sustain the authority of the founding ideals of rights by subjecting them to the ongoing interpretational vigilance of critique and revision.

Many of the essays in this volume build their arguments around moving targets of ontological and geographical mobility—distance, diaspora, relationality, portability, itinerancy—that repeatedly configure the "homeland" as an enigma of arrival. Being-at-home is an anxious striving for accommodation unsettled by cycles of loss and disoriented by processes of social transition and cultural translation. These essays do not dismantle the hegemonic architectures of national authority or regional territoriality only to replace them with overarching constructs such as the transnational or the global. There is little doubt that these post-Westphalian concepts are riven by a critical consciousness composed of spatial displacements, temporal disjunctions, and relational networks. However, global vocabularies of mobility and contingency frequently become victims of their own curricular success. As these keywords of global discourse develop a ubiquitous methodological currency *across* the disciplinary map, the articulation of disjunction and displacement established in any specific case oftentimes loses its critical edge, and "contingency" becomes canonized in the disciplinary interests of the legitimation of "global studies." This is not a matter of critical "bad faith" operating in the self-interest of turf wars. In establishing their presence in the enlarged mapping of institutional knowledge, emergent disciplines develop a mimetic medium of recognition that retroactively projects a mirror image of the discipline as a master trope. The effects of contingency—disruptive causalities, indeterminate meanings, disjunctive connections—lose their complexity when they are "scaled up" and assume the authoritative legitimation of a meta-critical discourse. The claims of critique are frequently normalized in the interests of maintaining disciplinary authority.

The hermeneutic of the "homeland" reveals the site of domestic affiliation to be a space of iterative and belated return, not a springboard of identitarian authenticity from which cultural narratives of selfhood and statehood must naturally begin as if emerging from a centered point of national origin. The "difficult mobilities" of social stratification and unequal opportunity, to say nothing of political oppression and structural discrimination, explode the myth of a singular and sovereign "origin" of the nation's people. The homeland, as I conceive of it, is a destination at which you arrive beset by the anxiety and anticipation of an extraneous geographic consciousness and a contingent sense of cultural history narrated through passages of life shaped by itinerancy and exile—conditions of being that are as vividly present within the internal lifeworlds of nations and regions, as they are crucial forces in shaping inter-cultural global relations. An unsettled sense of a "homeland" is not a place of domestic habitation or habituality—no local comforts of home here; no "homeland security" even when you are at home. Anxiety and anticipation, as they dwell together in the homeland, resonate with the uncanny feeling that Heidegger associates with the ontology of *Dasein*:

> In anxiety one feels uncanny. . . . But here "uncanniness" also means "not-being-at-home" . . . [in] our clarification of the existential meaning of "Being-in" as distinguished from the categorical signification of "insideness." Being-in was defined as "residing alongside . . . ," "Being familiar with. . . ." This character of Being-in was brought to view more concretely through the everyday publicness of the "they," which brings tranquillised

self-assurance—"Being-at-home" with all its obviousness—into the average everydayness of Dasein. On the other hand, as Dasein falls, anxiety brings it back from its absorption in the "world." Everyday familiarity collapses. . . . Being-in enters into the existential "mode" of the "*not-at-home.*" Nothing else is meant by our talk about "uncanniness."[6]

For our purposes, I am straying from the purely ontological implications of Heidegger's argument to suggest that practices of mobility must negotiate the anxiety of the uncanny—the ambivalence between "being-at-home" and "being-*not-at-home*"—in the everyday life of disciplines. Each of these essays has a home discipline that becomes, after its diverse accretions and divagations, a belated and translated destination: an uncanny homeland.

Let me illustrate my argument with a few random examples from the volume. Musicology is Kay Shelemay's home discipline, and her particular interest lies in exploring the diasporic "destination" of Ethio-jazz—a fusion of Ethiopian music, Latin jazz, and bebop. Loss, distance, longing, separation, and relocation come together in an affective constellation to provide an anxious medium—not merely a theme—that makes possible the iterative performance of "restorative nostalgia" (56). The anxiety of nostalgia lies in a diasporic syncopation between "being-at-home" and "not-at-home," and it is the mobile quest for a haunting homeland that gives diasporic fusion its uncanny curricular accommodation within the home discipline of musicology.

Karen Thornber writes from the complex curriculum of world literature, into which she introduces the field of the medical humanities. In exploring the "world" to which the Japanese novel belongs *as literature*, she initiates a philological inquiry into the affective vocabulary associated with *medical ethics*—vulnerability, caregiving, responsibility. The worldliness of world literature is explored in a comparison of word choices as they appear in eight translations of the novel *The Equations the Professor Loved*. Thornber turns to translation as a critical method and a thematic trope—a practice of cultural translation—as she engages with the distinctive foreign "homelands" of diverse language communities. The uncanniness of translation lies in a mobility that engages, in Benjamin's formulation, with the foreignness of languages: "This, to be sure, is to admit that all translation is only a somewhat provisional way of coming to terms with the foreignness of languages. An instant and final rather than a temporary and provisional solution of this foreignness remains out of the reach of mankind; at any rate, it eludes any direct attempt."[7]

Indeed, there can be no "direct attempt" to come to terms with "foreignness," for the destination of translation is neither the original language nor a secondary one. The work of translation lies in articulating the itinerant transitions "through which the original can be raised there anew and at other points of time." The productive irony of translation resides in the process by which what is "raised anew" returns from its foreign wanderings to establish, on native terrain, the anxiety and the creativity of being at once "at home" and "not at home." Let me turn again to Benjamin's endlessly productive essay on translation: "Pannwitz writes: 'Our translations, even the best ones, proceed from a wrong premise. They want to turn Hindi, Greek, English into German instead of turning German into Hindi, Greek, English. Our translators have a far greater reverence for the usage of their own language than for the spirit of the foreign works.... The basic error of the translator is that he preserves the state in which his own language happens to be instead of allowing his language to be powerfully affected by the foreign tongue.'"[8]

The detour through "the foreignness of languages" does not return us to the home discipline of world literature to celebrate its power of accommodation or its englobing disciplinary horizon. The uncanniness of translation, emerging as it does through the practice of turning German into Hindi, Greek, and English, starts with an essential resistance to the "preservation" of the priority and hegemony of the native language and its cultural sovereignty. Translation is an iterative process of revision that moves back and forth in geographic circulation and discursive mobility, each time motivated by what is "untranslatable"—from one language to another, from one culture toward others—and therefore *must* be the cause for starting again from another place, another time, another history. A destination comes from the realization of the foreignness that constitutes what is regarded as normative and native: being at home with what is un-homely.

This is the sense in which I earlier proposed that the homeland is a belated, even displaced, destination that relocates objects and revises ideas through an uncanny rendering (uncanniness in the Heideggerian sense) of what seems, at first sight, to be local and familiar. Alina Payne's view of the "portability of art" is a fine instance of the hybrid aesthetic of "ultimate destinations." Payne writes: "Most of these artworks found their ultimate destinations in Venice, Rome, Vienna, or Lvov. But along the way, in the passage from one settlement to another, from one culture to another, they left traces: muqarnas in Romanian churches... Mongol costumes in Poland... mosques transformed into Genovese churches in Crimea only to be returned to mosques in later years.... [A hybrid aesthetic] would also have to envisage material shifts or translations—the effects of textile patterns upon architecture; the dialogue between pottery techniques and *sgrafitto façades*" (104). Beginning *again* is another kind of foreign destination found uncannily in the very space of being-at-home.

II

Mobile inquiries do not simply pit themselves against larger settled geographies of nation, area, or region or set themselves up in opposition to them. Itineraries and networks are part of an ambulant mode of critical analysis that cuts across, or runs athwart, precincts of disciplinary priority and discursive permanence. Mobility changes the *scale* of inquiry and interpretation by introducing new speeds of digital communication and enlarged measures of global convergence.

Such shifts in scale are often represented as contrasts in size and condition pitted against each other: the macro and micro, the global and local, homogeneity and heterogeneity, linearity and discontinuity, immediacy and incrementality. These measures of space and time often follow a binary logic of comparison and connection that represents two sides of the same mimetic coin. Mobility, however, adopts a temporal scale of transmission—a time and travel line—where differences are envisaged not as polarities or binaries but as dynamic trajectories. The measure of "difference" lies in the value attributed to the very process of circulation—the *shift* in direction, the *angle* of displacement, the *intersection* of academic and cultural itineraries. The analytic protocol associated with circulation is the practice of *convergence* rather than the method of comparison and connection.

Circulation takes a measure of mobility—the movement of languages, ideas, meanings, cultural forms, social systems—as it converges in specific and singular spaces of representation negotiated through a *dialogue of difference*. Incommensurable customs, disjunctive symbolic structures, itineraries that are diverse and yet proximate, continuities that become contingent over time—these *disproportionate* convergences generate an energy of interdisciplinary circulation. Instead of the binary logic of comparison and connection, we now have a logic of convergence launched by a kinetic burst of energy that, metaphorically, has a certain ballistic tendency. I use the term "ballistic" for the limited purpose of designating a form of motion whose trajectory is shaped by contending and competing forces. In the words of the OED: "Of motion, a trajectory . . . involving gravity, inertia, and the resistance of a medium. . . . Also (in wider sense): designating motion or change, or its course, etc., initiated by a brief input of energy and continuing as a result of momentum."[9]

For a critical strategy attuned to convergences, the ongoing momentum of a trajectory is more significant than its terminus. Convergence is initiated by an input of kinetic energy—an initial burst of velocity—that extends its arc of movement and articulation as a result of the initial momentum. A ballistic process is not an endlessly fluid, indeterminate exercise; nor is its aim linear.

Progress is determined by conditions and resistances—such as gravity, inertia, and the "resistance of a medium." For the medium of portability—be it marble, script, figure, or code—is a site of virtual and conceptual resistance that preserves the historic memory and cultural provenance of aesthetic form (sculpture, literature, painting, or digital art) as it encounters the force field of intermediatic mobilities or the networks of intercultural geographies. I am reminded here of Bruno Latour's terms of art—shifts, folds, nested translations—in his description of the "*differential* of materials": "What counts each time is not the type of material but the difference in the relative resistance of what is bound together."[10]

Convergence, then, is not about a practice or project as an *end in itself*, even if that end is an entangled encounter of diverse thoughtways and institutional intersections. The aim of convergence as critique is to track the spatial and temporal territories that open up within, and through, the act of circulation. The iterative dynamics of circulation and convergence reveal lateral meanings and interstitial spaces produced *in transit*. And if transition is the temporal dimension of circulation-cum-convergence, then its formal mode of articulation is the act of *translation* in its encounters with foreignness.

The aim of convergence, then, is not to establish comparisons on the scale of similitude—be it identity or difference—but to measure the surface tension, spatial and temporal, to decipher new, revisionary forms of agency that emerge in the interaction of subjects and objects. Scale, now, is less a matter of comparative advantage or disadvantage than it is a complex process of *mediation*—the mediation of meaning, value, power, authority, performance, identification—as it comes to be negotiated in the freedom of linguistic (or symbolic) flux or deliberated in the necessity of historical and political contingency. Convergence emphasizes a "movement toward"; it is a dynamic and dialogic process toward the meeting of minds and interests, a meeting place in a diachronic time frame. Such an argument resonates with what the philosopher Bernard Williams ascribes to the contingent and convergent condition of "thick ethical concepts" as the mainstay of the humanities: "Thick ethical concepts [crucial to the humanities] are contingent phenomena, whose histories typically do nothing to vindicate them, whose contributions to our lives are continuously being modified by all sorts of shifting social forces, and whose very futures may be open to question."[11]

The complex question of the "value" of the humanities is as philosophically urgent as it is central to the professional evaluation of the discipline. Williams provides us with a sage and salient insight. The humanities are contingent not because they are accidental, unstable, or profligate in their plurality of meaning and reading. Their systemic and semiotic contingency is a sign of their foundational concern with "process" and "duration"—as aesthetic, ethical, and social practices—in the lifeworld of their vocations.

The humanities have a rich pedagogical history rooted in philological traditions, archival canons, aesthetic movements, and ethical conceptions. However, it is contingency that keeps alive the work of literary and conceptual transformation, what Williams describes as the canon "continually being modified by all sorts of shifting social forces." It is contingency that makes the humanities translational, transactional, transitional, transcultural. And all of these practices contribute to the potentiality for curricular convergence. The shaping conditions of the sciences and social sciences, Williams argues, produce values that are frequently *vindicatory*—open to justification by proof in the name of progress. Vindication, in the sciences, is the establishment of proof (or "truth") through the proven methods of quantification, randomization trials, verification by the repetition of results; at other times, vindication is achieved through the evidence of statistical surveys, matrices, models. Representation and interpretation, two exemplary axes that produce "thick concepts"—aesthetic, ethical, cultural—in the curriculum of humanities on a global scale create values that are slow, iterative, accumulative, incremental.

In contrast to Williams's concept of the vindicatory, I would suggest that the humanities are driven in their quest for the truth by the search for veracity. Veracity is truth that is attributive and agential (not instrumental); the OED defines it as "a quality or character of truthfulness. . . . it is truthfulness *as manifested* in individuals."[12] Veracity is "truth" as a quality of attribution; a reflective judgment of value; a representational quality of *poiesis*—the making of metaphor, figure, form, meaning—achieved through creation and interpretation. Veracity bears the contingent thumbprints of the shaping hand of cultural choice and political interest; veracity is the insignia of mediation and intervention. The aim of veracity is tropological rather than taxonomic. It is less interested in classification and ordering than in exploring processes of translation through which disciplines, in diverse historical contexts and social conditions, acquire vocabularies of intelligibility and interpretation.

These thoughts on the scholarly labor of cultural translation and disciplinary convergence suggest, as Latour would have it, that it would be more accurate for us to speak of ourselves as *homo fabricatus* rather than as *homo faber*.[13] It may, however, be more provocative to suggest that it is only by grasping the endlessly complex cohabitation of the two—the contingent convergence of homo fabricatus and homo faber—that we can, in truth, exclaim, "Oh what a piece of work is Man."

III

Mobility, distance, and dissemination have always played a large part in evaluating the object of knowledge that lies close at hand, within the remit of our intellectual locality. Making knowledge contemporary requires a scholarly process of retrieval from a space of anteriority or externality—a foreignness, so to speak—that is a crucial part of the authorization of the scholarly imaginary. It is not so much that we have never been modern but that we are always trying to make ourselves contemporary with the lifeworlds of other peoples or other times, either by drawing invidious comparisons between *them and us* or forging coeval convergences among ourselves. The alterity of time, people, and things is part of the inner life of our disciplines, without which there would be no borders to traverse or boundaries to cross. Making present the enigmatic historical past; revealing the obscure archive; throwing light on a hidden meaning or the buried image; bringing to life dead languages and forgotten traditions; using digital media to make accessible what was once arcane, remote, or ephemeral—these are the tangents at which we encounter the foreignness of our own discourses in the process of translating the languages of others.

There is an inherent *elsewhere* that haunts the site of all disciplinary knowledge. As the alterity of difference and distance—meaning, time, place, or tradition—plays its role in the creation of hybrid disciplinary convergences, translation becomes the testing ground for the authorization of new knowledge. This is an issue as crucial to the institutional realm as it is critical to the community of interpretation. The circulation of knowledge and the mobility of disciplines represent something more significant than an emancipation from conceptual boundaries or institutional rigidity. Despite the productive agency of circulation, mobility has to face the problem of gravity and groundedness: *who* speaks, from *where* and under *what* conditions of authorization? These are questions of power—political, pedagogical, discursive—as well as trials of legitimation. To adapt Benjamin's insight on authority, power exists "not only in what it represents, but also in what it does."[14] And it is what the mobile "object" of knowledge *does*—and what is *done* to it—in the process of authoring convergent disciplines that gives authority to the diverse individual itineraries and global trajectories that traverse the pages of this book.

NOTES

Epigraph: Benjamin, "N/On the Theory of Knowledge, the Theory of Progress," 463.
1 Anderson, *Imagined Communities*, 260–61.
2 Greenblatt, *Cultural Mobility*, 252.

3 Said, "History, Literature, and Geography," 470.
4 Williams, *The Country and the City*, 196.
5 Said, *After the Last Sky*, 61–62.
6 Heidegger, *Being and Time*, 233.
7 Benjamin, "The Task of the Translator," 78.
8 Benjamin, "The Task of the Translator," 82.
9 Oxford English Dictionary Online, s.v. "ballistic, *adj.*," accessed November 16, 2016, http://www.oed.com.ezp-prod1.hul.harvard.edu/view/Entry/14960?redirectedFrom=ballistic.
10 Latour, *An Inquiry into Modes of Existence*, 228.
11 Williams, "Philosophy as a Humanistic Discipline," 111.
12 Oxford English Dictionary Online, s.v. "veracity, *n.*," accessed November 16, 2016, http://www.oed.com.ezp-prod1.hul.harvard.edu/view/Entry/222345?redirectedFrom=veracity.
13 Latour, *An Inquiry into Modes of Existence*, 230.
14 Benjamin, "Karl Kraus," 440.

BIBLIOGRAPHY

Anderson, Benedict. *Imagined Communities: Reflections on the Origin and Spread of Nationalism*, rev. ed. London: Verso, 1991.

Benjamin, Walter. "Karl Kraus," trans. Edmund Jeffcott. In *Walter Benjamin: Selected Writings, Volume 2, Part 2, 1931–1934*, ed. Michael W. Jennings, Howard Eiland, and Gary Smith, 431–58. Cambridge, MA: Harvard University Press, 1999.

———. "N/On the Theory of Knowledge, the Theory of Progress." In *The Arcades Project*, trans. Howard Eiland and Kevin McLaughlin, 456–88. Cambridge, MA: Harvard University Press, 2000.

———. "The Task of the Translator: An Introduction to the Translation of Baudelaire's Tableaux Parisiens," trans. Harry Zohn. In *The Translation Studies Reader*, 2nd ed., ed. Lawrence Venuti, 75–85. New York: Routledge, 2004.

———. "Theses on the Philosophy of History." In *Illuminations*, ed. Hannah Arendt, trans. Harry Zohn, 253–64. New York: Schocken, 1968.

Greenblatt, Stephen. *Cultural Mobility: A Manifesto*. Cambridge: Cambridge University Press, 2009.

Heidegger, Martin. *Being and Time*, trans. John Macquarie and Edward Robinson. New York: Harper Perennial, 1962.

Latour, Bruno. *An Inquiry into Modes of Existence: An Anthropology of the Modern*, trans. Catherine Porter. Cambridge, MA: Harvard University Press, 2013.

Said, Edward. *After the Last Sky*. New York: Faber and Faber, 1986.

———. "History, Literature, and Geography." In *Reflections on Exile*, 453–73. Cambridge, MA: Harvard University Press, 2001.

Williams, Bernard. "Philosophy as a Humanistic Discipline." In *Philosophy as a Humanistic Discipline*, 180–99. Princeton, NJ: Princeton University Press, 2009.

Williams, Raymond. *The Country and the City*. London: Chatto and Windus, 1973.

Editor's Introduction

Alternative Geographic Mappings for the Twenty-First Century

DIANA SORENSEN

The impetus behind the essays in this collection is the shift of the study of people and things away from notions of fixity and sedentarism in order to rediscover transnational space connections based on diffusion and mobility, heightening the academy's awareness of an institutional transformation that must unfold alongside scholarly practices.

Taking distance from older notions of stability and containment derived from the nation-state and the area studies model, this book explores and develops alternative ways of thinking about space and mobility and prompts us to rethink identity (whether individual or national) as the result of circulation and exchange and, therefore, as essentially relational. It is a shift with potential ethical consequences: if we become aware of the constitutive nature of interconnections (whether commercial, cultural, ethnic, or political), we may tend to be less essentialist in our notions of self and society and more aware of the ways in which we are the result of circuits of interaction. It may make us more hospitable to what may appear to be alien and altogether nimbler in our dealings with alterity. Just as important, it will give us the opportunity to discover productive lines of transmission that are no longer bound to fixed space categories.

As it is, our times have been witnessing realignments of spatial thinking in terms of scale, principles of organization, and stability. The conceptual models we are employing to map our global topographies have been expanding and contracting, as well as reorganizing along shifting, often incommensurate, logics. As Gilles Deleuze and Félix Guattari observed, we are "at the crossroads of all kinds of formations" in which the ordering patterns produce shifting, fractal terrains.[1] The area studies paradigm established during the Cold War can no longer provide the central organizational structure that reflects our institutional cultural mappings, producing instead contradictory alignments.[2] A crisis of understanding has resulted from the inability of old categories of space to account for our diverse cartographies, as if our geographies had become jumbled up. Even the global–local dyad that helped to rearticulate our mappings a few decades ago is proving inadequate to deal with the multiple and dynamic understandings of transactions across space: cultural formations are shifting in ways that need less a bimodal understanding along the local versus global paradigm than the circulatory one, which provides an interface that is truly relational, connecting interlocked, even if potentially disparate, points in the globe. We could echo Arif Dirlik's observation that while modernist teleology gave the local a derogatory image that helped justify the forward movement of scientific rationality, later critics of modernity argued for a return to the local as a site of resistance, heterogeneity, and the repudiation of capitalist teleology. What remains is less the anchoring site of locality than the unprecedented mobility of exchanges—material and cultural. As it becomes increasingly difficult to discern the center of global capitalism, fragmentation sets in to call into question established structures of regional coherence.[3] What we have instead, as Homi Bhabha points out in his introduction to this volume, are multicentered circuits that transcend the local–global binary and call for a different kind of understanding in which dynamic trajectories help open up temporal and spatial territories, as well as interstitial spaces. In his introduction, Bhabha calls this a "ballistic" process, marked by a mobility that engenders convergences as well as disjunctures.

In literary and cultural studies, we observe the instability of regional coherence models as the world is remapped along differing principles of organization: a very capacious world literature initiative is becoming the prominent paradigm in a number of comparative literature departments; it goes hand in hand with the rising interest in translation studies and bilingual studies. This kind of model has produced significant tensions around the role of vernacular languages, the potentially flattening gaze of translation, and the totalizing force of Anglo-globalism. Other—quite different—ways of thinking about contemporary space tend to privilege regional comingling that may be expansive or contractive in their gravitational force. Other initiatives further areas of study such as Mediterranean studies and the Global South—itself seen more as a condition than a place, and, in several ways, an heir to the now outmoded Third World as a designation for non-hegemonic areas. Orientations such as Global South are parceling up the larger field of postcolonial studies, representing a reordering of the geographic to focus on the parts of the world marked by the highest degree of political, social, and economic upheaval. In a different alignment of forces, North and South are brought together in the hemispheric studies of the Americas, which are modifying the configuration of some history and literature departments. The globe is reshaped in yet other regimes of representation in transatlantic studies, whose gravitational pull is west-east and which are thriving in departments of history, history of science, English, comparative literature, and Spanish or Lusophone Studies, often ruled by the logic of colonial affiliations. A case in point is Hispanic transatlantic studies, originally supported by the Spanish government as it sought to renew old ties severed by independence movements in the nineteenth century and by the shift of power alignments that took place in the twentieth century.

Forces of contraction are also at work. Regional studies such as Catalan, Galician, Czech, Mapuche, and Aymara are taking root across the academic landscape. This is not new in itself, but it is significant as a response to the perceived risk of overgeneralization, homogenization, and the flattening of specificities. The power of local languages is emphasized in these groupings, and they are seen as the backbone of the scholar's understanding of the cultural world in question. In this mapping, the nation-state is eschewed in favor of the region, the city, or the village, reminding us, with K. Anthony Appiah, that "humans live best on a smaller scale."[4] In a loosely connected way, I have been struck by the rising interest among young linguists in dying languages, which implies studying groups of five or six speakers and their disappearing cultural universe in tightly circumscribed areas.

What is local and vernacular is in constant transformation as our epistemologies respond to the unstable politics of community of our time. Borders are confounded by diasporic peoples who actually inhabit or make present their vernacular cultures in the midst of a foreign state, so that, for example, within California we may have parts of Mexico or India. Cultural flows in these contexts are both homogenizing and heterogenizing: some groups may share in a global culture regardless of where they are; they may be alienated from their own hinterlands, or they may choose to turn back to what may once have been seen as residual, very local cultures that deliberately separate themselves from global culture. As Bhabha has pointed out, we need to turn to paradox to name the ever rearticulating formulations of our geographic imaginaries: we have coined such oxymoronic phrases as "global village," "globloc," "vernacular cosmopolitanisms," and "transcultural localisms."[5]

The different movements of expansion and contraction operate with logics of their own, so that the overall effect is similar to the movement of tectonic plates. While this is known to be characteristic of the era of globalization,[6] several interlocking and even contradictory views may be at work in these liminal moments, made all the more unstable by the current global financial scene. I would claim that rather than the oft-cited process of de-territorialization, what we are witnessing is intense re-territorializations, obtaining in spatial figurations and models that are often incommensurate. Confusing as it may appear, this is an opportunity to work out new frames of understanding; to rethink identities; to eschew conventional distinctions; and to produce new, relational articulations between area studies and global studies.

The divergent processes I have sketched unify or fragment the object of study and its explanatory force. Different logics of understanding are produced by some of the current geographic models, enabling multidirectional regional and global kinds of knowledge. A maritime emphasis privileges crossings and exchanges, movement and distances to be traversed, as well as migration and multi-local networks. The vast geopolitical reach of the oceans embraces imperial histories, the slave trade, scientific and biomedical exchanges, biogeography, and cultural geography, all in multiple directions of movement in space and historical periodicity. Prasenjit Duara's work makes us keenly aware of the ways in which global networks of exchange have spatialized and respatialized divisions in the Asian context, where imperial histories once led to regional formations connected with maritime trade. Rivers and seas constituted circulatory regions, as did the much earlier Silk Road. Yet Duara reminds us that even Asia as a cartographic image does not represent unity of any kind, having been named to designate territories to the east of the Greek ecumene.[7] If we consider transatlantic studies, we note that they are also predicated on the logic of colonial histories and their effects, whether English or Spanish, North or South. We read about the Red Atlantic of revolutions, the Black Atlantic of the slave trade, and the Green Atlantic of Irish migrants; Cis-Atlantic and Circum-Atlantic studies are introduced into the broader transatlantic realm. We see efforts to reinterpret empires such as Portugal's according to the extent to which the Atlantic may or may not fully represent Portuguese holdings beyond Africa and Brazil. On a different, North-South axis, hemispheric studies take stock of indigenous commonalities and differences, neglected cross-border exchanges, and the comparative structures that united and separated the Americas with the arrival of the Europeans. The hemispheric turn in American studies may be a step toward furthering inter-American scholarly relations, and so far it has operated by tackling such projects as comparing different appropriations of European culture or tracing the presence of Spanish-speaking groups along borders that separate the United States and Mexico today. The hemispheric turn is receptive to notions of hybridity, creolization, and *mestizaje*, which are especially productive in the study of the heteroglossic Caribbean. In hemispheric studies, considerable tensions exist around the direction of the gaze in a historically fraught North-South relationship. These different ways to assemble geography and culture produce epistemological realignments that need to reach institutional structures of organization.

The oscillation between expansion and contraction mentioned earlier is subject to varying senses of distance and movement as constitutive of cultural production and understanding. The awareness of distance presents the need for cultural and linguistic specificity: what is understood as being far is perceived as different, linguistically and culturally. In its fullest expression, the focus on difference can provide specificity and contextual richness; it can also produce a certain exhaustion of difference whereby, as Dirlik has pointed out, our recognition of previously ignored aspects of cultural difference, while countervailing the pitfalls of essentialization, may have the undesirable effect of producing a conglomeration of differences that resist naming and the postulation of collective identity. In Dirlik's terms, "The dispersal of culture into many localized encounters renders it elusive both as a phenomenon and as a principle of mapping and historical explanation."[8] Even when one nation is studied as a discrete unit, the spatial logic of explanation and the function assigned to distance will produce different accounts of the object of study—that is to say, different geographic imaginaries. To help flesh out these concepts, a couple of illustrations may be helpful. One is offered by Dirlik in a study of Chinese culture that rethinks the intersection between space and historical explanation. For Dirlik, distance is not so much a measure between two or more bounded cultural worlds as a "potentiality, a space of indeterminacy inherent to all processes of mediation, and therefore inherent to the social process per se."[9] When distance is brought into play, new ways to conceive social and cultural space follow. In the example of China, it would call into question the traditional account of the formation of Chinese civilization as radiating from a Han monarchic center toward peripheries in which barbarism ruled under the aegis of fifty-six recognized ethnic nationalities. Dirlik sees in the current condition of migration and displacement ("living in a state of flux") an opportunity to relinquish static, traditional notions of cultural formation and replace them with paradigms that stress distance and mobility over "stable containers."[10] Such alternative spatialities would instantiate a more productive understanding of the role of boundaries in the formation of Chinese culture, which would become the product of "multiple contact zones of a people in constant motion." In this reversal, the Chinese would be global in reach "because they have been formed from the outside.... The inside and the outside become inextricably entangled in one another."[11] It is important to note the emplacement of explanation and its bearing on the geographic imaginary it produces: an identity that emanates from a centrally located origin (the Han) is transformed when the border becomes the intellectual perch, the place from which the scholar looks.

In fact, the border is not only the focus of current border studies; it is also the nodal point that represents the convergence of geography and mobility. It is emblematic of new identity formations and, at the same time, of the current politics of national security, surveillance, and containment. Yet the border is not exclusively situated in the national periphery. Boundaries are dispersed in cosmopolitan cities, marking exchanges of technology, objects, and people. Their plurality contains the dilemma of contemporary citizenship and belonging, as is clearly argued by Jacqueline Bhabha's chapter in this volume. The subject position that stems from the boundary is the refugee or the immigrant, who represents the reality of internal exclusion.

Shifting from the center to the border produces an alternative geographic epistemology; so does an explanatory logic displaced from a territorial center to the sea. Consider the role of the heartland in an agrarian American tradition invented in the nineteenth century, when the notion of Manifest Destiny evoked a drive west and the move of European settlers toward the interior, with its rolling, grain-producing plains and imposing mountains. There is an emerging countervailing model that does not emanate from the heartland: it displaces its stable centrality and opts instead for maritime studies as fluid spaces of movement and multiple engagements that eschew closure and operate with different causal systems. Within the fluid parameters of the maritime imaginary we would have to make distinctions between the Atlantic and the Pacific, the North and the South. If the border or contact zone—be it China or the U.S.-Mexico border—de-essentializes the logic of explanation by taking stock of transborder forces while assailing notions of belonging, citizenship, and cultural homogeneity, the fluid notion of the seas eschews confinement and tracks multiple directions of contacts and crossings. In Lindsay Bremner's chapter in this volume, the sea engenders epistemological confusion that borders on unknowability.

In sum, important distinctions emanate from each epistemological location, whether it is the sea or the interior, the North or the South, the East or the West, the center or the border. The global system can be mapped from different locations, and it is being drawn and redrawn in structures of various kinds both within the academy and in the geopolitical order.[12] Echoing the many rewritings of Marx's *Communist Manifesto* and his reference to the deterritorializing effects of capitalism, we might advance the claim that our intellectual projects are hyperterritorial and in constant transformation.

The reorientation we are discussing is not the same as the discourse of globalization: the cognitive impulse that drives us has a strong sense of directionality, arguing for alternative vectors of movement that imply transit, transmission, and exchange, often detecting conversations that have gone unnoticed. It requires attentiveness to the singularity and uniqueness of each encounter and then, in a concomitant move, an attempt to draw appropriate generalizations. While the dominant forces of globalization today tend to deal with economic flows and communities wired together through financial networks, the flows we trace here have more to do with the effects of translation, travel, diaspora, transportation, pilgrimage, relationality, and, more generally, the ways in which space (maritime and land-based) inflects our ability to produce knowledge. The directionalities that interest us are not regulated by the conventionally established paths of hegemony, from North to the Global South, from West to East. Instead, they shift according to a reorientation of the gaze: at times from East to West and back, or from South to South; at times circulating along maritime pathways or settling in the borders to observe the displacement in more than one direction and, through it, to discern linkages, many of which may be unexpected. As each individuated network of mobility is studied, it contributes to the variegated vision of a relational conception of the world. In a book that anticipated what we are trying to accomplish in this one, Stephen Greenblatt eloquently advocates for what medieval theologians called *contingentia*, the sense that things are unpredictable and subject to chance. Greenblatt urges us to pursue the study of mobility by remaining attentive to the peculiar, particular, and local, to "the strategic acts of individual agents and by unexpected, unplanned, entirely contingent encounters between different cultures."[13]

There is a long history to the work we are doing—one that I will not revisit in detail. In the twentieth century, as the historian Lynn Hunt observes, globalization emerged triumphantly after the fall of the Berlin Wall and the collapse of the Soviet Union, when it seemed to be, as she put it, "the one sure thing."[14] In fact, some have argued that the fall of the Soviet Union was not unrelated to the inability of the state-run economy to adjust to the electronic global economy that gained ground in the 1980s. Before 1989, Fernand Braudel, Immanuel Wallerstein, and Andre Gunder Frank wrote important books derived from a transregional, world-based perspective.[15] Following in Braudel's perambulatory footsteps, Wallerstein did influential work on the "world system," whose beginnings he located in the sixteenth century and which he associated with a capitalist world economy. Other transnational thinkers, such as Frank, not only located the origins much earlier (as early as 4000 BC) but advanced the concept of dependency theory to study the world from a different vantage point, perched on Asia and Latin America. Yet the articulating principle remained, at most, regional, and a global political consciousness remained elusive.[16] Indeed, scholarship has tended to reify contained units of analysis: here we are trying to produce entanglements that exceed those units through the power of transit across established notions of spatial coherence. It is a realignment derived from concrete trajectories exemplified in each chapter and with a variety of disciplinary angles.

The geographic consciousness of the past few decades strains and tugs at inherited notions of space conceived as absolute and fixed. While immovable, absolute space is the space of standardized measurement, cadastral mapping, Euclidian geometry, and Newtonian mechanics, relative space, as David Harvey points out, is associated with Einstein and non-Euclidean geometry; it is predicated on process, motion, relationality.[17] This leads to different mappings organized around spatial discontinuities and unexpected connections. In this collection, we will find geometries that illuminate different lines of influence and fluid, indeterminate engagements across space and time. To cite just one example, we can observe such mappings in Finbarr Barry Flood's chapter, which suggests a reconsideration of aniconism through the study of the neglected relationship between Islam and Protestantism in the sixteenth century. The nature of the relations depends on disparate footprints drawn by travelers from Brazil to China and monuments from ancient Pergamon to nineteenth-century Berlin or by the journeys of diasporic musicians. The trajectories themselves become productive lines of reflection. Human practice is followed across space-time, recognizing the effects of hegemony but without letting it dictate the conversation about the units of analysis or the agency of those engaged in transit. In its very heterogeneity, the space of representation and analysis calls for collaborative scholarship, since our institutions are still anchored in absolute space—the nation or, at best, the area studies unit. Laboratory-like workshops such as those engaged in the study of world or global literature and history are leading the way in the study of exchange and relationality. This volume itself emerged from an exploratory seminar made possible by the Radcliffe Institute for Advanced Study, and it included an interdisciplinary array of scholars.

Revising sedentarism requires a different imaginary in terms of space and time—one that is infused with what Homi Bhabha calls "the scattering of the people."[18] Significantly, this phrase appears in the concluding essay of the influential collection he edited in 1990, which, together with Benedict Anderson's *Imagined Communities*,[19] did much to advance the study of nations in those decades. "DissemiNation" offers a salutary skepticism about national discourses, pointing to their sliding ambivalence, their internal contradictions, and their obsessive fixation on boundaries. That important essay and the volume in which it appeared made us deeply aware of the internal contradictions of the discourse of the nation: "Quite simply, the difference of space returns as the Sameness of time, turning Territory into Tradition, turning the People into One."[20] In the very ambivalence discerned by Bhabha lies the possibility of other narratives, some of which this volume seeks to open up as it explores alternatives to the nation and its boundedness through networks of dissemination that crisscross the globe in directions that have received insufficient notice.

In their diversity and range, the essays collected here question the assumption that the local is fixed, independent of displacement, migration, and exchange. Instead, we want to open up areas of knowledge through the paradigms of exchange, motion, and geographic porosity. Each of the chapters in this collection unveils connections that have remained hidden, whether in the field of musicology or literary and art history, the study of the seas and the environment, or the question of citizenship.

Furthering the productive power of the mobility paradigm is its constitutive interdisciplinarity: it allows cultural geographers, historians, art historians, anthropologists, architects, urban planners, literary scholars, cartographers, and students of religion and of sociology to work together. As objects, ideas, and people circulate, they transform and are transformed. It is not a question of studying influences—which used to flow along the channels established by hegemony, usually in a North-to-South direction—but of observing the profound effects of intercultural contact. Instead of focusing on the stasis of nations and civilizations, with their sense of boundedness, the group I have gathered in this volume thinks about networks of encounter and exchange, of geographies in motion. Transmission is enmeshed in multidirectional networks, in a fluid, Deleuzian mode. Conjuring new and shifting localizations, we trace footprints and boundaries, land and water as complex media not only of orientation but also of disorientation. Units of geographic coherence are rethought, and the located nature of our knowledge is brought to the forefront. A glance at the chapters that follow may throw light on the actual practice of our relational views.

The chapter on musicology is an ideal point of departure because, paradoxically, music, as Kay Shelemay notes, is "at home in circulation" (47). Indeed, airwaves live in movement. They are transformed when they are propelled by exile, but they also, in turn, transform the musical forms they encounter. Drawing on the case study of diasporic Ethiopian music, Shelemay shows how a new form, Ethio-jazz, was created in the United States in the 1960s as a fusion of Ethiopian music, jazz, bebop, and Latin jazz. Emerging as the result of the accretions and transformations of exile, it also allows for the processing of nostalgia, for diasporic communities connect through songs that mediate loss, and new genres emerge as loss and distance are expressed. Mulatu Astatke's music exemplifies this process, reaching out to the longed-for home and even returning to Ethiopia to reconnect homeland and exile. Shelemay also studies a kind of song (*tizita*) that obtains in various renditions to express what might be called restorative nostalgia, which enables multiple performative iterations of the feeling of loss. The chapter shows how distance and separation can be at the root of aesthetic productivity and how the national is reconceptualized through itinerant performances.

Xiaofei Tian's chapter also turns to distance and mobility as the condition of possibility for knowledge and insight. Her chapter charts how venturing out into unknown territories can lead to discovery, as well as to a renewed understanding of the homeland. Departure and return are productive, as in a circle that gets closed when the homecoming takes place: within the circle drawn by travel and return lie both discovery of the unknown and rediscovery of the known. Studying the first Chinese text about travel in foreign lands, written by a Buddhist monk in the fifth century BC, Tian traces the construction of rhetorical tropes and conceptual categories that have guided Chinese travel writing. Through the study of a Buddhist pilgrim who ventured outside the empire before there were maps, Tian shows how movement itself allows for a change in vision and understanding while also creating links as the pilgrim strings together the places he visits. The Buddhist injunction to travel reminds us of the role played by pilgrims in cultural exchange; in the case of Faxian, we can see an inaugural venture into uncharted territory. An added significance of this injunction is its impact on women, who, thanks to it, were given the opportunity to travel independently. Movement itself changes what Tian calls "self-positioning," as well as the understanding of the related concepts of center and periphery. As we saw in the case of Ethiopia, movement also produces emotional states that intensify affect: the pain of separation and the longing for community play a productive role in this travel narrative.

Rosario Hubert's chapter also dwells on the insights generated by travel. The mappings she traces are not the usual ones that move from center to periphery, or vice versa. Instead, she studies Brazilians who are not entirely bound to the imperial categories of ethnographic exploration and cultural superiority. Here again, national identity is formulated and reformulated in relation to observations made while traveling. In the South-South encounters Hubert examines, the peripheral location seems to open up other ways of seeing, evaluating, and judging. A memoir from 1888 by a member of the first Brazilian Diplomatic Mission to China, Henrique Carlos Ribeiro Lisboa, reads like a defense of the Chinese against European stereotypes: Lisboa argues for the need to observe details of physiognomy and type and to question arbitrary, received notions. Even if this vigilant stance may have been motivated by his desire to promote Chinese immigration to Brazil, Lisboa's four-hundred-page volume is a significant alternative to the prevalent discourse produced by the Age of Empire. Hubert also studies the great Gilberto Freyre's travel writings and finds in them yet another take on the question of cultural encounter: Freyre opts for a form of kinship based on the combination of a shared Lusophone genealogy (anchored in the area around Goa), material exchanges, and the affinities of the tropics. In Freyre, then, the impulse to detect common traits produces South-South affinities through a shared Luso-imperial genealogy. Brazil and India, far apart as they may be, are drawn closer together by the gaze of travelers from the periphery, where power relations obtain in other ways.

It is this very attention away from the centers of power and to what she calls "minor sites" that makes Shu-mei Shih's focus on world art also yield a "non-centrist" (that is to say, neither Eurocentric nor China-centric) perspective. Shih sets out to offer a relational study based on nodal points of artistic production. She opts for relation as the concept that points to "the state of world-wide entanglements of cultures and peoples," to a way of studying the world. In many ways, we could say that this very volume is part of *relational studies*: arts practices from different parts of the globe are brought into relational comparison by Shih, opening up connections that exist within trajectories inflected by power relations. Shih's relationality steers clear of geographic hegemonies: neither the West nor the East is privileged in her study of three female visual artists. The arc drawn in her chapter connects a Taiwanese, a Cambodian, and an Asian American whose work shares concerns for women's issues, the environment, and sociopolitical questions stemming from the historical legacies of twentieth-century conflicts. With a decentered perspective that is not ordered along a primary geographic axis, Shih maps fluid cartographies of relationality linked by an ethos of critique, care, and awareness. Wu Mali, Marine Ky, and Patty Chang are diasporic artists whose work addresses memory, trauma, sexual politics, and community work in a manner that is at once local and mobile, eschewing exclusively national definitions. Seeing the three of them relationally offers a sense of world arts practices linked by ethical impulses.

The ethical dimension is powerfully at work in the study of serious global problems as they are represented in the novel. Karen Thornber's essay generates multiple relationalities derived from archives that are opened up by her reading. Her path to mobility draws a line that connects languages from different regions: as she engages in what she calls global world literature, Thornber studies *The Equations the Professor Loved*, a Japanese novel published in 2003 that deals with traumatic brain injury. Through the lens provided by illness, and thanks to her access to Asian and European archives, she explores diverse worldviews and mobilizes cultural contacts. New pathways are cleared by this scholar's immersion in vernacular languages: one can almost visualize the globe crisscrossed by the voices of diverse societies in a multilingual conversation. Thornber's contribution to the enterprise of world literature and the health humanities adds not only specific linguistic immersion but also an awareness of how the nuances of translation play a part in our understanding of texts that we do not read in the original. Tracing the effect of word choices in eight versions of *The Equations*, Thornber makes us aware of the subtleties produced by translation decisions around notions of responsibility, caregiving, agency, and vulnerability. She inflects world literature and the health humanities with the effects of linguistic particularity by considering what it means to read a Japanese novel in multiple languages, moving between linguistic regions to show meaning shifts as well as inter- and intra-regional interactions. Expanding the map allows her to connect the materials she unearths with problems the whole world needs to face, such as environmental degradation and disease. Thus, Thornber's enterprise moves around the globe to give the literary the ring of pragmatic urgency: the critic reads across cultural divides and linguistic registers to call attention to questions that require global attention.

Ethical urgency is at the core of Jacqueline Bhabha's chapter on a problematic consequence of mobility: the predicament of displaced peoples. Our era of globalization produces not only capital flows and cultural exchanges but also diasporic communities and refugees that are stripped of rights. Bhabha's chapter forces us to think about the legal importance of the stationary correlative of mobility: emplacement. Studying circulation and its consequences becomes particularly telling in the case of the history of discrimination of the Roma, a group whose lack of legal identity has meant not only discrimination but also deportation, removal, and lack of suitable housing, education, and health care. Bhabha calls attention to belonging as a key element of migratory communities, no matter how post-national our times may appear to be. Borders, then, remain real forces of exclusion, and diasporic communities need the protection of civil emplacement and the care of the state if they are to avoid falling prey to the deprivation attendant on the absence of residential status. Even as we strive to think in a post-Westphalian, global way, it is imperative to aver that only legal permanence guarantees legal personhood and that until borders disappear—

and with the notable exception of cosmopolitan elites—displacement and migration tend to cause hardship. Bhabha's work pays special attention to the plight of children in these circumstances, and it is sobering to read that one-third of the world's children lack birth registration. Such a compromised connection between an individual and citizenship (with its attendant rights) is one of the most negative aspects of the subject we are studying. Human movement and encounter produce cultural exchange and circulation of ideas, but we cannot turn a blind eye to the very real consequences of residential displacement and discrimination. Thriving in dynamic geographies is predicated on the root of belonging: at some point, the mobile subject needs to find legal emplacement under the protection of the state.

The two chapters devoted to the history of art and architecture open up new questions that have remained occluded by conceptions of immobility and rootedness dear to the discipline. Here we should do well to remember with Heidegger that things never reveal themselves in static isolation; they are always part of a complicated network of flexible relations to which they provide access through their own disclosure.[21] Alina Payne's contribution alerts us to the surprisingly restless life of architectural materials, objects, and even buildings themselves. Her chapter calls attention to displacement narratives that open up a different way to think about material culture, one that is enriched by following the lives of objects and buildings as their paths are traced. Portability, the concept she puts forward to articulate her approach, invites us to rethink the discipline. Understanding the effects of transportation and arrival transforms our understanding of the process of making itself, and it includes a broad range of connected agents, such as artists, craftsmen, middlemen, buyers and sellers, scholars and patrons, the public at large, and the agents of the state. As she puts it, the "vicissitudes of the road" would generate another way to study the vast context within which an art object or a building generates its force field. Payne's chapter stuns us with surprising instances of colossal feats of transportation. It starts with the obelisk of St. Peter's in Rome, with its 326 metric tons, transported from Egypt to Rome during Nero's time, and then makes us aware of the provenance of the materials with which several monuments have been built. The impact of such transplantations cannot be underestimated, as is proved by the fascinating effect of the arrival in Berlin of the Hellenistic Pergamon Altar in the 1870s. In addition to the daunting efforts of transportation, we need to trace the footprint of objects because the stories they tell bear on related cultural, economic, social, and political forces. Transit histories can have a transformative effect on the discipline of art history, freeing it from its nineteenth-century dependence on the nation as a foundational cult (à la Renan), which is the principle at work in the spirit of *patrimoine* and in the enclosed space of the museum. Instead, Payne advocates for a mode of study that is not contained within static borders; rather, it seeks the mobility of territorial expanses and the flow of rivers as conduits of connections. Instead of national purity, we have territorial hybridity, derived from tracing paths such as *riverine ties*, which enrich the study of the seas and the hinterland with attention to rivers as conveyors of combination, assimilation, and transformation. The effect of this unveiling is to discover fluid and fluctuating networks of transmission that transform the history of art and architecture.

The impulse of unveiling is literally and symbolically central to the chapter by the other art historian we feature in this volume, Finbarr Barry Flood. Taking as his point of departure the whitewashing of 115 feet of gold-ground mosaic decorations of the Great Mosque of Damascus completed in 715, Flood traces the complex debates around the question of aniconism in the sixteenth century. The debates chart a vast discursive map crossing boundaries by which scholarship has tended to abide. Around the question of images, Flood builds a fascinating network of exchanges that reveal recognized or occluded commonalities between Islam and Protestantism on the issues of idolatry and images. As was the case with the pastoral scenes that were whitewashed from the Damascus mosque, we have disregarded propinquities that would remap cognitive frontiers. In Flood's symbolic removal of the plaster that has blinded us to these discursive shifts, we learn about the early polemical exchanges surrounding Protestantism and the extent to which Arabs, Jews, Turks, Protestants, and Native Americans were implicated in the heresy of iconoclasm. Heretics though they were considered to be, Turks and, in general, Islam were not entirely other. They were part of the intense Christian polemics of the time. Here is a geographic and symbolic imaginary to which we need to return. Flood takes it all one step further as he concludes his breathtaking itinerary, delineating the ethical implications of the rhetoric of whitewashing, which point to the moral resonances of rejecting worldly embellishments for the sake of moral purity and interior beauty.

Thinking differently about units of geographic coherence and the effects of mobility also means giving consideration to parts of the globe that have been less noticed by cultural and historical scholarship. In our mobile cartography, land, air, and water are seen as conductors of questions and knowledge. How does the world look from other locations, other points of entry? Oceans and rivers have not received their due in the nation-bound scholarly agenda until recently, when we have seen some very interesting work on rivers and on oceans.[22] Waterways help us move beyond national boundaries and area studies contours. They touch on distant lands and make for multidirectional contacts. The study of oceans is offering very productive interregional models: the eastern coast of Africa, for example, is linked to many points in the western reaches of the Indian Ocean; the turn to the Pacific Rim in the study of the Americas is turning the gaze away from the dominant paradigm organized around Europe. These reorientations may have the power to shift the prevailing principles of spatial organization and retrieve all sorts of cross-fertilizing exchanges that we had tended to neglect.

Yet while oceans offer opportunities for different regional configurations, they can confront us with the limits of the knowable. As Lindsay Bremner's chapter attests, the deepest recesses of the ocean floors may well be impenetrable, as the case of the missing Malaysia Airlines Flight MH370 leads us to conclude. Bremner's fascinating retracing of the international search for the disappeared airplane makes us aware of the uncertainty that no amount of technological or scientific expertise managed to dispel. "Theory machines" deployed for the study of the oceans yielded inconclusive results: ACARS, pings and pinger locators, data visualization, satellite systems, and Inmarsat technologies were pressed into action, with inconclusive results. Narrating the complex history of the search, Bremner's chapter traces the arduous gathering of data and evidence, the positing and re-positing of hypotheses, the modeling of data, the interpretation of sightings. Examining a vast scopic system based on the most advanced technologies brings Bremner to the conclusion that, as she puts it, "making the ocean comprehensible" is a daunting enterprise that defies vast scientific and technological resources. At the heart of the problem is the very question of mobility: the ocean's fluid nature is made up of moving forces. No place is still in the ocean, and that means that dispersion rules. In other words, the material reality of water limits our cognitive efforts, regardless of our scientific prowess. Bremner's essay is about mobility as a regime of knowledge and about the impact of the emplacement of the research effort: locating a study in the ocean determines the limits of our understanding.

Diana Sorensen's chapter is built as a study that seeks to find a balance between the specificity of a given case and the general insights that can be derived from it. It deals with Bernard Berenson as a connoisseur who orchestrated the sale and transportation of a great number of early Italian Renaissance paintings from Italy and the United Kingdom to America between the end of the nineteenth century and the early decades of the twentieth century. In this case, the study of mobility converges with the study of material culture: the circulation of artworks engaged different regions and their historical complexities, and they invoke questions of taste, value, esthetics, and society. Art objects as luxury goods have the capacity to convey complex social meanings: their value is rhetorical and social, as well as economic. Cultural and material factors enabled or hindered the circulation of artworks. At each step along the way, we find revealing intersections of regimes of explanation, ranging, for example, from the value of British land to the history of taste, from the symbolic value of the Medici in the late nineteenth century to the meaning of collecting and connoisseurship. Central to the enterprise is the impulse to trace routes of exchange that can be understood only in a dynamic, transnational order, in contexts of understanding that are anything but local.

Our goal in the pages that follow is to further a relational worldview in which there are multidirectional influences and sometimes unexpected engagements. The historical vision opened up by the study of minorities, the rearticulation of proximities and distances, we hope, will erode boundaries that have made us blind to the linkages that enable a new understanding of the difference inherent in identity. Eventually, this should reach the static institutional structures by which universities are hindered and help open up fluid trajectories that are better suited to the needs of our times.

NOTES

1 Deleuze and Guattari, *A Thousand Plateaus*, 20.
2 This is stated in lapidary form in the introduction to Miyoshi and Harootunian, *Learning Places*, 8: "Paradoxically area studies has now become the main custodian of an isolating system of knowledge, which was originally ranked near the bottom of the academic hierarchy. By the same measure, it is committed to preserving the nation-state as the privileged unit of teaching and study. In this sense, it was the perfect microcosmic reflection of the liberal arts curriculum that since the nineteenth century has been focused on the nation-state as the organizing principle for teaching and research."
3 See Dirlik, "The Global in the Local."
4 Appiah, *The Ethics of Identity*, 246.
5 See Bhabha, *The Location of Culture*; Bhabha, "Unsatisfied," 191–207.
6 This has been observed by numerous scholars. As Rosi Braidotti has noted, late postmodernity functions through the paradox of simultaneous globalization and fragmentation: see Braidotti, *Metamorphoses*; Braidotti, *Nomadic Theory*.
7 See Duara, *The Crisis of Global Modernity*. For the Indian Ocean, see, among others, Bose, *A Hundred Horizons*.
8 Dirlik, "Timespace, Social Space, and the Question of Chinese Culture," 5.
9 Dirlik, "Timespace, Social Space, and the Question of Chinese Culture," 14.
10 Dirlik, "Timespace, Social Space, and the Question of Chinese Culture," 14.

11 Dirlik, "Timespace, Social Space, and the Question of Chinese Culture," 11.
12 An interesting geopolitical illustration would be the different configurations of groups that gather to discuss the world financial crisis that began in 2008. Aside from the Group of Eight, we have a new Group of Twenty that reflects divergent notions of emerging power, as well as an array of local trade organizations such as the Association of Southeast Asian Nations and Mercosur. A revealing new group of recent formation is BRIC, constituted by Brazil, Russia, India, and China. Its agenda included an attempt to go beyond the dollar as the international currency.
13 Greenblatt, *Cultural Mobility*, 17. This book gathers a number of scholars that offer "microhistories" (I would call them "case studies," following Giorgio Agamben) that account for particular instances of mobility. See also the final "Manifesto," on pages 250–53, which presents five lucid recommendations for those that set out to do this sort of work.
14 Hunt, *Writing History in the Global Era*, 46.
15 Braudel, *Civilisation matérielle, économie et capitalisme*; Braudel, *La dynamique du capitalisme*; Braudel, *L'identité de la France*; Braudel, *La Méditerranée et le Monde Méditerranéen a l'époque de Philippe II*; Frank, *Capitalism and Underdevelopment in Latin America*; Frank, *Crisis in the World Economy*; Frank, *The European Challenge*; Frank, *Lumpenbourgeoisie, Lumpendevelopment*; Wallerstein, *The Modern World-System I*; Wallerstein, *The Modern World-System II*; Wallerstein, *The Modern World-System III*.
16 For a broad view of the relationship among the nation-state, colonialism, and globalization, see Miyoshi, "A Borderless World?"
17 See Harvey, *Cosmopolitanism and the Geographies of Freedom*, 134.
18 Bhabha, "DissemiNation," 291.
19 Anderson, *Imagined Communities*.
20 Bhabha, "DissemiNation," 300.
21 Martin Heidegger, *What Is a Thing?* 81.
22 Berry, *A Path in the Mighty Waters*; Bose, *A Hundred Horizons*; Cusack, *Framing the Ocean, 1700 to the Present*; Hoag, *Developing the Rivers of East and West Africa*; Klein and Mackenthun, *Sea Changes*; Mann and Phaf-Rheinberger, *Beyond the Line*; Matsuda, *Pacific Worlds*; Redford, *Maritime History and Identity*; Sheriff and Ho, *The Indian Ocean*; Sobecki, *The Sea and Englishness in the Middle Ages*.

BIBLIOGRAPHY

Anderson, Benedict. *Imagined Communities: Reflections on the Origin and Spread of Nationalism*. London: Verso, 1983.

Appiah, Kwame Anthony. *The Ethics of Identity*. Princeton, NJ: Princeton University Press, 2005.

Berry, Stephen R. *A Path in the Mighty Waters: Shipboard Life and Atlantic Crossings to the New World*. New Haven. CT: Yale University Press, 2015.

Bhabha, Homi K. "DissemiNation: Time, Narrative, and the Margins of the Modern Nation." In *Nation and Narration*, ed. Homi K. Bhabha, 291–322. New York: Routledge, 1990.

———. *The Location of Culture*. New York: Routledge, 1994.

———. "Unsatisfied: Notes on Vernacular Cosmopolitanism." In *Text and Nation: Cross-Disciplinary Essays on Cultural and National Identities*, ed. Laura Garcia-Moreno and Peter C. Pfeiffer, 191–207. Columbia, SC: Camden House, 1996.

Bose, Sugata. *A Hundred Horizons: The Indian Ocean in the Age of Global Empire*. Cambridge, MA: Harvard University Press, 2006.

Braidotti, Rosi. *Metamorphoses: Toward a Materialist Theory of Becoming*. Malden: Blackwell, 2002.

———. *Nomadic Theory*. New York: Columbia University Press, 2011.

Braudel, Fernand. *Civilisation matérielle, économie et capitalisme, XVe–XVIIIe siècle*, 3 vols. Paris: Colin, 1979.

———. *La dynamique du capitalisme*. Paris: Arthaud, 1985.

———. *L'Identité de la France*, 2 vols. Paris: Arthaud, 1986.

———. *La Méditerranée et le Monde Méditerranéen a l'époque de Philippe II*, 3 vols., 4th rev. ed. Paris: Colin, 1979.

Cusack, Tricia, ed. *Framing the Ocean, 1700 to the Present: Envisaging the Sea as Social Space*. Farnham, UK: Ashgate, 2014.

Deleuze, Gilles, and Félix Guattari. *A Thousand Plateaus: Capitalism and Schizophrenia*, trans. Brian Massumi. Minneapolis: University of Minnesota Press, 1987.

Dirlik, Arif. "The Global in the Local." In *Global/Local: Cultural Production and the Transnational Imaginary*, ed. Rob Wilson and Wimal Dissanayake, 21–45. Durham, NC: Duke University Press, 1996.

———. "Timespace, Social Space, and the Question of Chinese Culture." *Boundary 2* 35, no. 1 (2008): 1–22.

Duara, Prasenjit. *The Crisis of Global Modernity: Asian Traditions and a Sustainable Future*. Cambridge: Cambridge University Press, 2015.

Frank, Andre Gunder. *Capitalism and Underdevelopment in Latin America: Historical Studies of Chile and Brazil*. New York: Monthly Review Press, 1967.

———. *Crisis in the World Economy*. New York: Holmes and Meier, 1980.

———. *The European Challenge: From Atlantic Alliance to Pan-European Entente for Peace and Jobs*. Nottingham, UK: Spokesman, 1983.

———. *Lumpenbourgeoisie, Lumpendevelopment: Dependence, Class, and Politics in Latin America*. New York: Monthly Review Press, 1974.

Greenblatt, Stephen. *Cultural Mobility: A Manifesto*. Cambridge: Cambridge University Press, 2010.

Harvey, David. *Cosmopolitanism and the Geographies of Freedom*. New York: Columbia University Press, 2009.

Heidegger, Martin. *What Is a Thing?* Chicago: Henry Regnery, 1967.

Hoag, Heather J. *Developing the Rivers of East and West Africa: An Environmental History*. London: Bloomsbury Academic, 2013.

Hunt, Lynn. *Writing History in the Global Era*. New York: W. W. Norton, 2014.

Klein, Bernhard, and Gesa Mackenthun. *Sea Changes: Historicizing the Ocean.* New York: Routledge, 2004.

Mann, Michael, and Ineke Phaf-Rheinberger, eds. *Beyond the Line: Cultural Narratives of the South Oceans.* Berlin: Neofelis, 2014.

Matsuda, Matt K. *Pacific Worlds: A History of Seas, Peoples, and Cultures.* Cambridge: Cambridge University Press, 2011.

Miyoshi, Masao. "A Borderless World? From Colonialism to Transnationalism and the Decline of the Nation State." In *Global/Local: Cultural Production and the Transnational Imaginary*, ed. Rob Wilson and Wimal Dissanayake, 78–106. Durham, NC: Duke University Press, 1996.

Miyoshi, Masao, and Harry D. Harootunian, eds. *Learning Places: The Afterlives of Area Studies.* Durham, NC: Duke University Press, 2002.

Redford, Duncan, ed. *Maritime History and Identity: The Sea and Culture in the Modern World.* London: I. B. Tauris, 2014.

Sheriff, Abdul, and Engseng Ho, eds. *The Indian Ocean: Oceanic Connections and the Creation of New Societies.* London: Hurst, 2014.

Sobecki, Sebastian I., ed. *The Sea and Englishness in the Middle Ages: Maritime Narratives, Identity and Culture.* Cambridge: D. S. Brewer, 2011.

Wallerstein, Immanuel. *The Modern World-System I: Capitalist Agriculture and the Origins of the European World-Economy in the Sixteenth Century*, repr. ed. Berkeley: University of California Press, 2011.

———. *The Modern World-System II: Mercantilism and the Consolidation of the European World-Economy, 1600–1750*, repr. ed. Berkeley: University of California Press, 2011.

———. *The Modern World-System III: The Second Era of Great Expansion of the Capitalist World-Economy, 1730s–1840s*, repr. ed. Berkeley: University of California Press, 2011.

PART I

Travel and Transmission

. . . . .

Chapter 1

The Diplomacy of Exoticism: Brazilian Accounts of the Global South

ROSARIO HUBERT

In recent years, the signifier "Brazil" has gone through a radical set of branding makeovers. With the frenzy of the mid-2000s fueled by the confidence of Brazil, Russia, India, and China—known collectively as BRIC—in economic growth or the commitment to sustainable development of grassroots events such as the United Nations Conference on Sustainable Development (Rio+20), the label "Brazil" came to represent a global fantasy of neoliberalism and racial democracy, a fusion of a booming economy and Carnival culture. With the current economic crisis, political crisis, and controversial handling of the FIFA World Cup in 2014 and the Olympic Games in 2016, the celebratory image of the largest South American nation is being contested by different spheres of culture outside and within Brazil. At the opening ceremony of the Frankfurt Book Fair in 2013—that had Brazil as a guest of honor—the Mineiro writer Luiz Ruffato announced to the cosmopolitan audience of the largest publisher market in Europe that the fantasy of "savage capitalism" was by no means an irony in Brazil but, rather, the literal explanation of the historical clash of cultures that facilitated modernization:

> O maior dilema do ser humano em todos os tempos tem sido exatamente esse, o de lidar com a dicotomia eu-outro. Porque, embora a afirmacao de nossa subjetividade se verifique através do reconhecimento do outro, o outro é também aquele que nos pode aniquilar. E se a humanidade se edifica neste movimento pendular entre agregaçao e dispersao, a histo-

ria do Brasil vem sendo alicerçada quase que exclusivamente na negacao explícita do outro, por meio da violência e da indiferença.¹

The greatest challenge humans have faced throughout time has been exactly this: dealing with the self-other dichotomy. Our subjectivity may be confirmed by recognizing the other—it is alterity that grants us the feeling of existence—yet the other is also the one that can annihilate us. And if humanity builds itself through this pendulum movement between aggregation and dispersion, the history of Brazil has been built almost exclusively through the explicit negation of the other, through violence and indifference.²

Rather than conforming to a jingoist portrayal of the country, Ruffato condemned foundational instances of cultural intolerance (the extermination of the indigenous population by the Portuguese, slavery, dictatorships, racism, and so on) that lie in the roots of the tropical modern nation.

This scene is symptomatic of the anxieties of representation in a changing geopolitical scenario that does not necessarily encompass cultural change. In this chapter, I address Ruffato's critique of racial democracy as a façade—a fiction of multiculturalism that legitimizes economic modernization—to analyze Brazilian constructions of Otherness in the context of the Global South. By reconfiguring the framework of the nation-state to an ordering of the world that emerges from the map of the Third World allows us to consider strategies of transnational identification, solidarity, and, therefore, authority at a planetary scale. As Arif Dirlik observes, even if there are certain affinities between the societies of the Global South in terms of mutual experience with colonialism and neocolonialism, economic, political, and social (racial) marginalization, and, in some cases, memories of common struggle for global justice, there are still issues of global power at stake.³ In this sense, it is worth asking: how have Brazilian writers and intellectuals described and theorized *their own* inscription in this world map? How do the country's multiracial population and historical links to a transoceanic empire determine its access to a global scenario that no longer places the axis in the North? To what extent is the current distress with discourses of alterity a function of peripheral subjectivities in relation to foreign ones? When the modernist writer Oswald de Andrade states in the *Manifesto Antropofago* (1928), "Só me interessa o que nao é meu" (I'm only interested in what's not mine), he affirms an essential appetite for Otherness but leaves open the question of what exactly informs that *meu* (mine).⁴

To work through these questions that imply transnational negotiations of cultural difference, I propose to look into travel writing, a genre that supposes collective identities in confrontation under the assumption of geographical displacement. As Graciela Montaldo argues, reading texts that deal with spaces, territories, and geographies outside national borders illuminates a problematic zone opened by economic and cultural modernization: the reformulation of group identities in relation to others.[5] In the interest of exploring geographies situated in the margins of the developed world, the sources in question deal with Brazilian travels in Asia—namely, India, China, and Mongolia: *A China e os chins: Recordações de viagem* (1888), by Henrique Carlos Ribeiro Lisboa; *Aventura e rotina: Sugestões de uma viagem à procura das constantes portuguesas de carácter e acções* (1953), by Gilberto Freyre; and *Mongólia* (2003), by Bernardo Carvalho. Separated in time and written from different points of social and disciplinary enunciation within Brazil, these texts, I argue, employ a discourse of exoticism to eventually overcome it. If exoticism is the projection of a gaze that distances the Other by making it foreign (*exo* 'from the outside'), I contend that in the discursive economy of the Global South, exoticism becomes a token of both difference and identity, a rhetorical strategy that enables translation, continuation, and fragmentation of such a gaze. By "diplomacy of exoticism" I understand that these redefinitions of exoticism do not necessarily aspire to a universal ideal of global identity. Rather, they reveal particular agendas of the place of Brazil in a global scenario—namely in terms of immigration, lusophony, and world literature.

Far from the imperial and metropolitan place of enunciation that defines the gaze of "Orientalism"[6]—the predominant framework for reading East-West relations—the South-South paradigm casts new light on the relation between Brazil, or Latin America in general, and other peripheries, and thus facilitates an exploration of the literary potential of relative notions such as the primitive, the subaltern, or the exotic that still dominate the discourse of Otherness. This approach not only questions hegemonic representations of Latin America and Asia; it also revises the epistemological frameworks that account for difference.

Translation

Henrique Carlos Ribeiro Lisboa's *A China e os chins* is the travel memoir of the first Brazilian Diplomatic Mission to China. Defined by its author as a "conscious study of characters and customs of the Chinese," the four hundred-page volume deals with the events and observations of the mission's year-long stay in China in 1880.[7] As a resolute advocate of Chinese immigration to Brazil, Lisboa refutes the stereotypes of the Chinese that had gained widespread notoriety in the Americas after the introduction of Asian indentured labor (coolie trade) in Hispanic America, mainly in Cuba and Peru. In this respect, the narrative addresses not only a reading public anxious for depictions of a distant land about which no other Brazilian had ever written directly, but also addresses the agents directly involved in the "transformation of labor," mainly the pro-slavery planter class and the abolitionists, uneasy about the implementation of Chinese manpower.

In his description of the Chinese, Lisboa enumerates particular aspects of their culture that usually appall European voyagers: binding feet, eating dogs, gambling. Immediately, he mitigates their negative connotations by translating them to equivalent aspects of Western-French culture. For example, to alleviate the impression of the Chinese custom to bind women's feet, Lisboa argues that the corsets worn by European women follow the same principle of sculpturing the female body; against the claim of the lack of sanitation in the habit of eating dogs in China, Lisboa reminds readers that one of the most sophisticated delicacies in France are frogs, an equally unimaginably edible animal. Implied in this operation is the understanding that, regardless of its exterior radical differences, Chinese culture is essentially similar to that of the West; therefore, Chinese subjects are compatible candidates for immigration. Who are his readers, one might ask, considering that the equivalences he establishes define a backdrop of European culture? As a man of letters from an aristocratic background, Lisboa shifts his position of enunciation from the Europeanized elites of the court of imperial Brazil to the *criollo* landowners who are the main addressees of his narrative.

Addiction to opium is a recurrent topic of discussion throughout the text, mostly due to the effects of anti-Chinese propaganda after the Opium Wars (1839–42, 1856–60), which kindled the fears of the "Yellow Peril," but also due to controversial photographs of opium dens. In *Opium Regimes*, Timothy Brook and Bob Tadashi Wakabayashi note, "A small group of men, poorly or well attired, sprawled on an opium couch became the recognizable image of the 'Chinese' opium smokers—or more broadly, of 'Chinese' tout court—that Westerners liked to photograph."[8] In Brazil, this portrait was also used as a crucial argument against the introduction of Asian labor: the Chinese were just not fit for plantation work. At the Agricultural Congress of 1878, a detractor claimed: "Weak and lazy, exhausted by the depravation of customs and habits developed since the cradle, physically and morally narcotized by opium, they will never cope with the arduous and miserable coffee labor."[9] Lisboa attacks this argument from all fronts. First, he minimizes the relevance of opium in China by once again translating and comparing opium to alcohol consumption in the West. But he also calls for greater precision in the use of categories such as "the Chinese," quoting the work of the sinologist Abel-Rémusat: "Intellectual features and moral physiognomies are confused, and from this mixture emerges an imaginary product, a true creation of reason—that resembles nothing—which is praised or criticized arbitrarily. It is given the name of Asian or Oriental (or Chinese), and this dispenses with studying it in detail. This is a precious faculty granted by generic denominations to those who pay little attention to exact ideas and, when judging things, do not take pains to look deep into them."[10]

In what can be read today as a postcolonial gesture, Lisboa denounces the Orientalism in other travelers' depictions of the Chinese, but mostly he questions the legitimacy in the observation. In turn, he dedicates an entire chapter to spelling out the nuances of each of the ethnic groups that inhabit the Middle Kingdom and takes advantage of the new possibilities opened up by photography in the representation of cultures, using the lens of ethnography rather than tourism. In a plate captioned, "Types of Chinese Inhabitants," he presents upper-torso portraits taken in three-quarter profile organized by the sitter's nation of origin. This was a very popular genre in the late nineteenth century because it allowed immediate and analogical representation of physiognomies of race, typologies, and genes and was used extensively in Brazil in the study of African nations.[11] What is singular about the plate is the centrality attributed to the Mongol people and the effort Lisboa makes to rule out the derogatory theories emerging from criminological discourses that associated that particular group with idiocy and thus with the fear of "mongolization of the nation."[12] Thus, Lisboa's representation of the Chinese offers a change in the position of enunciation, not only in geographical terms (he differentiates himself from European tourists and, in turn, affirms his subjectivity as a Brazilian imperial diplomat), but also in the acknowledgment of the changing patterns of travel and in calling for a more critical and scientific examination of cultural difference.

Continuity

The Brazilian sociologist Gilberto Freyre's diplomacy of exoticism in India is far more categorical: he claims there is no difference whatsoever between India and Brazil. Invited by the Portuguese Ministry of Overseas Affairs in 1951 to issue a report about Portugal's colonial settlements in Africa and Asia, Freyre traveled for a year through the Portuguese-speaking regions of the world "with a sociological clinical eye" according to his own words in the prologue. In 1953, he published *Aventura e rotina*, writing, "Chegou a época de partirem do Brasil para as terras portuguesas, brasileiros que retribuem aos de Pêro Vaz de Caminha suas palavras de revelacao de *paisagens e valores ignorados*" (Now is time for Brazilians to travel through Portuguese lands and return to Pêro Vaz de Caminha their words of revelation of ignored landscapes and values).[13] The evocation of Pêro Vaz de Caminha, the author of the Letter of Discovery of Brazil (1500), at the start of his text not only places Freyre in a genealogy of Portuguese maritime explorers (together with other pioneer navigators in Asia mentioned in the text, such as Fernão Mendes Pinto and Pêro de Covilhã); it also transfers the agency of geographical discovery to South America, claiming thus to inaugurate a new historical stage of global lusophony.

Yet it is precisely because of his Brazilian provenance that he does not expect to discover anything new in India. He writes, "Minha impressão de Pangim, a hoje capital de Goa, é menos a de uma cidade exótica para olhos de brasileiro, que de uma pequena e velha capital do Norte do Brasil: São Luis de Maranhão, por exemplo" (My impression of Panjim, the current capital of Goa, is less of an exotic city to the eyes of a Brazilian than any small old capital of northern Brazil: São Luis de Maranhão, for example).[14] Later in the text we read, "Continuo impressionado com as semelhanças da Índia Portuguesa com o Brasil. Ou do Brasil com a Índia Portugesa, desde que, daqui, assimilou o português muito valor oriental, hoje dissolvido no complexo brasileiro de cultura: uma cultura luso-tropical tanto quanto a da Índia" (I am still impressed by the similarities between Portuguese India and Brazil. Or Brazil and Portuguese India, since so much from here was adopted by the Portuguese and later dissolved into Brazilian culture: a Luso-tropical culture just like India).[15] Freyre casts light on the global circulation of goods, thus reinterpreting myths of origin of the vernacular: from India, Brazil obtained "varandas canja, mangueira, coqueiros dos chamados da Bahia mas na verdade da Índia" (verandas, mango trees, coconut palms, which are thought to be originally from Bahia but are actually from India). In turn, India received "o cajueiro, a mandioca, o tabaco, o mamoiero, a rede" (the cashew tree, mandioca, tobacco, papaya, the hammock).[16]

While Henrique Lisboa's diplomacy of exoticism consisted in reading the visible aspects of Chinese culture as only apparently different but essentially similar, Freyre recognized identity with India from the start, with no need for further mediation. He attributes this to the benevolence of the Portuguese colonial experience: because of the long history of miscegenation with peoples from North Africa, a lax religious missionary spirit, and a stronger opening to the sea, Lisboa argues, the Portuguese were more human, more civilizing, and thus less resisting/resistant than the English and Spanish.[17] This is one of the central premises of Freyre's main work, *Casa-grande e senzala* (*The Masters and the Slaves*; 1933), and one of the most contested ones, too, since it is precisely this idea that gave way to the myth of racial democracy that survives in Brazil to this day.[18]

In addition to the historical experience of Portuguese colonialism, Freyre cites the geo-cultural convergence of the tropics as an explanation for the continuity between Brazil and Portuguese India. In this respect, *Aventura e rotina* serves as a draft for what Freyre will institutionalize later as Lusotropicology, an interdisciplinary area study of the economic, ecologic, and cultural phenomena of tropical regions of the Portuguese world.[19] Since Freyre defines Lusotropicalism both as an epistemological project and a sensibility, we ought to wonder what he actually meant when he referred to it as "a way of being tropical." His own memories of his meeting with the Bengali poet Rabindranath Tagore at Columbia University in the early 1920s hint at a possible answer:

> Some of what I had found in his poems, reading them, myself, I now found in his Oriental person, in his gestures, in his voice. He sounded to my ears with a sound that was not entirely exotic in its way of giving vowels in English a value not usually given to them by Anglo Saxons. And I suddenly felt: there is something in the way of this East Indian speaking, as there is something in his written lyrical poetry, that makes a part of his person, and a part of his poetry, strangely familiar to me: to a Latin American. To a Brazilian. To a son of the tropics.[20]

The affirmation of a tropical empathy with Tagore shifts the cartography of Orientalism, transferring the locus of exoticism from Asia to northern Europe. In this operation resounds Victor Segalen's own critique of the uses of cultural diversity. In his *Essay on Exoticism*, Segalen pledges to avoid exclusive and familiar associations of exoticism with tropicality and the regime of geographic adventure: "Throw overboard everything misused or rancid contained in the word exoticism. Strip it of all its cheap finery: palm tree and camel; tropical helmet; black skins and yellow sun."[21] While Segalen's critique is against exoticism as escapism from contemporary capitalist society to a primitive tropical paradise, Freyre's emancipation of the tropics affirms their modernity. In other words, tropicality is the reason that Brazil is to occupy a central role in a reconfigured global scenario. In the metonym that closes the passage about Tagore—"strangely familiar to me: to a Latin American. To a Brazilian. To a son of the tropics"—Freyre extends his immediate northeastern Brazilian particularity (Pernambuco) to a larger definition of Brazil and even Latin America. This is why it is so productive to look at representations of collective identities transnationally. What is at stake here is Freyre's personal stance in the debates about the interpretation of Brazil from the 1920s and 1930s and their relation to foreign cultures in general.

As opposed to avant-garde intellectuals from São Paulo, such as de Andrade, who used the tropical particularity of Brazil as a metaphor in their relation to the foreign "cannibal culture," Freyre takes tropicalism at face value and, in the *Manifesto regionalista* (1926), argues that the tropical northeastern Brazil is the region that most faithfully embodies Brazilian identity as such. In other words, Freyre's map of Lusophony is defined in his own map of Brazil, which strives to revive the predominance of the decadent northeast in contrast to the booming industrial southwest.

Fragmentation

The last case is Bernardo Carvalho's *Mongólia*, one of the most accomplished novels published in Brazil in recent years. Carefully blurring the boundaries between fiction and history, the main narrator of *Mongólia* speaks from a position of critical consciousness regarding the traps of ethnographic discourse, a position of awareness of the contingent, and of the dangers of ethnocentrism.[22] The narrative juxtaposes three texts: the memoirs of a retired ambassador who is back in Rio de Janeiro; the travel journals of another Brazilian diplomat sent in a consular mission to Mongolia in search of a missing photographer; and the journal of the Brazilian photographer who had gone missing. These three documents reproduce itineraries and descriptions of "the Westerner" and "the misfit," as the two characters become identified in the text. The dialogue among the entries of the journals written at different moments in time portrays a double and contradictory representation: "É impossível que a pessoa que veio aqui e que falou que isso era de tal jeito não tenha visto que não era. Isso é irritante. O sentimento é de que você está sendo enganado a distância" (It's impossible that the person that came here and spoke like this wouldn't get it. It's so annoying. The feeling is that you are being cheated from a distance).[23]

Apart from questioning the photographer's entries, the Westerner writes against other Western stereotypes of Mongolia as a place forgotten by time and untouched by progress ("me pergunto se ele de fato esperava encontrar bons selvagens" [I wonder if he really was expecting to find good savages]). The most evident refutation of the diplomat is the deconstruction of nomadism: "A graça de visitar as iurtas é a surpresa do que se vai encontrar, a diversidade dos indivíduos que ali estão fazendo as mesmas coisas. O nomadismo em si não tem nenhuma graça. A mobilidade é só aparente" (The whole point of visiting the yurts is the element of surprise, the diversity of individuals always doing the same things. Nomadism as such is completely dull. Mobility is only apparent).[24] The Westerner does not ultimately deny the previous notion but does denounce the poverty in its observation: it is only in appearance that nomadism can be considered a dynamic state, since as much movement as there might be in a mobile lifestyle, the routines of mobility become considerably more systematic and monotonous than sedentary life. This inversion of meanings also occurs in relation to Buddhism, for after visiting several shrines and interrogating monks, the Westerner concludes that the transcendental silence of the monasteries actually conceals sexual abuses, perversions, and crimes. This discrepancy between what is exposed at a superficial level and what is ultimately revealed is not resolved by translation (as in Lisboa); rather, it yields to catastrophe: "Fico na impressão de que, na paz dessas paisagens despovoadas, a qualquer momento pode explodir a violência mais sangrenta, do atrito entre indivíduos alterados" (I have the impression that, in the peacefulness of these desert landscapes, the bloodiest violence can explode at any moment from the friction among these restless individuals).[25]

Throughout the novel, Mongolian identity is presented not in terms of its quaint, primitive traits but through the flattening effects of external influence, mainly Russian imperialism, which, as the narrators mention, forced rejection of the local religion, language, and education. Tourism has its flattening effects, too. There are several moments in one of the journals in which the authors express distress when Mongolians see Westerners and rush to put on their typical dress and offer them photographs, a gesture the Argentinean writer Cesar Aira describes as "ready-made exoticism," the moment in which the "Persian sells the Parisian the Persia the Parisian is expecting to see."[26] It is not only the traveler who goes in search of this automated experience (as in the case of photographers of the opium dens described in Lisboa's text), but also the local culture that changes to accommodate the expectations of an exotic gaze.

The polyphonic narration of *Mongólia* complicates the framework to read forms of diplomacy of exoticism, since the point of enunciation of such a gaze is no longer a unified voice. According to Pedro Erber, in Carvalho's ability to expose the subject's schizoid split, to dwell on the symptoms rather than conceal them, lies perhaps one of the privileges of literature as a discursive mode vis-à-vis the scientific discourse of anthropology.[27] So this leads us to wonder: to what extent are Lisboa's and Freyre's texts not eminently literary works, too? It is not just the narrative and essayistic quality of his prose that secured Freyre's work such a large audience in Brazil. It is also its oblivion, since later generations of Brazilian social scientists discarded his work as a mere apology for reactionary agrarian society. Also, to what extent is the access to "foreign" difference and the discussion of ethnography in Brazil necessarily mediated by the institutions of diplomacy? It seems that in all cases mentioned, the access of Brazilians to other regions of the globe is facilitated by an Imperial Mission of Friendship, Trade, and Navigation (in the case of Lisboa), a form of international cooperation between a Brazilian intellectual and Portugal (Freyre), or simply a novel about embassies, consuls, and diplomacy in general (Carvalho). It should be added that *Mongólia* was facilitated by a fellowship from the Portuguese Fundação Oriente to promote cultural exchanges between Portugal and Asia.

Even if Brazil has a long-standing tradition of diplomat writers, the fact that diplomacy is the practice of conducting negotiations among representatives of states supposes that it will inevitably operate at a level of discourse that implies fictional mediations. This brings us back to the starting point of the discussion of exoticism as a gaze that defines an exo or outside. It may appear that in their proposals of the "compatible" Chinese, the "familiar" Indians, or the "impenetrable" Mongolians, Lisboa, Freyre, and Carvalho operate within their own boundaries of cultural difference and thus reveal that exoticism is not so much the gaze of cultural difference as the negotiation of an unstable geographic and epistemological standpoint—in other words, a "fiction of identity."

NOTES

1. Luiz Ruffato, speech at the opening ceremony of the Frankfurt Book Fair, October 8, 2013, http://veja.abril.com.br/blog/rodrigo-constantino/cultura/o-discurso-de-luiz-ruffato-em-frankfurt.
2. Nielson, "Dispatch from Brazil," 91.
3. Dirlik, "Global South," 16.
4. De Andrade, "Manifesto antropófago," 4. Unless noted otherwise, all translations are mine.
5. Montaldo, *Ficciones culturales y fábulas de identidad*, 66.
6. Said, *Orientalism*.
7. Lisboa, *A China e os Chins*, 3.
8. Brook and Wakabayashi, *Opium Regimes*, 2.
9. Dezem, *Matizes do "Amarelo,"* 43.
10. Lisboa, *A China e os Chins*, 284.
11. I am referring to the paintings of Johann Moritz Rugendas (1802–58) and Jean Baptiste Debret (1768–1848).
12. Lesser, *Negotiating National Identity*, 14.
13. Freyre, *Aventura e rotina*, xxxii.
14. Freyre, *Aventura e rotina*, 255.
15. Freyre, *Aventura e rotina*, 259.
16. Freyre, *Aventura e rotina*, 256. The Mexican writer Octavio Paz follows a similar exercise in *Vislumbres de la India* by tracing the circulation of chili pepper from

Mexico to India and in *El signo y el garabato* by comparing the Portuguese architecture of Goa and Mexico City to formulate a theory of "Indo-American baroque."

17   The idea that Portuguese colonization experienced more miscegenation than other European forms of empire was also advocated by other interpreters of Brazil, such as Sergio Buarque de Holanda and Paulo Prado, yet in another tone. What Freyre understood as a peaceful—and loving—racial coexistence within the patriarchal structure, other historians read as violence and lust between the masters and the slaves: see Buarque de Holanda, *Raízes do Brasil*; Prado, *Retrato do Brasil*.
18   Freyre, *Casa-Grande e senzala*; Freyre, *The Masters and the Slaves*.
19   Freyre, *Portuguese Integration in the Tropics*, 10.
20   Freyre, "Tagore," 7.
21   Segalen, *Essay on Exoticism*, 18.
22   Erber, "Contemporaneity and Its Discontents," 34.
23   Carvalho, *Mongólia* 52.
24   Carvalho, *Mongólia*, 138.
25   Carvalho, *Mongólia*, 60.
26   Aira, "Exotismo," 75.
27   Erber, "Contemporaneity and Its Discontents," 32.

BIBLIOGRAPHY

Aira, César. "Exotismo." *Boletín del Centro de Estudios de Teoría y Crítica Literaria* UNR 3 (1993): 73–79.
de Andrade, Oswald. "Manifesto Antropófago." *Revista de Antropofagia* 1, no. 1 (May 1928): 3–7.
Brook, Timothy, and Bob Tadashi Wakabayashi, eds. *Opium Regimes: China, Britain, and Japan, 1839–1952*. Berkeley: University of California Press, 2000.
Carvalho, Bernardo. *Mongólia*. São Paulo: Companhia das Letras, 2003.
Dezem, Rogério. *Matizes do "Amarelo": A gênese dos discursos sobre ps orientais no Brasil (1878–1908)*. São Paulo: Associação Editorial Humanitas, 2005.
Dirlik, Arif. "Global South: Predicament and Promise." *Global South* 1, nos. 1–2 (2007): 12–23.
Erber, Pedro. "Contemporaneity and Its Discontents." *Diacritics* 41, no. 1 (2013): 28–48.
Freyre, Gilberto. *Aventura e rotina: Sugestões de uma viagem à procura das constantes portuguesas de carácter e acções*. Lisbon: Livros do Brasil, 1953.
———. *Casa-Grande e senzala*. Rio de Janeiro: Schmidt Editor, 1933.
———. *The Masters and the Slaves (Casa-grande e senzala): A Study in the Development of Brazilian Civilization*, 2d ed., trans. Samuel Putnam. New York: Knopf, 1956.
———. *Portuguese Integration in the Tropics: Notes Concerning a Possible Lusotropicology Which Would Specialize in the Systematic Study of the Ecological-Social Process of the Integration in Tropical Environments of Portuguese, Descendants of Portuguese and Continuators of Portuguese*. Lisbon: Realização Grafica da Tipografia Silvas, 1961.
———. "Tagore: A Brazilian View of His Lyrical Poetry." *Mosaic* 15 (1976): 7–11.

de Holanda, Sérgio Buarque. *Raízes do Brasil*. Coleção documentos brasileiros, 1. Rio de Janeiro: José Olympio, 1936.

Lesser, Jeffrey. *Negotiating National Identity: Immigrants, Minorities, and the Struggle for Ethnicity in Brazil*. Durham: Duke University Press, 1999.

Lisboa, Henrique Carlos Ribeiro. A China e os Chins, Recordações de viagem. Montevideo: A. Godel, 1888.

Montaldo, Graciela. Ficciones *culturales y fábulas de identidad*. Rosario, Argentina: Beatriz Viterbo, 1999.

Nielson, Rex P. "Dispatch from Brazil: Translation of Luis Ruffato's Speech at the Opening Ceremony of the Frankfurt Book Fair 2013." *Mester* 42, no. 1 (2013): 91–95.

Paz, Octavio. *El signo y el garabato*. Mexico City: Joaquin Mortiz, 1973.

———. *Vislumbres de la India*. Barcelona: Seix Barral, 1996.

Prado, Paulo. *Retrato do Brasil: Ensaio sobre a tristeza brasileira*. Rio de Janeiro: José Olympio, 1928.

Said, Edward W. *Orientalism*. New York: Vintage, 1978.

Segalen, Victor. *Essay on Exoticism: An Aesthetics of Diversity*. Durham, NC: Duke University Press, 2002.

Thomson, John. *Illustrations of China and Its People: A Series of Two Hundred Photographs, with Letterpress Descriptive of the Places and People Represented*, vol. 1. London: Sampson Low and Searle, 1873–74.

Chapter 2

Hearing Geography in Motion:
Processes of the Musical Imagination in Diaspora

KAY KAUFMAN SHELEMAY

Music can be said to be at home in circulation. Both through human movement and through virtual channels, music travels easily, including when unheard, embedded in human memory. When sounded, music's presence is temporal and spatial, moving through time and space simultaneously and carrying with it a surprising capacity to reaffirm and level boundaries, whether they are physical, social, or symbolic. Music might be described as a sonic chameleon as it adapts in the context of performance to new circumstances and settings. In sum, music occupies an exceedingly flexible position that permits both real and virtual boundary crossing in human sensory and social experience.[1]

Discussions of musical mobility and geographical border crossing have provided challenges to musical scholarship due to the strong grounding of the study of music in specific geographical areas and bounded national settings. Historical musicology long approached music through a dual conceptual frame: chronology (the heritage of art-history work) and nation (the heritage of nineteenth-century nationalism). Ethnomusicology brought to the broader musicological conversation the exploration of music beyond the boundaries of Europe, as well as new methods of musical ethnography. But the gravitational pull of the hierarchical national divisions of historical musicology, along with deep local cultural engagement, was strong enough to insure that ethnomusicology emerged with its own geographical hierarchies—notably, court music traditions of East Asia and Southeast Asia, along with West African drumming traditions. While the global circulation of popular music raised a challenge to conventional geographies in the late twentieth century, musical scholarship has been slow to explore the realm of the geographic imaginary and music's relation to it.

This chapter departs from the assumption that music is always malleable and vulnerable to transformation, even when anchored in stable settings. It seeks to move beyond stability to query what transpires when music travels, especially under circumstances of forced migration and exile. Later I explore music of the rapidly proliferating Ethiopian diaspora to understand the roles that music plays in both shaping and giving voice to the geographical imagination. I suggest that if we have failed to *see* the dynamic geographies that link seemingly separate domains, we might try instead to *hear* these geographies in motion. It is the imaginative geographies created by and expressed through music that are my subject, and it is on these acts of musical imagination that I focus.[2]

Edward Said is generally credited with introducing the concept of imaginative geographies in his classic volume *Orientalism*, bringing together notions of distance and difference in the regard to "others" from perspectives of the West.[3] But what transpires when both difference and distance are manifested within the individual experience, apart from relational perspectives conveyed through comparison with others? Here I explore imaginative geographies as processes that are in constant flux *within* a given community, foregrounding an awareness that "distance—like difference—is not an absolute, fixed and given, but is set into motion and made meaningful through cultural practices."[4] While most discussions of the geographic imaginary have been located in the domain of visual perception,[5] it is necessary here to write against conventional understandings of the word "imagine" as a process of forming a mental *image* of something that is not present.[6] I argue that music offers a striking case study of sound's imaginative capacities and that it offers models for interrogating its own geographic circulation.

The Background for Ethiopian Geographical Dispersion

Diasporic communities provide rich subjects for exploring geographic imaginaries: they bring into play simultaneously past and future, with the former homeland juxtaposed against the new home in ways that can coexist only in the imagination. Any present locale, including transit itself, may be said to exist on an intermediary, even liminal, plane, providing a flexible link in the transition from homeland to the next place of repose, mediating among different locales, as well as with the historical homeland.

Beyond these frequent spatial juxtapositions there are also marked temporal dimensions to musical imagining: while musicking at home, the sonic imagination may drift outward toward worlds yet to be explored.[7] Similarly, while musicking in diaspora, the imaginative ear and voice often turn back toward home. Over time, music can embed and link these sites as geographical imaginaries, creating sonic landscapes that could have emerged only over periods of time, generated through processes of travel and displacement. In addition, music becomes not just a carrier of real and imaginary places, as well as overlapping time continua; it becomes a locus of personal agency. Indeed, music achieves its greatest power as a register through which an individual can exert a measure of emotional control, however fleeting, over the unstable time and space of his or her existence by merging aspects of both in musical performance.

In the following pages we will consider musicking drawn from the diasporic experience of Ethiopians who left their homeland and went into exile after the beginning of the Ethiopian Revolution.[8] Here, the Ethiopian experience resembles that described by other artists and writers in diaspora, such as the Indian writer Salman Rushdie:

> It may be that writers in my position, exiles or emigrants or expatriates, are haunted by some sense of loss, some urge to reclaim, to look back, even at the risk of being mutated into pillars of salt. But if we do look back, we must also do so in the knowledge—which gives rise to profound uncertainties—that our physical alienation . . . almost inevitably means that we will not be capable of reclaiming precisely the thing that was lost; that we will, in short, create fictions, not actual cities or villages, but invisible ones, imaginary homelands.[9]

As the Ethiopian example demonstrates, the pathway toward imaginary homelands can take shape suddenly. In early 1974, Ethiopia was shaken by a wave of urban protests against famine and social inequality that soon led to widespread armed conflict. Within six months, these events ended the long reign of Haile Selassie I, who had begun his rule as regent in 1916 and assumed the throne as Ethiopian emperor in 1930. The revolution of 1974 replaced not just a longtime ruler; it also overturned the long-standing hegemony of the Orthodox Christian Amhara ethnic/religious community, which, although only about a third of the population, had for centuries dominated Ethiopian political, religious, and economic life.

By 1975, the emerging military dictatorship was headed by Mengistu Haile Mariam, an officer who ruthlessly jailed and killed opponents and oversaw the nationalization of all urban and rural land and buildings. Revolutionary violence forced hundreds of thousands to flee Ethiopia, some to refugee camps in Sudan and others to start new lives as exiles elsewhere in Africa and in Europe,

Australia, the Middle East, and North America.¹⁰ Musicians were part of this forced migration, among the earliest to depart as their livelihoods were disrupted by curfews and suspicion of political activism surrounded their activities.¹¹

In 1991, the province of Eritrea won its independence after a protracted civil war, and Mengistu was himself overthrown and exiled by forces from northern Ethiopia's Tigray Province.¹² This government has maintained its sway over Ethiopia for the more than two decades that have passed since the revolution's official end.¹³ One vital change was that after 1991, stringent travel restrictions imposed during the revolution were relaxed somewhat, opening the possibility for voluntary migration abroad, as well as for processes of return and visitation from diaspora to the homeland. Building on ethnic divisions that emerged during the revolutionary period, the post-1991 Tigrayan government restructured the Ethiopian regional map, dividing it according to ethnic groups (termed "nations") and introducing a multiethnic policy many viewed critically as a means to pit one community against another. The large number of Christian Amhara émigrés of the revolutionary years continued to grow in the 1990s, as did migration by members of other ethnic/religious groups, many of whom sought to escape both ethnic tension and economic hardship. Thus, political upheaval in 1974 initiated a period of population outflow from Ethiopia that continued under the post-revolutionary state. The outcome has been the establishment of an extended network of Ethiopian diaspora communities worldwide.

There may appear to be some irony in invoking Ethiopian subject matter as an example of a transnational geographic imaginary, given that the country often has served historically as a metaphor for geographic isolation by virtue of its nearly impassable Rift Valley topography crosscut by huge chasms. But Ethiopia did not "sleep for a thousand years," as some historical sources have proposed.¹⁴ Ethiopians were often on the move, if not in large numbers, as individuals and in small groups to other parts of Africa, to the Middle East, and, over time, to Europe. Yet there is no doubt that the mass population outflow since 1974 challenged the imagination of most Ethiopians, who were forced to reconceptualize their relationships to one another at home, as well as to their many friends and relatives now living in widely scattered locales internationally.¹⁵

These networks of new Ethiopian communities are linked by communications media of the late twentieth century and twenty-first century.¹⁶ They are also joined by sound recordings and by musicians who travel from place to place, performing at weddings, concerts, and community events. Since the early 1990s, too, migratory movements have come full circle, as many "diasporas,"¹⁷ especially musicians, have begun to travel back to visit Ethiopia, refreshing traditions there and carrying new Ethiopian styles worldwide. Although for some Ethiopians who are still at home this new, global Ethiopia remains both an imaginary and a mystery, for many in both urban and rural settings, the new mobility touches their lives frequently through family visits from abroad, repatriation of funds from diaspora to homeland, and the naming of newly constructed homeland sites that commemorate these new realities, such as Addis Ababa's Diaspora Square.[18]

Thus, beginning in the mid-1970s, Ethiopians moved from a relatively bounded locale in Africa's Horn to one of global dispersion and constant motion. In this compressed period of little more than four decades, the broader world moved from the position of a distant unknown to sites at the center of the Ethiopian experience. But the Ethiopian imagination has been further challenged both at home and abroad: at home, changes now include, beyond the new provincial mappings, massive growth of urban areas and new alliances with a series of countries that range from Cuba to China. In diaspora, Ethiopian immigrants inhabit many different and widely dispersed environments from which they must also reimagine the rapidly changing homeland they left behind. Nowhere are these disparate and disorienting experiences mediated more directly than through musical performance.

Two brief case studies can illustrate different aspects of the interactive and imaginative relationships between music and processes of Ethiopian diasporization. The first draws on the creativity of a single musician, while the second charts the course of a single song over a period of about twenty-five years. In offering these examples, I hope to clarify some of the interacting sonic and social dimensions that shape diasporic musical circulation—and that simultaneously command the Ethiopian imagination worldwide.

Case Study 1: The Music of Mulatu Astatke

The life and music of Mulatu Astatke provides our first example of the close and interactive relationship between the geographical imagination and musical processes. Born in Ethiopia around 1940, Mulatu has spent much of his life in transit between his homeland and the wider world, even before the formal advent of the global Ethiopian diaspora in 1974. Sent abroad by his parents as a teenager for schooling in England, Mulatu next decided to pursue jazz studies in the United States.[19] Having returned after nearly a decade abroad to build his career in Ethiopia, Mulatu has maintained his primary residence in Ethiopia while touring much of the time. While he did not become part of the permanent Ethiopian diaspora, one of his children lives in the United States.[20]

Mulatu Astatke is best known for innovating the musical genre named "Ethio-jazz," a style that he created while studying and playing jazz in the United States during the 1960s. Building on a foundation acquired in England, Boston, and New York and grounded in the modal jazz, bebop, and Latin jazz, Mulatu joined traditional melodies and modes from his Ethiopian homeland with these global styles. Thus, Mulatu's instrumental jazz is constructed of sonic content from his Ethiopian past fused with the musical styles and melodies he acquired over time and in different places.[21] For instance, Mulatu's best-known composition, "Yekermo Sew," quotes and transforms as its refrain a melody borrowed from "Song for My Father," a piece composed in 1964 by the Cape Verdean American jazz musician Horace Silver.[22] Melodic quotations and stylistic borrowings thus tie Mulatu's music simultaneously to the sonic world of his Ethiopian past and to the American jazz worlds of Boston and New York of the late 1950s and 1960s. Sound also implicitly acknowledges the sources of its own borrowings. For instance, "Yekermo Sew," which dates to the late 1960s,[23] foregrounds in solo passages both the instruments and the technology that came into prominence during that period, including the Fender Rhodes electric piano and the "fuzz box" pedal that creates distortion in electric guitar sounds.[24] The sound of Mulatu's music thus locates itself both temporally and spatially in particular times and places, its prominent ostinato implying motion. One devotee of Mulatu's music, the American film director Jim Jarmusch, perceived the imaginative geography of Mulatu's music so clearly that he referred to "Yekermo Sew" as "traveling music" and used it to accompany scenes of travel on the soundtrack for his film *Broken Flowers* (2005).[25] Mulatu's music does not map place in a cartographic or visual sense. Rather, through processes of musicking, it re-creates a sonic image of times and places that inspired its composer/performer's creativity and style.

Case Study 2: The Song "Tizita"

Music created and performed by an individual can encode a number of different times and places,[26] as well as imply movement between them over the course of time. The circulation of the same song by different musicians across boundaries of homeland and diaspora communities can provide grist for a more linear, though equally imaginative, embedding of both time and place through music. While Mulatu's music provides a site in which musical content and sound sources are absorbed within an individual's style over time, we can trace the imprint of different times and divergent spaces in five different versions of the same song. The spatial purview of this song is as global as that of the diaspora musicians who perform it, and once again, the song itself inevitably incorporates and sounds the temporal and spatial dimensions of its own mobility as experienced and imagined.

The song in question is titled "Tizita," which is usually translated as "Nostalgia" or "Longing."[27] Both its textual content and its melody signify deeply felt remembrance. Through its text, a rendition of "Tizita" can express powerful sentiments by the singer and elicit strong emotions from knowledgeable listeners. The textual content of the song varies, with most individual singers performing their own pre-composed text or, more rarely, improvising a text during a performance. Each "Tizita" conveys multiple layers of verbal meaning, employing the Ethiopian literary device of wax and gold to refer ambiguously to a beloved place or person, whether it is a site or individual left behind or one as yet to be experienced.[28]

In terms of its musical form, "Tizita" generally adheres to a modified strophic form that reflects the cadence of the "free poetry" (*sǝd gǝt'ǝm*) that the melody conveys. Each textual stanza has two lines of roughly equal length, with the melody of the rhymed second line contrasting to the first; most "Tizita" songs have a total of six to ten verses. A series of melodic patterns carry each line of the textual verse and return, often in different orders, in subsequent verses. Vocables are sung at the beginning of the song, usually following an instrumental introduction; they anticipate the opening melody of the lead verse and may recur during and at the end of the song, implying a type of refrain.[29]

The five renditions of "Tizita" discussed here illustrate the broad potential of the song to convey different aspects of the Ethiopian temporal and spatial imagination. I have purposefully selected both vocal and instrumental versions of the song because in the case of "Tizita," signification is conveyed by both text and tune. That is, "Tizita" is not just the name of the best-known Ethiopian song of longing; it is also the name of one of the four major categories of melody or mode employed within Ethiopian highland secular music. The tizita mode is based on an anhemitonic pentatonic pitch set,[30] which in its most straightforward form can be translated into Western scale degrees C-D-E-G-A.[31] Whatever the content of its accompanying text, should there be one, this pitch set and its characteristic melodic contours and ornaments convey a feeling of nostalgia and longing. Thus, a rendition of "Tizita," whether vocal or instrumental, embeds and conveys a strong sentiment of nostalgia to the listener. That this nostalgia may cut across both temporal and spatial domains is part of the song's ambiguity—and its power.

The five "Tizita" examples considered here are divided among homeland and diaspora renditions in a manner calculated to reveal the potential of the song's expressive capabilities.[32] They include renditions by the following artists, each of which is briefly described.

1 ASTER AWEKE (*Aster*, Columbia Records, Washington, DC, 1990, track 3)

Aster's traditional rendition of "Tizita" is accompanied by *krar* (six-stringed lyre) and was the first recording of the song to circulate globally. Aster, a popular Ethiopian singer, left Ethiopia for the diaspora (England, then the United States) in 1982. She provides a translation of her "Tizita"; the text is provided and discussed later. Aster's performance was recorded for and distributed on a Columbia Records CD in the early world music period. It is a traditional rendering of "Tizita" on a CD that otherwise contains popular numbers in a variety of styles, drawing on African American soul, funk, and rhythm and blues.

2 BEZAWORK ASFAW (*Tizitawoch Tizita [Tizita of Tizitas]*, Nahom Favorites, Washington, DC, 2010, track 5)

Having previously visited the United States on concert tours, Bezawork arrived in Canada from Ethiopia in 1990 and subsequently received asylum in the United States. She is known in Ethiopia as "the Queen of Tizita" and is featured singing "Tizita" in the BBC film *Under African Skies: Ethiopia* (1989). Bezawork's rendition is included on a compilation disc that presents performances of "Tizita" by different singers. Her recording for the CD was made in Washington, DC, with accompaniment by Ethiopian immigrant musicians, including the virtuoso Eritrean guitarist Selam (Selamino) Seyoum Woldemariam, and others on drums, synthesizer, and bass. In terms of its genre, Bezawork's recording of "Tizita" is a good example of the style known to Ethiopians as *bahel zemanawi* (traditional popular music)—that is, the tune and text are traditional, but the accompaniment is provided by a popular band.

3 GETATCHEW MEKURIA (*The Ex and Guests*, *Moa Anbessa [Conquering Lion]*, Terp Records, Amsterdam, 2006, track 8)

The saxophonist Getatchew Mekuria is a jazz legend in Ethiopia, where he lived in between concert tours until his death in 2016. Getatchew's recording of "Tizita" is one track on a CD with other Ethiopian repertory produced and performed by Getatchew in collaboration with the

Dutch band The Ex. The recording is titled "Conquering Lion," alluding to the Lion of Judah, the historical symbol of Ethiopia's Emperor Haile Selassie I. In the recording, Getatchew performs "Tizita" as a virtuoso saxophone solo.

4 VIOLIN (*Instrumental Music*, Asatamina Akafafay Master Sound, Addis Ababa, 2008, track 12)

A female violin trio trained at Ethiopia's Yared School of Music, a division of Addis Ababa University, performs "Tizita" in a 2008 recording made in Ethiopia. The impact of Western art music on this interpretation of the song reflects the longtime influence in Ethiopia of the Western bands and orchestras that proliferated under imperial sponsorship beginning in the 1920s. Today, the Yared School offers instruction in both Ethiopian traditional music and Western art music. The musical style and content embeds aspects of the last century of Ethiopian music history, presenting an imaginative transformation of "Tizita." The performance implicitly draws on decades of musical exchange with foreign styles in the Ethiopian homeland.

5 MICHAEL BELAYNEH WITH THE EITHER/ORCHESTRA (*éthiopiques*, *Volume 20: Live in Addis*, Buda Musique, Paris, 2004, track 6)

The Either/Orchestra of Somerville, Massachusetts, has been actively performing Ethiopian music since about 2000. This rendition of "Tizita" was recorded live at the Either/Orchestra's appearance at an international music festival in Addis Ababa, where one can hear the enthusiastic response of the Ethiopian audience in the background. The track appeared on volume 20 of the *éthiopiques* CD series, an ironic publication venue given that Russ Gershon, the leader of the Either/Orchestra, was first exposed to Ethiopian music (including the song "Tizita") through encounters with the earliest *éthiopiques* CDs released in the late 1990s. The vocal part is performed by a respected Ethiopian singer, Michael Belayneh.

Three vocal versions of "Tizita" are included here: performances by Aster Aweke, Bezawork Asfaw, and Michael Belayneh. Aster provides a translation of her Amharic text in the notes that accompany the recording. She translates "Tizita" as "memories," a common gloss of the word among Ethiopians:

You are my memory, I have no other memory.
Promising to come, yet breaking this promise yourself.
Please let him come by horse, softly,
A man of his kind never uses a mule.
My cry for your love has become music to your ear,
Music to your ear.

Please remember I am haunted by love and affection.
Look at me, I've grown thin because of your love.
I only wish I could be free of your love.
I imagined baking bread in an oven of moonlight.
How could people start gossiping about things I haven't done?
I see him every day in my daily dream.
My obsession with him has become my only food.
I am restless and sleepless in the middle of the night,
I am sleepless.

I wonder where my love is.
I wonder where my love is.
I wonder.

In this version of "Tizita," Aster appears to be singing to a male lover, for whom she pines and from whom she simultaneously desires to be free. The traditional images in the text—a lover of high social status riding a horse instead of a mule, the suggestion of gossip about a pregnancy only imagined—link her love to a personal attachment in Ethiopia. Yet at the same time, other verses of the song strongly imply an attachment to the homeland itself, which in diaspora can be said to have become the only memory and to have led to obsession, bad dreams, and the inability to eat. Given that much of Ethiopian traditional poetry—as well as daily speech—is replete with double meanings, Aster's "Tizita" can be argued to be purposefully ambiguous.

In the text, Aster sings, "My cry for your love has become music to your ear." Here "Tizita" embeds both a longing separated in time and space from the object of its affection and an effort to recover memories through a process of musical expression. Aster's text constitutes a classical expression of nostalgia, which has been defined as a longing for a home that no longer exists or, perhaps, may never have existed.[33] It has been suggested that the word "nostalgia" can convey two very different tendencies toward nostalgia, an argument predicated on the word's two roots. The first is a restorative nostalgia (from the Greek *nostos* "to return home"), which puts emphasis on restoring the past and proposes to rebuild the lost home or patch up memory gaps. The second, a more reflective nostalgia (from *algos* "pain" or *algia* "longing"), is proposed to encode longing and loss but through an imperfect process of remembrance.³⁴ Nostalgics of the restorative kind generally do not acknowledge their own nostalgia; they believe their project to be about truth and to manifest itself in the reconstruction of monuments of the past. Reflective nostalgics, in contrast, linger on ruins, the patina of time and history, and embed longing in the dreams of another place and another time. One can find aspects of both types of nostalgia in the three vocal renditions of "Tizita" discussed here, along with evidence of shifting times and places of performance. Aster's "Tizita" seems to express a restorative nostalgia, constructing a replica of the song with a traditional text as performed with lyre accompaniment in the distant Ethiopian past, a perfect aural imagination of an original from another time and place.

The rendition by Bezawork is less faithful to traditional homeland musical models, given its accompaniment by a modern band; it is also more reflective in its textual content.³⁵ Bezawork's lyric from 2010, composed by the poet Nigussie Te'amwork, "deals with an overall comparison of life in the past, versus the present, emphasizing changes observed in human relations and characters. . . . [The lyricist] portrays *təzəta* as everyone's faithful friend, a way of looking back to yesteryears in which more wisdom and maturity had prevailed. According to Bezawork, all these facts noted in the lyrics are related to her personal life and to her decades-long experience in exile."³⁶

Beyond the relationship of this song to temporal interactions of the past with and in the present, as well as in different locales, Bezawork has discussed the emotional impact induced by the song and its modal setting. She links the song to personal agency, describing how it enables her to express and manage her emotions about distance and diaspora even though she does not understand fully the song's power:

> When I sing "Tizita," I feel so many things, and then every time, if I miss something, I'm gonna sing "Tizita." And when I sing, I'm just crying. For when I miss my Mom, I'm just singing about my Mom. Every time, I'm just crying about what I feel like back home, feeling lonely. I'm just singing, and then, when I sing with the *tizita* melody, I'm gonna cry. And every time when I'm happy, or I love somebody, or I miss somebody, I can tell. And then, I don't know how to explain the *tizita* feeling. I wish somebody could explain it to me.³⁷

Michael Belayneh performs his "Tizita" with a text written by the lyricist Getinet Eniyew. The beginning of the text translates:

> *Təzəta* is poetry; *təzəta* is melody
> *Təzəta* is art; *təzəta* is life
> Something to live on during times of nostalgia
> Life and hope, dreams and reality
> Work and incident, living and destiny
> At times of conflict between the body and soul
> *Təzəta* is a treasure one is adorned to memorize the past.[38]

This "Tizita" song text links nostalgia for the past with dreams of the present and future, sentiments closer to the reflective performance discussed earlier. But while Belayneh performs "Tizita" in a very traditional vocal style and melody line in the recording made live in Addis Ababa with the Either/Orchestra, another version of his included on the recording *Tizita of Tizitas* (the same volume that contains Bezawork's solo), distributed in the United States, is accompanied by solo guitar and incorporates considerably more deviation from tradition.

These examples demonstrate both the global circulation of this Ethiopian song and the myriad ways in which it has been performed and reimagined in different times and settings. From Ethiopia to North America and Europe and back to Ethiopia, "Tizita" echoes in new renditions through the performance and agency of mobile Ethiopian musicians, as well as others who now perform the song. "Tizita" makes it clear how emotions of separation and loss can be conveyed through music and how a cry for love and land lost can indeed become "music to the ear."[39]

Conclusion

As Ethiopian musicians have crossed spatial and temporal boundaries, both their music and their lyrics have engaged repeatedly with places and times traversed, as well as with other music and even other versions of the same song. Mulatu Astatke's "Yekermo Sew" compresses decades of musical listening and performing both at home and abroad within the framework of a single composition. The music continues to travel and to change through both Mulatu's live performances and channels of technological mediation, extending the possibility of continued reinterpretations and new performances.[40] "Yekermo Sew" expresses nostalgia for places and times past while communicating a subtly articulated hope for the future through its title, which references the "new year" yet to be experienced.

In contrast, "Tizita" sustains a dual identity as song and mode, becoming a remarkably flexible vessel for many musical styles. "Tizita" song texts, purposefully ambiguous, are able to incorporate ideas that at once intertwine and contradict. The musical content of the song lends itself to stylistic colorings that are as diverse as those of a traditional folk song with lyre, a popular ballad, a saxophone improvisation, a Western violin trio, and a rendition accompanied by jazz band. Despite their differences, all of these versions of "Tizita" share elements of mode and form that trigger deeply felt emotions from performers and listeners. The song allows one to both sing and cry, as Bezawork has commented.

But here we can interrogate ways in which these examples speak more broadly to music's role in processes of migration and how these life-altering experiences are expressed and assimilated musically. Beyond the allusion to melodies and instruments from different times and places, it is clear that "Yekermo Sew" also conveys movement, sounding an ostinato that recurs and propels the music forward yet moves energetically in a direction that remains undefined, embedding multiple possibilities simultaneously. In "Tizita," both song text and melody overflow with expressions of longing and nostalgia but at the same time remain purposefully ambiguous, encouraging associations with whatever may be absent from the particular time and place in which it is heard. Both "Yekermo Sew" and "Tizita" share Ethiopian musical processes of repetition that can be discussed with attention to their relationship to repetitive musical structures of considerable cross-cultural significance.[41]

Here we can turn to late twentieth-century critical theory for additional insights. In *A Thousand Plateaus*, Gilles Deleuze and Félix Guattari propose the now well-known concept of the rhizome, defined as a system based on principles of connection and heterogeneity that at any point can be connected to anything other.[42] The notion of rhizome, with its unpredictable contents and constant movements, embraces multiple, heterogeneous elements but at the same time embeds aspects of consistency, that can be transformed by a new motion path, termed "a new line of flight."[43] Germane to this discussion is that the rhizome admits semiotic chains from every possible domain that can accommodate diverse modes of coding, making room for the interaction within it of music, text, and social and political history.[44] The rhizome framework further acknowledges that there will be breaks and ruptures between "regimes of signs and their objects," with the system proceeding to "start up again on one of its old lines, or in new lines."[45]

We find a great deal of resonance between the concept of the rhizome and the diasporic music of the modern Ethiopian diaspora discussed at length earlier. Beyond the clear presence of multiple and heterogeneous elements, principles of repetition—especially refrains and refrain-like structures—provide points of entry and exit through which content may be reconfigured to produce new trajectories on different levels. Here, theory meets indigenous Ethiopian practice in a most felicitous manner. For Ethiopian listeners, a predilection for repetition pervades most repertoires of both their secular and sacred music, providing a supportive framework for variation in multiple dimensions. In Ethiopian highland daily life, where the tizita mode is so central, most musical phrases and virtually every verse return to and reiterate a central pitch at their endings. So pervasive is this pitch that it is named the *melash*—literally, the "returning tone." In Ethiopian Christian chant, one finds this same, frequent return to a central pitch, with repetition realized on a broader plane of the entire ritual through multiple repetitions of the same chant in as many as five contrasting performance styles.[46] These deeply embedded patterns of repetition in Ethiopian Christian music and liturgy are also embedded in secular styles at the level of the individual strophe, which often returns as a refrain. It is not coincidental that *əzmatch*, the term in Amharic for a refrain, shares a root that translates as "to sing or intone." Repetition on different levels reinforces the impact of each chant and song, deepening their associations in the present moment with performances past. In this way, repeated performances of songs such as "Tizita," whether conveyed through live or mediated channels, reinforce the song's nearly universal power among Ethiopians, wherever they may hear it, while allowing new styles of musicking to arouse nostalgia for other places and other times.

In the essay "Of the Refrain," Deleuze and Guattari write about the territorializing role of the refrain and the ways in which the refrain (at this point of their discussion, the glass harmonica)

> is a prism, a crystal of space-time. It acts upon that which surrounds it, sound or light, extracting from it various vibrations, or decompositions, projections, or transformations. The refrain also has a catalytic function: not only to increase the speed of the exchanges and reactions in that which surrounds it, but also to assure indirect interactions between elements devoid of so-called natural affinity, and thereby to form organized masses. . . . It is of the nature of the refrain to become concentrated by elimination in a very short moment, as though moving from the extremes to a center, or, on the contrary, to develop by additions, moving from a center to the extremes, and also to travel these routes in both directions. . . . The refrain remains a formula evoking a character or a landscape, instead of itself constituting a rhythmic character or melodic landscape.[47]

Modes of expression such as musical repetitions and refrains allow musicians both to articulate place and time and to reference that which continues to exist only fleetingly within the lives of displaced and fractured communities. Musical performance, at least for a few moments, has the capacity to weld these fragmented worlds of diaspora into a fragile whole. Whether through the repetition of one song that unites many places and times or the repetition of a single song traveling across time and space clothed in different styles, these musical expressions become, for a time, more than music. They embrace and link what is otherwise separate and detached from one another, from the homeland, from all that was once assumed to be stable and connected. Here we arrive at the place of the musical imaginary within diaspora music making, where one indeed "ventures from home on the thread of a tune."[48]

NOTES

1 Here music may challenge the assertion that "language is the slipperiest of human creations; like its speakers, it does not respect borders, and like the imagination, it cannot ultimately be predicted or controlled": Greenblatt, "Racial Memory and Literary History," 62.
2 Derek Gregory has suggested that imaginative geographies are not only accumulations of time, sedimentations of successive histories; they are *performances of space* and that an act of performance serves to produce the effects that it names. Surely musical performance falls comfortably within this performative framework, simultaneously defining both temporal and spatial dimensions, and producing the effects it articulates: see Gregory, *Imaginative Geographies*, 18.
3 Said wrote, "For there is no doubt that imaginative geography and history help the mind intensify its own sense of itself by dramatizing the distance and difference between what is close to it and what is far away": Said, "Imaginative Geography and Its Representations," 55.
4 Gregory, *Imaginative Geographies*, 18.
5 Most notably, through the emphasis on visual skills in mapping and cartography: see Reder, *Kartographisches Denken*. For instance, in an exploration of travelers' texts, maps, pictures, and illustrations, Emma Teng suggests that these sources created a "new imagined geography of the expanded Qing empire": Teng, *Taiwan's Imagined Geography*, 5.
6 The word is derived from the Latin verb *imaginare*, which implies a visual element: see Merriam-Webster Dictionary Online, http://www.merriam-webster.com/dictionary/imagine.
7 The term "musicking" was coined by Christopher Small, who defines it as "tak[ing] part, in any capacity in a musical performance, whether by performing, by listening, by rehearsing or practicing, by providing materials for performance (what is called composition), or by dancing": Small, *Musicking*, 9. Small suggests that using the gerund "musicking" enables one to capture the temporal and social processes that music instantiates.

8 For additional information about this migration history, see Shelemay and Kaplan, "Introduction." This special double issue of the journal *Diaspora* (first published in 2011) was later published as Shelemay and Kaplan, *Creating the Ethiopian Diaspora*. We also incorporated examples that speak to the impact of diaspora and social changes under conditions of migration on homeland music traditions.

9 Rushdie, *Imaginary Homelands*, 10.

10 By the early 1990s, virtually the entire community of Beta Israel, formerly called Falasha and known since the 1980s as Ethiopian Jews, had left Ethiopia for Israel. The Ethiopian Jewish population in Israel today exceeds 125,000, the second largest Ethiopian diaspora community internationally after that of North America.

11 Musicians had a long history of political activism in Ethiopia, most particularly the *azmari* (minstrels), as they both spread news via oral tradition and sang songs with double meanings embedded in their texts, a traditional poetic device in the Ge'ez and Amharic languages known as *sem-enna werq* (wax and gold).

12 Ethiopians are traditionally called by their first names.

13 The date Genbot 20 (falling in late May of the Roman calendar, in contrast to Ethiopia's Julian calendar) has been celebrated annually in Ethiopia to mark the victory over the revolutionary government in 1991 and the establishment of a new regime under the leadership of the Ethiopian People's Revolutionary Democratic Front. May 28, 2014, marked the twenty-third observance of Genbot 20. The Ethiopian government was led by Meles Zenawi until his death in August 2012.

14 After Edward Gibbon's famous phrase, "The Aethiopians slept near a thousand years, forgetful of the world by whom they were forgotten": Gibbon, *The History of the Decline and Fall of the Roman Empire, Vol. 2*, 159–60.

15 The redrawing of longtime provincial boundaries into districts defined by ethnic identity represented a dramatic reordering of homeland space and identity; it also injected heated issues of ethnic boundaries and religious difference into diaspora politics worldwide. Ethiopian diasporic identity has been further challenged by encountering new concepts of racial difference, especially in the North American and Israeli diasporas.

16 See Hafkin, "Whatsupoch on the Net."

17 Ethiopians who live in diaspora are generally called "diasporas" by those in the homeland. "Ethiopian Americans in particular are referred to in Amharic-English as 'Whatsupoch' because of how they greet Ethiopians; *och* is the plural form of a noun in Amharic. In full English, they are called WhatsUps or Wassups": Hafkin, "Whatsupoch on the Net," 242.

18 Diaspora Square is located in the Bole area near the Addis Ababa airport alongside the Ring Road; by fall 2015, the Light Rail Project had opened two lines linking outlying areas of Addis Ababa to the city center: see Lidz-Ama Appiah, "Ethiopia Gets the First Metro System in Sub-Saharan Africa," CNN, October 14, 2015, http://www.cnn.com/2015/10/14/tech/addis-ababa-light-rail-metro.

19 See Shelemay, "Ethiopian Musical Invention in Diaspora," 306–9. I thank the Radcliffe Institute for Advanced Study at Harvard University for a cluster fellowship during 2007–2008 that brought the musician Mulatu Astatke, the historian

Steven Kaplan, and me together for a year's residency. To summarize briefly Mulatu's global trajectory, he switched from studying engineering in Wales to studying music in London, gaining broad exposure to an array of world music traditions. In 1959, Mulatu became the first African musician to study at the Schillinger School, the antecedent of the renowned Berklee College of Music in Boston. He resided and performed in New York City from 1960 until his return to Ethiopia later in that decade. Throughout his career thereafter, Mulatu traveled frequently for periods that ranged from months to a year, performing for global audiences, as well as for the new and growing communities of the Ethiopian diaspora.

20 Ethiopians and Eritreans are said to number at least 250,000 in the Washington, DC, metropolitan area, while more than a million immigrants from the African Horn reside in multiple urban locales across the United States and Canada, including Los Angeles, Atlanta, Dallas, Minneapolis, New York, Boston, Toronto, and, increasingly, western Canada. Sizeable Ethiopian and Eritrean populations reside permanently in the United Kingdom, Italy, the Netherlands, Australia, and New Zealand and in many locales across the Middle East and Africa.

21 For example, the composition "Yekermo Sew" is based heavily on the Ethiopian tizita mode. Mulatu was familiar with traditional music of the Ethiopian highlands, as well as with Ethiopian Orthodox ritual music from his childhood exposure. Instrumental jazz was also performed in Ethiopia as a result of the close alliance among Ethiopia, the United States, and Europe during and after World War II. Brass instruments of Western manufacture were introduced into Ethiopia much earlier, just before the turn of the twentieth century, and a distinctive style of Ethiopian big band music was already quite popular in Ethiopian urban settings by the 1950s. Although Mulatu surely conceived a creative, new, hybrid jazz style in the form of Ethio-jazz, he was not the first to perform jazz in his native land.

22 "Yekermo Sew" is an instrumental piece that uses a common jazz form that begins with a distinctive head—in this case, a transformation of both the melodic phrasing and rhythm of Silver's melody, along with expansion of its accompanying ostinato figure to reiterate the interval of an octave. The head is followed by a contrasting bridge, after which the head is repeated; the head and bridge together serve as a refrain with an A-B-A form. This refrain is followed by a series of solo improvisations, after which the refrain returns. For a lengthier discussion of "Yekermo Sew," see Shelemay, "Traveling Music." "Yekermo Sew" is also sung occasionally with a solo voice part. For a history of Horace Silver's "Song for My Father," the instrumental composition from which Mulatu quoted, see Rosenthal, *Hard Bop*, 48; Silver, *Let's Get to the Nitty Gritty*. Silver died in New York on June 18, 2014: Peter Keepnews, "Horace Silver, 85, Master of Earthy Jazz, Is Dead," *New York Times*, June 18, 2014, http://www.nytimes.com/2014/06/19/arts/music/horace-silver-85-master-of-earthy-jazz-is-dead.html.

23 "Yekermo Sew" was composed at the invitation of the Ethiopian poet and playwright Tsegay Gabre-Medhin (1936–2006) for his play of that name. Succinctly translated as "A Man of Experience and Wisdom," "Yekermo Sew" derives from a colloquial phrase in the national Ethiopian language, Amharic, with Orthodox

Christian associations: *Yekermo sew yəblan* (May He [God] make us people of the next year), a traditional New Year's blessing that prays the speaker and those addressed will live to see the next new year: Thomas Leiper Kane, *Amharic-English Dictionary*, vol. 2 (Wiesbaden, Germany: Otto Harrassowitz, 1990), 1384.

24 See Bacon, "Electric Guitar," 56–57; Bacon, "Fender."

25 Jim Jarmusch, dir., *Broken Flowers*, Focus Features Studio, 2005. "Yekermo Sew" can be heard on Mulatu Astatke, *éthiopiques 4. Ethio-Jazz and Musique Instrumentale, 1969–1974*, compact disc, Buda Musique, Paris, 1998. Most of the music mentioned in this article can be accessed through commercial recordings or on YouTube in multiple renditions.

26 Here Foucault's notion of heterotopia—heterogeneous spaces that are also heterochronies—seems congruent with the juxtapositions found in Mulatu's music and other diasporic musical creations: see Foucault, "Des espaces autres," 46–49.

27 The name of the song can be transliterated in different ways, although the spelling *təzzəta* properly represents the sixth-order vowels (pronounced like the "e" in roses), as well as the gemination of the consonant "z." For sake of simplicity and to avoid confusion for the reader who may wish to locate numerous recordings of the song on the Internet, the title hereafter will be transliterated as it is most commonly represented internationally: "Tizita."

28 As noted earlier, the "wax and gold" metaphor is applied to double meanings in Ethiopian poetry and speech, alluding to the lost wax process of gold casting during which the wax mold is melted by the gold inside it. There are different types of wax and gold literary constructions in the Ge'ez and Amharic languages. Some separate the wax and gold into successive couplets, while in others the wax and gold are combined in the same word or phrase, as in a pun. The most obscure type of double meaning provides only the "wax," with the "gold" to be unearthed by the listener. For a more detailed discussion of this poetic device of double meanings, see Levine, *Wax and Gold*, 5–9. In sum, Levine suggests that the wax-and-gold complex, if at odds with the ethos of modernity, constructs "a cult of ambiguity": Levine, *Wax and Gold*, 10.

29 Kebede, "The Music of Ethiopia," 100–103.

30 That is, a five-note scale without half-steps.

31 Mulatu's "Yekermo Sew" is also based in tizita mode but in a realization that today is termed its minor form (C-D-Eb-G-Ab). Various permutations of *təzəta* are discussed in great detail in Teffera, "Canvassing Past Memories through *Təzəta*."

32 Teffera, "Canvassing Past Memories through *Təzəta*." There she presents comments from fellow Ethiopians about the emotional impact of the song, discusses its musical characteristics, and compares a number of performances of "Tizita." Teffera's discussion overlaps with my inclusion of "Tizita" by Bezawork Asfaw, whom we have both interviewed. Teffera's article contains a particularly valuable appendix listing many additional traditional, modern, and instrumental versions of the song.

33 Boym, *The Future of Nostalgia*, xiii.

34 Boym, *The Future of Nostalgia*, xiii.

35 However, there does exist in the literature a colorful description of another performance by Bezawork that was not recorded but is said to have been an improvised, deeply painful, and reflective "Tizita." It took place in 1984 at a nightclub in Washington, DC, that hosted visiting Ethiopian performers and was described by Amha Ashete, the nightclub's owner, who recalls Bezawork's song as a "memorable and heartrending version. Visibly smarting from her recent romantic breakup, Bezawork improvised for 45 minutes on the torments of lost love, never repeating a single verse, as if pain heightened her inspiration. The audience was transfixed, somewhere between enchantment and fear": described by Francis Falceto in Francis Falceto, "Tezeta dans la musique populaire éthiopienne," in *Sentiments doux-amers dans les musiques du monde*, ed. Michel Demeuldre (Paris: L'Harmattan, 2004), 43. I thank Timkehet Teffera for bringing this source to my attention.
36 Teffera, "Canvassing Past Memories through *Tǝzǝta*," 9.
37 Bezawork Asfaw, interview by the author, Washington, DC, June 24, 2008.
38 Teffera, "Canvassing Past Memories through *Tǝzǝta*," 5.
39 Aster Aweke, *Aster*, CD, Columbia Records, NY, 1990, track 3.
40 Indeed, Mulatu himself continues to revise and alter this composition as it has traveled with him. "I have another idea also for '[Ye]Kermo Sew' to change it as well. I haven't finished with it yet!": Mulatu, quoted in Shelemay, "Traveling Music," 365.
41 For a nuanced discussion of repetition of short segments of sound (riffs) in jazz and the manner in which their deployment in various ways in African and African American music speaks to broader issues of global musical circulation and the need to engage with multiple levels of analysis, see Monson, "Riffs, Repetition, and Theories of Globalization."
42 Deleuze and Guattari, "Introduction," 7.
43 Deleuze and Guattari, "Introduction," 9.
44 Deleuze and Guattari, "Introduction," 6.
45 Deleuze and Guattari, "Introduction," 9.
46 For holiday rituals, an individual chant is sung first as plainchant without accompaniment in antiphonal style by two solo singers; second, in unison by all the musicians accompanied by rhythmic motions of their prayer staffs; third, by all musicians accompanied by rhythmic patterns sounded on sistra; fourth, by all musicians accompanied by rhythmic patterns of sistra and drums; and fifth, by all of the musicians, who sing and dance accompanied by drums, which eventually shift to double the pace, and clapping.
47 Deleuze and Guattari, "11.1837," 348–49.
48 Deleuze and Guattari, "11.1837," 310.

BIBLIOGRAPHY

Bacon, Tony. "Electric Guitar." In *The New Grove Dictionary of Music and Musicians*, vol. 8, 2nd ed., ed. Stanley Sadie, 55–58. London: Macmillan, 2001.

———. "Fender." In *The New Grove Dictionary of Music and Musicians*, vol. 8, 2d ed., ed. Stanley Sadie, 668. London: Macmillan, 2001.

Boym, Svetlana. *The Future of Nostalgia*. New York: Basic, 2001.
Deleuze, Gilles, and Félix Guattari. "Introduction." In *A Thousand Plateaus: Capitalism and Schizophrenia*, trans. Brian Massumi, 3–25. Minneapolis: University of Minnesota Press, 1987.
Deleuze, Gilles and Félix Guattari. "11.1837: Of the Refrain." In *A Thousand Plateaus: Capitalism and Schizophrenia*, trans. Brian Massumi, 310–50. Minneapolis: University of Minnesota Press, 1987.
Falceto, Francis. "Tezeta dans la musique populaire éthiuopienne." In *Sentiments doux-amers dans les musiques du monde*, ed. Michel Demeuldre, 43–44. Paris: L'Harmattan, 2004.
Foucault, Michel. "Des espaces autres. Hétéropies (1967)." *Architecture, Mouvement, Continuité* 5 (1984): 46–49.
Gibbon, Edward. *The History of the Decline and Fall of the Roman Empire*, 2 vols. Chicago: Encyclopedia Britannica, 1952.
Greenblatt, Stephen. "Racial Memory and Literary History." *Proceedings of the Modern Language Association* 116, no. 1 (2001): 48–63.
Gregory, Derek. *Imaginative Geographies: The Colonial Present; Afghanistan, Palestine, and Iraq*. Malden, MA: Blackwell, 2004.
Hafkin, Nancy. "Whatsupoch on the Net: The Role of Information and Communication Technology in Shaping of Transnational Ethiopian Identity." *Diaspora* 15, nos. 2–3 (2011): 221–45.
Katz, Mark. "The Rise and Fall of Grammophonmusik." In *Capturing Sound: How Technology Changed Music*, 109–123. Berkeley: University of California Press, 2010.
Kebede, Ashenafi. "The Music of Ethiopia: Its Development and Cultural Setting." Ph.D. diss., Wesleyan University, Middletown, CT, 1971.
Levine, Donald. *Wax and Gold: Tradition and Innovation in Ethiopian Culture*. Chicago: University of Chicago Press, 1965.
Monson, Ingrid. "Riffs, Repetition, and Theories of Globalization." *Ethnomusicology* 43, no. 1 (1999): 31–65.
Reder, Christian, ed. *Kartographisches Denken*. Vienna: Ambra, 2012.
Reyes Schramm, Adelaida. "Music and the Refugee Experience." *World of Music* 33 (1990): 3–21.
Rosenthal, David H. *Hard Bop: Jazz and Black Music, 1955–1965*. New York: Oxford University Press, 1992.
Rushdie, Salman. *Imaginary Homelands: Essays and Criticism, 1981–1991*. New York: Penguin, 1991.
Said, Edward W. "Imaginative Geography and Its Representations: Orientalizing the Oriental." In *Orientalism, 25th Anniversary Edition*. New York: Random House, 1994.
Shelemay, Kay Kaufman. "Ethiopian Musical Invention in Diaspora: A Tale of Three Musicians." *Diaspora* 15, nos. 2–3 (2011): 303–20.
———. "'Traveling Music': Mulatu Astatke and the Genesis of Ethiopian Jazz." In *Jazz Worlds/World Jazz*, ed. Goffredo Plastino and Philip V. Bohlman, 351–57. Chicago: University of Chicago Press, 2015.

Shelemay, Kay Kaufman, and Steven Kaplan, eds. *Creating the Ethiopian Diaspora: Perspectives from across the Disciplines.* Los Angeles: Tsehai, 2015.

———. "Introduction: Creating the Ethiopian Diaspora." *Diaspora* 15, nos. 2–3 (2011): 191–213.

Silver, Horace. *Let's Get to the Nitty Gritty: The Autobiography of Horace Silver*, ed. Phil Pastras. Berkeley: University of California Press, 2006.

Small, Christopher. *Musicking: The Meanings of Performing and Listening.* Middletown, CT: Wesleyan University Press, 1998.

Teffera, Timkehet. "Canvassing Past Memories through *Tǝzǝta*." *Journal of Ethiopian Studies* 46 (2013): 31–66.

Teng, Emma. *Taiwan's Imagined Geography: Chinese Colonial Travel Writing and Pictures, 1683–1895.* Cambridge, MA: Harvard University Asia Center, 2006.

Chapter 3

A Chinese Fan in Sri Lanka
and the Transport of Writing

XIAOFEI TIAN

This essay is a study of the mobility of people, things, and texts in an early period in East Asian history. Specifically, it is about a fifth-century Chinese traveler who spent more than a decade traveling through India and Southeast Asia and came home to tell his tale to an enraptured audience and about the world, or worlds, in which he lived. By examining this traveler's tale I intend to explore the issue of travel and identity, not just how seeing others and being seen by others produce the self, but also how going away creates a sense of home that enables the self to suddenly acquire an origin in both temporal and spatial terms. In other words, I am interested in how moving is conditioned by and, in turn, helps locationing; how moving from one point to another changes one's self-positioning with regard to the world and enables one to chart the world in different ways. I am also interested in the related question of how one orients oneself and navigates in the world outside empire, in the unknown territory where there are no preexisting roadmaps, signposts, and way stations. How does one position oneself in such a world and, upon encountering such a world, map it and articulate it?

The travel text under discussion, best known as *A Record of the Buddhist Kingdoms*, was written by a Buddhist monk named Faxian (ca. 340–422).[1] At Faxian's time, the Chinese empire was split between northern and southern rival states, with the north ruled by non-Han ethnic peoples. In the year 399, Faxian, along with several other monks, started out from Chang'an (modern

Xi'an), the capital of the northern state at the time, and embarked on an arduous journey to India in search of the complete Vinaya Pitaka—that is, texts outlining rules and regulations for Buddhist monks and nuns. The journey by land took him through nearly thirty kingdoms of Central Asia and India. Thirteen years later, in 412, he finally returned to China via the sea route from Sri Lanka. In the following year, he arrived at Jiankang (modern Nanjing), the capital of the southern state, and wrote an account of his travel. Although this was not the first travel text in the Chinese tradition, it is the first written Chinese account about traveling to foreign lands outside the traditional confines of the Chinese empire. As such, it appeared more than two centuries earlier than, and set a model for, the famous account of India written by the monk Xuanzang (ca. 602–64), which inspired the beloved sixteenth-century novel *Journey to the West* or, in Arthur Waley's masterly translation, *Monkey*.

The immense interest of Faxian's account primarily lies in the fact that it is the first extant first-person narrative about traveling to a foreign world. If a map is a peculiar sort of visual text, then his text is a peculiar sort of textual map for a world that had had no map. People knew that world existed because they saw people coming and going from there; although there were surely many oral reports, no traveler had told his tale quite in the same way as Faxian did. Prior to Faxian's work, accounts of foreign lands had usually appeared in dynastic histories as a sort of ethnographic record, written in a dispassionate, objective style, organized by kingdoms in terms of their distances from the Chinese empire. In contrast, Faxian's account is given as a first-person linear narrative, beginning with the initiation of his journey and ending with his return. In it, time is an important organizing principle: space is arranged on the axis of temporal progression as the author negotiates political geography, religious geography, and cultural geography in the multilingual and cross-cultural worlds further complicated by political boundaries. Faxian's account provides the first guidebook for an unmapped world at a time when seeing the foreign world was not yet preconditioned by a textual tradition with fixed conceptual categories and rhetorical tropes. His account subsequently became one of the foundational texts that helped establish those conceptual categories and rhetorical tropes in the Chinese tradition. Its influence can still be seen in Chinese writings about the encounter with the foreign in the nineteenth century, a period in Chinese history that forms a parallel with Faxian's age because of the unprecedented scale of encountering the foreign—in this case, the Western nations. But Faxian's age recedes farther back in time, and, to use a metaphor of travel, distance offers a better perspective on how encounters between different worlds are played out.

Peripatetic Body and Kinetic Vision: Faxian's Time

Faxian's account, which has been studied mainly by historians and scholars of religion but whose significance goes far beyond these fields, is emblematic of an age characterized by mobility and dislocation. The fourth century through the seventh century is usually referred to as the "early medieval period" or the "early Middle Period" in Chinese history. During this period, people were engaged in more physical movement than ever before, traveling both within China and beyond.[2] Within China, the constantly shifting and highly permeable border between the northern and southern states led to significant mobility. This fluid territorial boundary was mainly traversed by three categories of people: members of the Buddhist clergy; diplomats and emissaries going back and forth between the northern and southern states; and merchants. Traders and members of the Buddhist clergy also went far beyond China, by land and by sea, to South, Southeast, Central, and Western Asia, as well as to Europe. Exuberant contact existed among China, the Sassanid Empire, and the Byzantine Empire, as testified by the remains of material culture—for instance, the exquisitely crafted artifacts that bear Roman, Greek, or Sasanian influence, as well as the Sasanian and Byzantine coins and bracteates excavated from the tombs of Chinese aristocrats in North China.[3] At the same time, many foreign traders and foreign monks and nuns also came to China.

Not only were people and goods moving around, but texts and images were in constant traffic during this period. Buddhist texts and images were pouring into China from India, as well as from various Central Asian states. The translation of Buddhist literature from Sanskrit into Chinese was either sponsored by the state or undertaken privately; its vast scale was unprecedented in world history at this point. From the fourth century onward, China also became a clearinghouse that further transmitted Buddhist texts and images to East Asian states. The Chinese monk Tanshi was credited with spreading Buddhist teachings in Goguryeo (Gaogouli in Chinese records), the ancient Korean kingdom whose territory encompassed the northern and central parts of the Korean Peninsula, in the last decades of the fourth century. A hundred years later, Tanchao followed in his footsteps.[4] Diplomatic missions from Baekje or Baiji, another Korean kingdom located in southwestern Korea, had sought Buddhist images and texts from the Chinese court in the south, and it was from Baekje that Buddhism was introduced into Japan in the early sixth century.[5] Apart from trade, Buddhism seems to have been the most important link among the different cultures and regions in Asia.

A religion of peripatetic bodies and kinetic vision, Buddhism has had an influence in China that far exceeds the spiritual realm. The life of the Buddha himself proves exemplary. By traditional account, the Buddha was born as a royal prince and was prophesied to become either a great monarch or a great holy man; his father, the king, thus confined him to the palace to shield him from the outside world and keep him content with sensual pleasures. But the Buddha went out, saw an old man, a sick man, a dead man, and a monk; he was awakened to the suffering of human life and decided to pursue a religious path. Except for the famous period of forty-nine days of sitting in meditation under the Bodhi Tree to obtain enlightenment, the Buddha spent his life traveling from place to place, first in pursuit of enlightenment and, once he had attained it, teaching.[6] Movement is the key in the Buddha's life. The body in meditation is contrasted with and conditioned by the body in motion, and yet meditation is only another form of moving, as the meditative mind goes on an inner journey, figuratively and literally. A common form of meditation in early medieval China was to visualize oneself being transported to the Buddhist paradise known as the Pure Land presided over by Amitābha Buddha in the west.[7] This particular meditative practice was an important part of the foundations for the Pure Land Sect, which, in Arthur Wright's words, "was eventually to become the most popular form of Buddhism in eastern Asia."[8]

Various forms of motion thus characterize early medieval Chinese Buddhism: translation of texts, practices, and ideas; transposition of Buddhist monks and nuns; transportation of the meditative mind to alternative states of being. There was a great emphasis on mobility among the Chinese Buddhist clergy. The Chinese term for entering the Buddhist religious order is *chujia*, which literally means "leave family/home." The term *youhua* (*cārin* in Sanskrit), which means "travel around to transform or convert," is a key term in the massive *Gaoseng zhuan* (Lives of the Eminent Monks), written by the scholar-monk Huijiao (ca. 497–554), which includes the life stories of more than 250 Chinese and non-Chinese monks who lived from the second century until Huijiao's time.[9] The action frequently associated with *youhua* is *guan feng* or *guan fengsu* (observing the [local] customs) during one's travels. "Observing the customs" refers to the observation of the manners of the folk and has a strong Confucian association; in a Buddhist context, it is used, along with *guan hua* (observing [life's] transformations), to indicate a monk's or nun's observation of the world's vicissitudes to achieve enlightenment.[10] The motifs of *youxue* (traveling around to pursue one's studies) or *youfang wendao* (traveling around in quest of the Way) and of seeing holy sites also appears repeatedly in the accounts of the "eminent monks" of early medieval China.[11]

Many anecdotes in the *Biographies of Eminent Monks* attest to the importance explicitly attached to travel. The monk Baoliang (ca. 444–509), for instance, planned to travel around and propagate Buddhist teachings, but he was so attached to the monastery where he had been staying since childhood that he could not bring himself to leave. His teacher urged him to go, saying, "How can you be so trapped by the net of affection and not contribute to the dissemination of our Way?" At this Baoliang was moved to begin his extensive travels.[12] Sometimes the urging came in dream visions. Dharmayasas (fl. early fifth century), a monk of Kashmiri origin, dreamed that Virūpākṣa, the three-eyed guardian king of the west, had chided him for staying in one place to work on his own spiritual progress without roaming in the world of men to bring salvation to others. When he awoke, he decided to embark on his journey. He had traveled in various countries of Central Asia before he reached China in the early fifth century and became well known as a great translator of Buddhist scriptures.[13] Similarly, the Chinese monk Tanbin (ca. 409–475), troubled by questions about the Buddhist scriptures, had a dream in which he was told by a Buddhist deity to set out on a journey: "The questions you have about the doctrine will be resolved of themselves during your travels." Tanbin subsequently traveled to several monasteries in South China to study with different teachers before he returned to his native region.[14]

Buddhism offered women a legitimate opportunity to travel on their own initiative and independently of their families—notably, their husbands or fathers. This was something that Chinese women, especially elite women, had not been able to do until the spread of Buddhism. *Biqiuni zhuan* (Biographies of Buddhist Nuns), composed by the monk Baochang (ca. 460s–530s?) in the year 517, records sixty-five prominent nuns living from the fourth century through the early sixth century, and nearly one-third of them had traveled extensively.[15] Daoyi (fl. late fourth century), for instance, was so attracted to the many religious activities in Jiankang, the capital of the southern Chinese state, that she traveled a considerable distance to take up residence there in the 390s.[16] Daoyi was accompanied by her nephew, who was a monk.[17] Senggai (ca. 430–93), by contrast, seemed to have no travel companion other than the fellow nun Fajin, with whom she journeyed from north to south China in 473 and took up residence in Jiankang.[18] In 429, a group of nuns from Sri Lanka arrived at Jiankang. A few years later, another group of eleven Sri Lanka nuns, led by Tiesaluo (whose name is also rendered as Tessara and Devasārā from the Chinese transcription) reached Jiankang and joined the earlier group, who by this time had learned to speak Chinese. They carried on many exchanges with the local community of Chinese nuns.[19] A Chinese nun, Sengjing (ca. 403–86), was so inspired by meeting these foreign nuns that she, too, desired to travel overseas, although unfortunately she was unable to undertake the journey.[20]

As we can see, the time and the world in which Faxian lived and wrote his travel account were characterized by various forms of motion in artifacts, images, texts, practices, and ideas. It is perhaps worth mentioning here that fortuitously, the first travel narrative in the Christian European world was produced around the same time that Faxian wrote his travel account; it was written by a Christian woman named Egeria, who went on a pilgrimage to the Holy Land and from there wrote a letter to her "sisters" at home.[21] Little is known about this Egeria beyond her writing. While some scholars speculate that she was a nun, others express doubt on the ground that mobility was not encouraged in early Christian monasticism. As one scholar states, "Egeria's unusual freedom of movement and obvious affluence point away from a strictly organized monastic circle, that would have curtailed mobility and expenses, in the direction of a bourgeois milieu," for "only urban wealth based on trade can plausibly account for what appears to be her contacts spread over the empire like a commercial network."[22] Indeed, the famous *Regula Benedictina* (Rule of Benedict), written in Italy in the mid-sixth century, advocates a life of stillness in a monastery under the authority of an abbot and denounces the "gyrovagues"—that is, monks wandering from one place to another. Granted, there is always a gap between prescribed and actual behavior, and the very vehemence with which early Christian writers denigrated religious wandering and sought to control it seems to point to the popularity of monastic movement. As Maribel Dietz's study shows, religious travel was a common phenomenon in the Mediterranean world during the late antiquity despite the denial of its value.[23] Nevertheless, the stipulated norms for proper conduct in the surviving monastic rules from this period form an interesting contrast with contemporary Chinese Buddhist practice that held "roaming" (*you*) to be an important religious duty for monks and nuns. This is a divergence that perhaps can be partially explained by the different stage of development of Buddhism in China from that of Christianity in the West.

Heaven and Hell, Center and Periphery: The Dialectics of Faxian's Travels

The story of Faxian in the sixth-century *Biographies of Eminent Monks* fills us in about Faxian's early life.[24] Born around the year 340, Faxian was a native of Shanxi, in North China, and his secular surname was Gong. He had three elder brothers who all died very young. Believing that joining a religious order would save Faxian from his brothers' fate, Faxian's father had him ordained as a śrāmaṇera (Sanskrit for novice monk) when he was only two, though he apparently still lived at home with his parents. One day, Faxian became violently ill. His parents sent him to the monastery, where he recovered overnight, and he henceforth refused to return home. His father passed away when he was nine, and his uncle was going to force him to abandon his religious vows. Faxian again refused, saying, "I did not 'leave home' because of my father's command. I wanted to stay away from the dust and the crowd of the world, and that was why I decided to enter a religious life."[25] Moved by the words, his uncle gave up his attempt.

The other anecdote about Faxian's early life relates how he confronted bandits who tried to take the grain he and his fellow monks were harvesting from the field. While the others ran away, Faxian stayed to face the bandits and reportedly told them that he was more concerned about their sin than about the grain, because they would have to pay for the robbery in the next lifetime. The bandits were so impressed by his words that they left the grain untouched.

From these accounts his biographer immediately moves to a general description of Faxian at twenty, when he was ordained as a bhikṣu: "He was bright and sagacious in his aspiration and conduct, dignified and somber in his bearing. He often lamented the incomplete state of the Vinaya Pitaka [in China] and vowed to seek it. In the third year of the Long'an era of the Jin dynasty [399], together with his fellow monks Huijing, Daozheng, Huiying, Huiwei and so forth, he set out from Chang'an."[26]

The way in which the narration is given makes it impossible to tell that Faxian actually did not embark on his journey until he was in his late fifties. Between his ordainment as a bhikṣu and his legendary journey there was a remarkable gap of nearly four decades, about which we know next to nothing. What happened to Faxian in those decades, and what motivated him to begin traveling at such an advanced age (by contemporary standards), are questions to which we will probably never find answers. What we do know is that Faxian undertook his journey with a specific purpose in mind, in contrast to many contemporary religious travelers, who traveled for the general purpose of spreading Buddhist teachings or seeing holy sites. Therefore, Faxian's travel account is not just a narration of what happened along the way but a teleological narrative, beginning with a quest and ending with the mission accomplished.

Underlying the linearity of the narrative are two types of movement: one is going through hell to reach heaven, and the other is going from the periphery to the center. The first type of movement was a cultural narrative familiar to Faxian's contemporaries. By a "culture narrative," I refer to a story that appears in different types of texts and is well known to members of the society, whose recognition of the structure of the story, however, needs never to be articulated as such.[27] In this cultural narrative, a person experiences much hardship to attain heavenly bliss, and yet, once in paradise, the person longs for the mortal world and chooses to return to it—hence, losing paradise. The most famous example of such a narrative is "Account of Peach Blossom Spring," written by Tao Yuanming (Tao Qian, 365–427), one of the greatest Chinese poets. It is justly called "one of the most beloved stories in the Chinese tradition."[28] In the account, a fisherman, lured by a forest of flowering peach trees, sails up a stream to find the end of the forest; at the end of the forest he finds a mountain, and, after passing through a narrow opening in the mountain, he comes upon a utopian land. There a small farming community enjoys life without a ruler, a state, or a sense of history. They ask the fisherman what time it is in the outside world, for "they didn't know of even the existence of the Han [dynasty], much less the Wei or Jin [dynasty]."[29] The fisherman is treated with hospitality; after he leaves, he marks the route at every step and reports his experience to the local magistrate. The magistrate sends people to follow the route, but they can never find the place. In a more fantastic reworking of the theme, popular paradoxographical writings known as *zhiguai* (accounts of anomalies) record mortal men's unexpected encounters with goddesses. In those writings, a mortal man typically meets a goddess, falls in love, and stays with her in the divine realm; one day, he feels homesick for the human world and takes leave of the goddess, and, as often happens, he is unable to find his way back to his immortal beloved.[30] Buddhist miracle tales flourishing during this period bring a religious twist to the theme, having the protagonist literally going through hell and witnessing hell's horrors before achieving enlightenment and salvation.[31] In this Buddhist variation, however, there is no going back once the protagonist finds faith.

In Faxian's account we can easily discern the plotline of progressing from hell to heaven and back. The treacherous terrains he traverses are often described in demonic terms, as Faxian recalls the "evil spirits and hot winds" of the desert where the only road markers were dead men's bones, or the gale, sleet, sand, and rocks spewed out by the "poisonous dragons" of the Pamir Mountains.[32] Once he reaches Central India, regarded as the Holy Land by Buddhists because it is where the Buddha obtained enlightenment, all perils and hardships vanish; we are presented with an ecstatic description of an earthly paradise. Although Faxian continues to travel after this point, the depiction of a dangerous and terrifying environment reappears only in his account of his return journey to China. Central India is thus the paradise surrounded by forbidding territory.

Faxian provides an idealized account of Central India, where there are no household registers, official code of law, or corporeal or capital punishment—in many ways, a reverse image of the Chinese regimes of the time. We are also told that the land there is flat and level, with no steep mountains or large rivers; the climate is temperate; and the people are perfectly happy.[33] The topography of Central India echoes not only the description of the Western Paradise in Buddhist scriptures—"the land, made of Seven Jewels, is all level and flat"[34]—but also that of Tao Yuanming's secular paradise in the "Account of Peach Blossom Spring," with its land "broad and level." The veracity of Faxian's account is not the issue here; rather, what he already knows and what he expects condition what he sees, and his representation of the Buddhist paradise is based on a discursive model he has already learned well from the sūtras.

What makes Faxian's travelogue particularly fascinating is that onto the account of going through hell to heaven he grafts the narrative of moving from periphery to center. Throughout his travelogue, Faxian explicitly refers to China as *biandi* (borderland) and Central India as Zhongguo (the Middle Kingdom), a term that traditionally had been used to indicate the northern Chinese heartland (and, in modern times, has been used to indicate China itself). The acknowledgment of Central India as the Middle Kingdom and the center of the world reflects the Buddhist perception of geography. As a devout Buddhist, Faxian clearly embraced this notion, which was still controversial among his Chinese contemporaries. The awareness of being someone from the borderland, however, seems to have been awakened in him and intensified when he became the object of scrutiny in his travels. In his account, Faxian noted two such occasions. The first occurred in the kingdom of Bhida, in western India, where the locals were amazed by the sight of Faxian and his companions. "When they saw us Qin monks, they were greatly moved," he writes. "They said: 'How could these men of the borderland become ordained as monks and travel such a great distance to seek the Buddhist Law?'"[35]

The second occurs at the Jetavānā Monastery in Central India: "The monks came out and asked us: 'Where did you come from?' We answered, 'We came from the land of the Han people.' The monks said with a sigh, 'How extraordinary is it that men from a border country should come to this place for the sake of seeking the Law!' They remarked among themselves, 'Our teachers and brethren have succeeded one another in this place for a long time, but none has ever seen a Han monk come here before.'"[36] These two passages forcefully call attention to the sign of racial difference inscribed on the bodies of the Chinese travelers and to their own sense of foreignness in encountering the foreign.

The construction of a new self-identity as the travelers penetrate deeper and deeper into the foreign territories is nowhere more apparent than in the shifted self-reference in the two passages quoted earlier. In the first, Faxian refers to himself and his fellow travelers as "Qin monks," Qin being the name of the northern region of China in which he started his journey; in the second, he states they "came from the land of the Han people." "Han" is the name of the Chinese empire that lasted from the second century BC to the second century AD; in Faxian's day, the term was used ethnically to refer to the native Chinese, in contrast to the nomadic people who ruled over North China at the time. The change from Qin to Han indicates a shift from a political to an ethnic construct. The traveler's identity is thus constantly being performed through motion, through seeing and being seen.

Significantly, the process of moving closer to paradise and center coincides with a gradual dispersal of his fellow travelers. Faxian had set out with four other monks, and soon afterward six more joined the expedition. Along the way, however, some left for another destination; some returned to China; and some died. The dispersal of the community culminated in the departure of the last of Faxian's fellow travelers, the monk Daozheng, who decided to stay in Central India and never go back to the "borderland." Faxian was alone when he embarked on his journey home. In a generally terse account, it is noteworthy that Faxian records with great care and precision each instance in which he was separated from his fellow travelers. As in a certain type of Hollywood movie, the last person left standing in a group of adventurers is the one who has penetrated the heart of darkness, solved the mystery, and won the battle against a hostile universe. The dispersal of the community is a powerful reminder that traveling in the fifth century was a rite of passage and a test of faith: the road offered a series of trials, and the travelers most certainly were, to reverse what John Ruskin implied about modern railroad traveling, *touched* by the space traversed.[37] The touching was both literal, as Faxian and his companions traveled on foot, and metaphorical, because a traveler, unlike a tourist merely skimming the surface of a culture, is always changed by the journey.

"Homeless at Home": The Transport of Writing

What, then, changed for Faxian? And how did the change occur? Change, I argue, began to take shape when the last of Faxian's fellow travelers made the decision to stay in Central India: "After he came to the Middle Kingdom, Daozheng witnessed the rules of conduct by which the local Buddhist clergy abided, and saw that the monks' dignified demeanor and behavior were worthy of observing under all circumstances. He recalled with regret that back in the borderland of Qin, rules and regulations in Buddhist monasteries were incomplete. He vowed never to be born in the borderland again until achieving Buddhahood. He thereupon stayed there and would not turn back."[38]

When one finally reaches heaven after going through hell, it is perhaps only natural to want to stay and enjoy the blank, writing-less state of "living happily ever after." The question is: what makes a person voluntarily leave such a state? In Faxian's case, the obvious answer is that he had a mission to accomplish: "My original aim was to seek the Vinaya Pitaka and have it circulated in the land of the Han people, so I went on the return journey alone."[39] But ending the blissful state of being in paradise requires an act of supreme willpower, and exactly when to head back is not as easy to decide as we might imagine. As we will see, the loss of his fellow travelers played a distinct role in Faxian's decision to take action, but, remarkably, the loss was brought home to him through a powerful visual image in a monastery at Sri Lanka:

> In the monastery there was a hall decorated with gold, silver and all kinds of precious stones. Inside there was a statue of the Buddha in green jade, which was about thirty feet tall, and shone forth with the fiery light of the Seven Jewels. Its majestic form was solemn and dignified beyond description. In the Buddha's right palm was a priceless pearl. I had been away from the land of the Han people for many years; all the people I associated with were foreigners, and my eyes had not seen familiar mountains, rivers, trees and plants for a long time. My fellow travelers were all gone: some stayed behind and some had died; there was only me left looking upon my own shadow. My heart was constantly filled with melancholy. Then, all of a sudden, in front of the Buddha's jade statue, I saw a white silk fan from the land of Jin, presented by some merchant as an offering to the Buddha. At that moment, I could not help my tears.[40]

Throughout his account, Faxian records no more than three occasion of shedding tears. The first comes when one of his fellow travelers, Huijing, dies crossing the Snowy Mountains; the second is when he witnesses the site of Buddha's preaching on Vulture Peak Mountain and is filled with longing for the long-departed Holy One; and the third is when he sees the white fan in the Sri Lankan monastery. Each time, tears are induced by the pain of separation, by an unfulfilled desire for connection to community. This passage is particularly striking in its stark contrast of the material splendor and opulence of the monastery and the plain silk fan: on the one hand, there are gold, silver, jade, pearl, precious stones, and the impressive height and weight of the Buddha's statue; on the other, there is a fan made of white silk, almost immaterial in its smallness and lightness, a humble offering to the Buddha from a Chinese merchant, perhaps taken directly from his stock of merchandise. Yet while the monastery and the statue of Buddha incite admiration, it is the plain little fan that provokes in Faxian an overwhelming emotional response. Significantly, the fan is from the "land of Jin," the regime in South China. Here it needs to be mentioned that the white silk fan is a quintessentially poetic image in early Chinese classical poetry. In the canonical poem known as "Yuan ge xing" (Song of Reproach) or more simply as "Shan shi" (Fan Poem), attributed to a court lady of the first century BC, the white silk fan, "fresh and pure like frost or snow," becomes a figure of a woman who fears she may be abandoned by her lover, just like the fan that is put aside in the cool autumn weather. The word for "silk" in Chinese, *si*, is a pun on "longing" (also *si*), which indicates either love-longing or homesickness; this pun figures prominently in contemporary popular songs from South China. Thus, after an epic journey that lasted fourteen years and crossed thirty kingdoms, Faxian takes comfort not in a religious icon but in a resonant cultural image that has been made accessible by a commercial network.

The network of trading played an instrumental role in Faxian's journey home in yet another way, for he returned via a sea route, boarding a merchant ship. After a long and perilous sea voyage, during which he almost lost his life, Faxian finally arrived in the Chinese territory ruled by the House of Jin. He describes the moment of homecoming:

> After going through perils and hardships, with days on end filled with worries and dread, we finally came on shore. Seeing pigweeds and beans, we knew it was the land of Han. But without seeing any human trace, we did not know where we were. Some said that we had not yet reached Guangzhou, while others thought that we had already passed it. No one knew for sure. Some sailors got into a little boat and sailed inland on a stream. They found two hunters and brought them back to the ship. They made me their interpreter and questioned them. After calming the hunters down with kind words, I asked them leisurely: "What sort of men are you?"
>
> "We are followers of the Buddha," they said.
>
> "What are you looking for in the mountains here?" I asked.
>
> They fibbed, saying, "Tomorrow is the fifteenth day of the seventh month, and we are going to pick some peaches as offerings to the Buddha."
>
> "What country is this?" I asked again.

"This," they said, "is the Prefecture of Changguang in Qingzhou, all belonging to the House of Liu."

When they heard this, the merchants were delighted.[41]

This is a remarkable passage for a number of reasons, not least because it is one of only a few vividly detailed anecdotes in a typically concise account, a fact that underlines the emotional importance of the event for Faxian. If his journey away from his native land is marked by nothing but dead men's bones through the desert, then on the return journey the edible plants—pigweeds and beans—become indices of home. Along with ethnicity, again indicated by "the land of Han," nature, now as a nurturing presence rather than a hostile force, precedes the markers of political boundaries.

The hunters specify for Faxian the administrative jurisdiction of the land to which the travelers came. "The House of Liu" has a textual variant in a few early editions, which is widely adopted by modern editions because scholars contend that Faxian returned home during the last years of the rule of Jin in South China and that the succeeding dynasty, founded by the House of Liu, had not yet been established. But Faxian's text soon reveals that the surname of the governor of Qingzhou, where the travelers came on shore, was Liu. The hunters may very well have been referring to their local governor. While the elite cared passionately about empire and dynasty, people in the lower strata of society in early medieval China have a local, not national, sense of place.

This, however, was not the case for Faxian, whose extensive foreign travels gave him a different sense of place altogether. This is the first instance in which he mentions "translation" in his account, and ironically it takes place in his native land. Apparently he was the only man on the ship who could speak Chinese, and the merchants from Sri Lanka needed his help to communicate with the hunters. The hunters, in turn, seem to have been brought to the ship by force—hence, their efforts to ingratiate themselves with Faxian, whom they recognized as a Buddhist monk, by claiming to be "followers of the Buddha." They also fibbed about what they were doing, saying that, rather than hunting animals, they were picking peaches as offerings to the Buddha during a major Buddhist festival. (The fifteenth day of the seventh lunar month is the Festival of Ullambana [Hungry Ghosts].) We hear echoes of Tao Yuanming's "Account of Peach Blossom Spring" in the references to boating upstream and peach picking. The people inside—the hunters—are greatly "shocked" by the sight of strange foreigners, just like the residents of the Peach Blossom Spring. Then, in an ironic twist from the famous story, the intruders from the outside ask about place and time. During his travels in foreign countries, Faxian was made aware of his foreignness by becoming the marvel of local monks, but when he finally came home after years of wandering, he again acutely felt his foreignness in the Chinese hunters' reaction, even though the feeling of alienation also must have been ameliorated by a sense of familiarity, as he was the only Chinese-speaker aboard the merchant ship. While the hunters tried to appeal to his religious identity, Faxian, who saw through their lie, took comfort in their ethnic and linguistic affinity instead. At the Festival of Ullambana, the spirits of the deceased come back to visit the world of the living; in many ways, Faxian, under the thrust of the narrative, functions as a long-lost ghost coming home.

Here, however, we encounter the most bewildering question. Instead of going on to North China, where he had started, Faxian decided to travel to Jiankang, the capital of the South Chinese regime: "Having been separated from my fellow Dharma masters for a long time, I wished to hurry to Chang'an. However, there was important business to attend to, so I traveled south to the capital [Jiankang], and worked with the *dhyāna* master there to translate the scriptures."[42] The "important business" refers to the enterprise of translating the scriptures he has brought back into Chinese. Why this had to be done in Jiankang rather than Chang'an is never explained. Perhaps it would have been self-evident to his contemporary audience, but it is not clear to modern readers, because Chang'an, too, was a center of translation at the time. Faxian did not quite "come home," but perhaps the very notion of home had changed for him.

At Jiankang, Faxian was a sensational figure. He wrote a brief account of his travels, no doubt at the request of the people in the southern capital, but this account was apparently too short to satisfy his readers' intense curiosity. A few years later, he was urged to relate his travels in greater detail, and this longer version has survived. Among those who were fascinated by his account was the poet Xie Lingyun (385–433), known as the father of Chinese landscape poetry, and Huiyuan (ca. 334–417), one of the most influential Chinese monks of early medieval times. Inspired by Faxian's eyewitness report of the legendary "Buddha's Shadow" manifested in a mountain cave south of Nagarahāra (in modern Afghanistan), Huiyuan had an image of the Buddha painted and commissioned Xie Lingyun, the famed writer of the day, to write an inscription.[43]

Faxian's account ends with a summary of his travels and an explicit statement about his intention in writing the account and his intended audience:

> I, Faxian, setting out from Chang'an, reached the Middle Kingdom in six years. I resided there for six years and arrived at Qingzhou in another three years. I had traveled through nearly thirty kingdoms. To the west of the great desert, in the land of India, the majestic bearings of the

Buddhist clergy and the influence of the Dharma cannot be adequately narrated in words. Because the various priests [in this country] had not yet heard of these things, I risked my insignificant life to cross the seas and encountered all kinds of danger to return home. Having been preserved by the divine power of the Three Honorable Ones [Buddha, Dharma, and Sangha], I was able to overcome the perils and came back. Thereupon I commit my experience to bamboo and silk, desiring that my worthy readers share what I have heard and seen. This is in the year of *jiayin*.[44]

Faxian came home bearing the Buddhist scriptures for which he had undertaken the journey to begin with, but he also says that he chose to come home to share his experience. The readers are invited to take a virtual journey to see what he saw and hear what he heard; thus, they become Faxian's new fellow travelers. In English, we would call them "armchair travelers"; in Chinese, the phrase is to *wo you* (take recumbent journeys). The dispersal of community that took place during Faxian's travels is countered, and recompensed, by the reconstitution of community, but this new community is a cultural one as much as a religious one.

Using the Chinese sexagenary cycle for time keeping, Faxian signs off by stating that the account is completed in the *jiayin* year, which is the year 414. At the opening of his account, Faxian has used the reign title of the ruler of the state of Qin—"the second year of the Hongshi era" (i.e., the year 399)—to record the commencement of his journey. The text begins with political time and political geography; it gradually shifts to religious time and religious geography, mapped by the temporal distance from the life of the Buddha, which is constantly evoked throughout the account, and by the Vedic measure of distance used in ancient India, *yojana*; it finally ends with cultural time and cultural geography, as Faxian develops a sense of cultural and linguistic home that transcends geopolitical boundaries. The traveler obtains a perspective on the world which he never would have obtained had he stayed at home.

Faxian never went back to Chang'an. It was not because he was too old and frail to travel; in fact, he left Jiankang in his seventies, and eventually died in Jiangling (in modern Hubei), a city about 500 miles to the west of Jiankang. The real reason for not going back might very well be that it simply did not matter anymore whether he returned to Chang'an or not. Like the numerous monks and nuns on the road in the fifth century, Faxian was a displaced person who mediated between the secular and religious worlds, homeland and foreign lands. As a man whose identity was defined by "leaving home" (that is, *chujiaren*, the Chinese phrase for entering the Buddhist order) and who did not want to return to his family home even when he was a child, he ended up discovering not so much a new home as a new notion of home during his transformative journey. In other words, instead of a closed-off space with fixed margins at a fixed place, home itself became a mobile, porous construct saturated with, for want of a better word, trans-local concerns.

Homecoming turns out to be crucial in telling his tale, because the people back home are the eager consumers of a world that otherwise would remain inaccessible to them, and because a new sense of home constitutes the essential part of Faxian's travel story. Home is also where the body in perpetual motion engages in a different sort of action: that of wielding a writing brush. Here we should recall that Faxian had traveled to seek writings in the first place: he tells us that after he reached northern India, he discovered that all Buddhist scriptures were transmitted orally, so what led him on was, quite specifically, the pursuit of written texts. He was a transporter of words who brought back not only Buddhist scriptures but also a story that, first related orally, was later written down not once, but twice. Faxian spent the rest of his days writing his story and translating; in doing so, he performed further acts of transportation and brought a foreign world home to readers not only in his own time but also in the future, to readers who occupy multiple points in space and time.

The writing material used by Faxian was most likely paper, but he chose to refer to it by the traditional Chinese terms, "bamboo and silk." Bamboo and silk were the very materials used to make the fan in Sri Lanka that evoked the image of home for Faxian, and fans in China at Faxian's time were frequently inscribed with calligraphy and paintings. The fan Faxian saw, however, was a plain one with no writing or image on it. The white silk fan, by virtue of the absence of inscription, silently and eloquently becomes luminous in the travel text as a thing that, like Faxian, has traveled to a foreign land and signifies with its material presence. A sign of the cultural home, of separation and desire, and of the materiality of writing, it provides an inscrutable, seductive blank space on which are inscribed infinite possibilities of the writing of home and writing as a mobile home.

NOTES

I am grateful to Diana Sorensen for organizing the Radcliffe Exploratory Seminar "Remapping Geographic Imaginaries," where I first presented this paper, and for her inspiring critical remarks. I thank my fellow participants in the seminar for their feedback, and I acknowledge with appreciation the graduate students in my seminar in the fall semester of 2012 for their enthusiastic discussions of the text analyzed in this chapter.

1. Faxian's work has been translated into English several times since the nineteenth century, as well as into Japanese, French, German, and Spanish. The Chinese edition used for this paper is Zhang, *Faxian zhuan jiaozhu*. The English editions consulted in writing this chapter include Giles, *The Travels of Fa-hsien*; Legge, *Record of Buddhistic Kingdoms*; Li, "The Journey of the Eminent Monk Faxian." Subsequent references to this text will be to Zhang's edition and Li's English translation. All translations are mine.
2. Tian, *Visionary Journeys*, 13–20.
3. Many stunning examples were on display at the exhibition "China: Dawn of a Golden Age, 200–750 AD," Metropolitan Museum of Art, New York, October 2004–January 2005. Images of these objects are in the accompanying catalogue: see Watt et al., *China*, 149–53, 254, 325–26.
4. Huijiao, *Gao seng zhuan*, 383, 424.
5. Yao and Yao, *Liang shu*, 805. *Nihon shoki* (also known as *Nihongi* or the *Chronicles of Japan*, completed in 720), the second oldest work of classical Japanese history, records the transmission of Buddhism from Baekje in the reign of Japan's Emperor Kinmei (r. 539–571). This is often considered the official introduction of Buddhism to Japan: see Sakamoto et al., *Nihon shoki*, 100; Aston, *Nihongi*, 65–66.
6. Aśvaghoṣa's *Buddhacarita*, one of the few complete biographies of the Buddha, was translated into Chinese in the early fifth century. E. H. Johnston's English translation was based in part on the Tibetan and Chinese versions of this beautiful work, which is no longer extant in entirety in its original Sanskrit version: Johnston, *Aśvaghoṣa's Buddhacarita*.
7. Zürcher, *The Buddhist Conquest of China*, 219–22. See also Tanaka, *The Dawn of Chinese Pure Land Buddhist Doctrine*.
8. Wright, *Buddhism in Chinese History*, 49.
9. Huijiao, *Gao seng zhuan*, 1, 4–5, 13, 41–42, 72, 107, 119, 121, 195, 230.
10. Huijiao, *Gao seng zhuan*, 33, 40, 70, 229.
11. Huijiao, *Gao seng zhuan*, 98–100, 103, 153, 166, 177–78, 190, 259, 290.
12. Huijiao, *Gao seng zhuan*, 337.
13. Huijiao, *Gao seng zhuan*, 41–42.
14. Huijiao, *Gao seng zhuan*, 290.
15. Wang, *Biqiuni zhuan jiaozhu*. This work has two English translations: Tsai, *Lives of the Nuns*, and Li, "Biographies of Buddhist Nuns." All references in this chapter are to Tsai's translation.
16. Tsai, *Lives of the Nuns*, 35.
17. Daoyi's nephew was Huichi (337–412): Huijiao, *Gao seng zhuan*, 229.
18. Tsai, *Lives of the Nuns*, 76.
19. Tsai, *Lives of the Nuns*, 53–54.
20. Tsai, *Lives of the Nuns*, 70.
21. See Wilkinson, *Egeria's Travels to the Holy Land*.
22. Sivan, "Holy Land Pilgrimage and Western Audiences," 534–35.
23. See Dietz, *Wandering Monks, Virgins and Pilgrims*.
24. Huijiao, *Gao seng zhuan*, 87.

25 Huijiao, *Gao seng zhuan*, 87.
26 Huijiao, *Gao seng zhuan*, 87.
27 This issue is explored in great detail in Tian, *Visionary Journeys*, 88–118.
28 Owen, *An Anthology of Chinese Literature*, 309.
29 Owen, *An Anthology of Chinese Literature*, 310.
30 The story of Liu Chen and Ruan Zhao is the best known: Kao, *Classical Chinese Tales of the Supernatural and the Fantastic*, 137–39.
31 See, e.g., the story of Zhao Tai, who died and came back to life with a sensational account of hell in 370 in Kao, *Classical Chinese Tales of the Supernatural and the Fantastic*, 166–71. See also Campany, "To Hell and Back," 343–56.
32 Zhang, *Faxian zhuan jiaozhu*, 6, 21; Li, "The Journey of the Eminent Monk Faxian," 163, 167.
33 Zhang, *Faxian zhuan jiaozhu*, 46; Li, "The Journey of the Eminent Monk Faxian," 175.
34 The *Sukhāvatīvyūha* or the *Sutra of Infinite Life (Wuliangshou jing)*, translated into Chinese several times between the late-second and early-fifth century. The version referred to here is in Takakusu and Watanabe, *Taishō shinshū Daizōkyō*, 12:283.
35 Zhang, *Faxian zhuan jiaozhu*, 44; Li, "The Journey of the Eminent Monk Faxian," 174.
36 Zhang, *Faxian zhuan jiaozhu*, 62; Li, "The Journey of the Eminent Monk Faxian," 182.
37 Schivelbusch, "Railroad Space and Railroad Time," 35.
38 Zhang, *Faxian zhuan jiaozhu*, 120; Li, "The Journey of the Eminent Monk Faxian," 203.
39 Zhang, *Faxian zhuan jiaozhu*, 120; Li, "The Journey of the Eminent Monk Faxian," 203.
40 Zhang, *Faxian zhuan jiaozhu*, 128; Li, "The Journey of the Eminent Monk Faxian," 204.
41 Zhang, *Faxian zhuan jiaozhu*, 147; Li, "The Journey of the Eminent Monk Faxian," 212.
42 Zhang, *Faxian zhuan jiaozhu*, 148; Li, "The Journey of the Eminent Monk Faxian," 213. The *dhyāna* master refers to Buddhabhadra (359–429) (or Fotuobatuoluo in Chinese transcription.
43 See Xie Lingyun's preface to "Inscription on the Buddha's Shadow," in Li, *Xie Lingyun ji*, 345.
44 Zhang, *Faxian zhuan jiaozhu*, 150; Li, "The Journey of the Eminent Monk Faxian," 213.

BIBLIOGRAPHY

Aston, W. G., trans. *Nihongi; or, Chronicles of Japan from the earliest times to AD 697*, vol. 2. London: K. Paul, Trench, Trübner, 1896.
Campany, Robert F. "To Hell and Back: Death, Near-Death, and Other Worldly Journeys in Early Medieval China." In *Death, Ecstasy, and Other Worldly Journeys*,

ed. John J. Collins and Michael Fishbane, 343–60. Chicago: University of Chicago Press, 1995.

Dietz, Maribel. *Wandering Monks, Virgins and Pilgrims: Ascetic Travel in the Mediterranean World, AD 300–800.* University Park: Pennsylvania State University Press, 2005.

Giles, Herbert A., trans. *The Travels of Fa-hsien (399–414 AD); or, Record of the Buddhistic Kingdoms.* London: Routledge and Kegan Paul, 1959.

Huijiao. *Gao seng zhuan* [Biographies of Eminent Monks], ed. Tang Yongtong. Beijing: Zhonghua Shuju, 1992.

Johnston, E. H. *Aśvaghoṣa's Buddhacarita; or, Acts of the Buddha.* New Delhi: Munshiram Manoharlal, 1995.

Kao, Karl S. Y., ed. *Classical Chinese Tales of the Supernatural and the Fantastic: Selections from the Third to the Tenth Century.* Bloomington: Indiana University Press, 1985.

Legge, James, trans. *Record of Buddhistic Kingdoms.* New York: Paragon Book Reprint, 1965.

Li, Rongxi. "Biographies of Buddhist Nuns." In *Lives of Great Monks and Nuns.* Translated by Li Rongxi and Albert A. Dalia, 69–154. Berkeley: Numata Center for Buddhist Translation and Research, 2002.

———, trans. *The Journey of the Eminent Monk Faxian.* In *Lives of Great Monks and Nuns*, trans. Li Rongxi and Albert A. Dalia, 157–214. Berkeley: Numata Center for Buddhist Translation and Research, 2002.

Li, Yunfu, ed. *Xie Lingyun ji* [The Collected Works of Xie Lingyun]. Changsha Shi: Yuelu Shushe, 1999.

Owen, Stephen, ed. and trans. *An Anthology of Chinese Literature: Beginnings to 1911.* New York: W. W. Norton, 1996.

Sakamoto, Tarō. *Nihon shoki.* Tokyo: Iwanami Shoten, 1967.

Schivelbusch, Wolfgang. "Railroad Space and Railroad Time." *New German Critique* 14 (Spring 1978): 31–40.

Sivan, Hagith. "Holy Land Pilgrimage and Western Audiences: Some Reflections on Egeria and Her Circle." *Classical Quarterly* 38, no. 2 (1988): 534–35.

Takakusu, Junjirō, and Watanabe Kaigyoku, eds. *Taishō shinshū Daizōkyō.* Taipei: Shihua Yinshua Qiye Youxian Gongsi, 1990.

Tanaka, Kenneth K. *The Dawn of Chinese Pure Land Buddhist Doctrine: Ching-ying Hui-yüan's Commentary on the Visualization Sutra.* Albany: State University of New York Press, 1990.

Tian, Xiaofei. *Visionary Journeys: Travel Writings from Early Medieval and Nineteenth-Century China.* Cambridge, MA: Harvard University Asia Center, 2011.

Tsai, Kathryn Ann, trans. *Lives of the Nuns: Biographies of Chinese Nuns from the Fourth to Sixth Centuries.* Honolulu: University of Hawaii Press, 1994.

Wang, Rutong, ed. *Biqiuni zhuan jiaozhu.* Beijing: Zhonghua Shuju, 2006.

Watt, James C. Y., An Jiayao, and Angela F. Howard et al., eds. *China: Dawn of a Golden Age, 200–750 AD.* New York: Metropolitan Museum of Art, 2004.

Wilkinson, John, trans. *Egeria's Travels to the Holy Land.* London: Ariel, 1981.

Wright, Arthur F. *Buddhism in Chinese History*. Stanford, CA: Stanford University Press, 1959.
Yao, Cha, and Yao Silian. *Liang shu* [History of the Liang Dynasty]. Beijing: Zhonghua Shuju, 1973.
Zhang, Xun, ed. *Faxian zhuan jiaozhu*. Beijing: Zhonghua Shuju, 2008.
Zürcher, Erik. *The Buddhist Conquest of China: The Spread and Adaptation of Buddhism in Early Medieval China*. Leiden: Brill, 1959.

PART II

Portable Materialities and Crossings

·····

Chapter 4

The Portability of Art: Prolegomena to Art and Architecture on the Move

ALINA PAYNE

I

When one thinks of portability one does not immediately think of the obelisk of St. Peter's in Rome or the Mona Lisa in the Grande Salle of the Louvre: one a grand monument, the other a grand painting, both seem embedded into their respective sites. The obelisk—weighing 326 metric tons—is firmly rooted, signaling immobility, strength, solidity, and weight. The Mona Lisa, surrounded by guards and tourists and encased in its place by wires, bulletproof glass, barriers, and ropes, seems just as permanently anchored to its soil. Yet their lives were much more complicated than this sedentary appearance may suggest. The obelisk, a piece of red granite, was transported to Rome, across the Mediterranean from Heliopolis in Egypt. Set up in the Circus of Nero on its *spina* by Caligula, it remained erect for more than a millennium, until Pope Sixtus V had it moved in front of the new basilica of St. Peter's, where it was finally raised in 1586 by the architect Domenico Fontana through a major feat of engineering involving hundreds of workers and spectators.

The other obelisks that dot the Roman urban landscape had similar and even more complex fates. The one that marks the entrance to the city at the Piazza del Popolo dates from 1200 BCE, has hieroglyphic inscriptions dating from the reigns of Sethos I and Ramses II, was moved to Rome and placed in the Circus Maximus by emperor Augustus, subsequently collapsed, and was covered by debris until the fifteenth century when the humanist and architect

FIGURE 4.1: Domenico Fontana, "Obelisk at the Circus of Nero prior to its Relocation to the Piazza of St. Peter in Rome." In *Della trasportatione dell'obelisco Vaticano* (Rome: Domenico Basa, 1590).

Leon Battista Alberti recovered it. Once more forgotten, it attracted attention again only in 1587—by then broken in three pieces—when Pope Sixtus V had it erected to mark the newly established circulation node at the entrance to the city from the via Flaminia (now Piazza del Popolo).[1]

The Mona Lisa had a similar, eventful path until it reached today's abode. Leonardo da Vinci packed it and took it with him when he left Italy for France in the service of the king and sold it to Francis I shortly before his death. The painting remained in the king's palace at Amboise; it was moved to Fontainebleau and finally to Versailles (by Louis XIV), whence it was brought to the Louvre. After a short stint in Napoleon's bedchamber it was eventually returned to the Louvre, from where it was stolen in 1911 by an Italian youth, Vincenzo Peruggia, to be returned to its homeland, although in the process of investigation both Picasso and Appolinaire were suspected of its theft. Brought to Florence and offered to a dealer who, with Giovanni Pozzi, then the director of the Uffizi, identified it and called in the police, it was then returned to France, but not before it went on tour in Italy, where it was exhibited in Florence, Milan, and Rome. During World War II the painting was hidden in Provence (Villefranche-la-Rouergue), and was returned to Paris in 1947. Its final trips were in 1963 to Washington, DC, and New York (against curatorial advice, as a personal gesture to John F. Kennedy), where it was rained on one whole night by a faulty sprinkler, and in 1973 to Tokyo and Moscow.

These are but two examples of the many convoluted histories that belie the apparent inevitable immobility and integrity of art objects that museums and prominent urban locations promote. Yet all too often the lives of objects—during which they change, for the Mona Lisa in Leonardo's house is not the same as the one we see today or the one in Napoleon's bedroom; nor are all of the people and sites that interacted with it along the way the same—are written out of their histories. Given and traded, stolen and shipwrecked, inherited and ransomed, art objects traversed space and time, encompassing a much larger geography than their current stability suggests. And it was not just the objects themselves that expanded in space in so many ways. The materials from which they were crafted also came from expansive geographies: porphyry, alum for dies, gold, silk, gems, precious woods and ivory, mother of pearl, granite, and marble came from the four corners of the world. To this dizzying geography one needs to add the most mobile component of all: the artist and the craftsman. By definition itinerant, particularly in the early modern period, moving where there was work, artists and craftsmen lived peripatetic lives that intersected with those of materials and art objects.[2]

A noted itinerant himself, Walter Benjamin had wanted to draw up a map of his life, a biography represented in space, as a cartographic object.[3] Bounded by the events and their locations that circumscribed his existence, this map would have given his life a physical territory, a visible and tangible geographic dimension. The project came to naught, yet the idea is a powerful one and goes beyond personal biography. The same cartographic exercise could be imagined for art objects: not only people have lives; objects do, too. While ruins contain and point to a narrative about time, an object such as an obelisk, for example, embodies a displacement narrative and makes it literally visible. From such a perspective, then, a whole range of different questions might be asked: how does the (art) object appear when its expansive geography is included in its history? Did those with whom it came into contact—people and things—also change along the way as result of contact? What are the narratives that are embedded and hidden inside its trajectories in space and time? In short, how does portability—the object's quality of being transportable—alter the way we think of art?

Paradoxical though it may seem, such an approach would not exclude architecture. Indeed, the phenomenon of portability does not stop at paintings and isolated monuments. For example, the remains of the Hellenistic Pergamon Altar were lifted in the 1870s from their Anatolian hilltop—where they had lain hidden as the foundation of a church and then a mosque—were crated, then shipped by sea and by trains after significant political negotiations, and finally reinstalled—indeed, staged—in a museum in Berlin.[4] So singular was this motion of architecture and its being parachuted down on one of the capitals of Europe that it caused a *mise-en-abîme* of a whole established aesthetic and ignited a reevaluation not only of ancient art but also of the much maligned Baroque, with which it was suddenly seen to stand in positive synergy.[5] Closer to our own time, that sacred site of modernism, Mies van der Rohe's Pavilion built for the International Exposition of 1929 in Barcelona, was dismantled after the event and shipped by sea. In the process it was lost. That architecture could be lost in transit really dramatizes the fact that architecture *can* behave as an object, *can* be portable, and *can* be a part of all manner of networks. Mies's pavilion was not the only one to be so treated. The equally famous and very much larger Crystal Palace by Joseph Paxton (with an almost 800,000 square foot footprint) built at Hyde Park for the Great Exhibition of 1851 was eventually dismantled and reassembled at Sydenham Hill in South London, where it stood from 1854 to 1936, when it was destroyed in a fire.

Buildings and architectural components are not the only travelers. Architecture's materials also and necessarily move and are (indeed, must be) portable, for few are the cases of local quarries that supply a building on its very site—the fifteenth-century Palazzo Pitti in Florence being one such exceptional case built almost on top of its quarry, as was the Hagia Sofia in Constantinople using the Sea of Marmara's white marble. Marble circulated across and around the Mediterranean: white Carrara marble from Tuscany went to Sicily and as far away as Shah Jehan's Taj Mahal in India; precious colored marbles and porphyry from North Africa and the Middle East went to Europe; large timbers from northern Italy circumnavigated the Italian peninsula aboard ships to reach Rome, where they were needed for large spans in massive buildings such as the Farnese Palace; giant marble columns collected from Roman sites dotting the Mediterranean were shipped in the sixteenth century to Florence (from the Baths of Caracalla) or to Constantinople to complete the great Suleymaniye Mosque.[6] Even more complicated assemblages were sent by sea to be reassembled when they reached their destination. This was the case of *Kleinarchitektur*, small architectures such as altars, funeral monuments, ciboria, and chapels intended for internal spaces—buildings within buildings—which were built as architecture and in the materials of architecture (stone, marble, and so on). One such example is the Brancacci monument by Donatello and Michelozzo, which traveled from Pisa (where the two artists had moved their workshop from Florence to be closer to the port from which the monument would be loaded onto a ship) to Naples in 1428 to be installed in the church of St. Angelo in Nilo; another is the monument for Cardinal Diego Hurtado da Mendoza carved by the Tuscan Domenico Fancelli, who had the marble shipped from Carrara to Genoa, executed the work there in the port city, then shipped it in pieces to Seville by boat and assembled it himself at its destination.[7] The monument of St. Francesco Saverio traveled even farther: made in Florence, it was dismembered and shipped to the cathedral of Bom Jesu in Goa by way of Lisbon in the 1690s, where it was reassembled on-site.[8]

Metaphors and fictitious removal and transport stories in connection with architecture abounded at all times. Like a seismograph, these metaphors turn up at moments of shifts in discourse. For example, a string of new metaphors starting with the architect and theoretician Gottfried Semper's mid-nineteenth-century connection between textiles and architecture to Le Corbusier's house as a car, plane, or ocean liner some sixty years later, across shells and snails as alternative analogies, signal both the anxiety and the enthusiasm attending the effects of the Industrial Revolution on the traditional reference system centered on the human body.[9] A similarly recurrent trope in the early modern imagination was the transportation by angels of the Holy House of the Virgin—the house in Nazareth where the Annunciation and hence the Incarnation were thought to have taken place—to Loreto on the Adriatic coast. Here, fact and fiction morphed into one: the stones of the house walls had been transported from the Holy Land at the time of the withdrawal of the Crusaders by a member of the Angeli family to the coast of today's Croatia. Given as dowry to his daughter who married a son of Charles of Anjou, King of Naples, it was transported once again, this time to the Italian Adriatic coast, to Loreto, where it became the second most important site of pilgrimage in Italy.[10] Although the angels said to have airlifted the house were in fact the Angeli family, the legend stuck and was invoked for miracles of engineering that permitted architecture to be miraculously lifted and relocated (such as the obelisks).

II

What this selection of examples suggests is that art objects—from paintings to architecture—have restless lives and, as a result, engage territory. That is, they have a geographical footprint. Put another way, the paths and itineraries art objects travel describe a field of impact or agency, a territory within which they generate and receive energy. Exchanges of techniques, invention of machines and instruments, and social and political obligations are created along the way among artists, craftsmen, middlemen, and contracting parties, not to mention aesthetic stimuli. An art object in transit modifies many registers that are generally left out of our histories. And, like Benjamin's life, the objects' biographies are not mapped.

Such a reading should not be confused with the new cultural geography that has been making a modified return in the field in the past decade or so or with the spatial turn that has refocused history-writing on the importance of location as a player equal to social and political factors.[11] The issue when considering portability is not—or not only—to acknowledge a geographical location, a place, for the art object, but also to focus on the *act* of portability and its consequences, on the trajectory through space and the multiple and varied encounters along the way.

Clearly there are reasons why portability disappeared in a blind spot of the field that have to do with the origin of art history as a discipline and its evolution. In the first place, like so many fields of academe, art history came to maturity in the nineteenth century and thus was much affected by the predominant nationalist narratives of the period. If literary studies came to be profoundly affected by nationalism—and language does indeed invite such clumping that works against seeing a transnational world literature—art and architecture certainly were its partners in the domain of culture.[12] The nationalist pull was such that art history inevitably became complicit in allowing a national identity to be constructed and claimed at a political level. National museums, a census of the *patrimoine* that included everything from vernacular art forms to historical monuments (the French Commission des Monuments Historiques not coincidentally was created in 1837) and even landscape preservation were among the most salient nineteenth-century institutional creations. Indeed, architectural monuments—declared as such—both of historical and artistic value became enhanced within the city through restoration to their original appearance, isolation from neighbors, and removal of encroaching later additions, almost as if they were in a museum setting with a spotlight trained on them.[13] Buildings were restored to their pristine state and even finished—witness the medievalizing work of Viollet-le-Duc in France and the completion of the Cologne Cathedral—removing the passage of time from them, their promiscuous pasts, and with it their tentacles reaching far and wide into time and space. The importance of this work was immense. Much was saved and researched, and, in fact, in France the *patrimoine* orientation (which remains a strong cultural undercurrent to this day) was initially a reaction to the destructive fervor of the Revolution.[14] But in France as elsewhere it also encouraged the study of art contained within its borders—and certainly within European borders—such that the larger movements across divides and continents remained peripheral to mainstream scholarship.[15]

A similar phenomenon was at work in the museum. Although for objects the arrival in the museum was the last of a series of displacements, ironically, once they were there, the location itself generated a static vision of artistic production. Objects had to be sorted out—the objects supplied by archaeology, anthropology, art collectors, and so on—and had to be entered into a fixed taxonomy that allowed everything else in that particular domain to exist in a relational and stable structure. Artists, patron, date, original place of installation, and, most important, style were the coordinates.[16] This process required fixity simply to be able to sort out the immense quantity of objects that the nineteenth-century state museums were collecting. Of course, not all art objects assembled in museums were local or national, as was the case for the Germanisches Nationalmuseum in Nüremberg (founded in 1852). Since much art came from far away—the enthusiasm for the distant and exotic being both pervasive and sustained—one might have expected this interest also to have generated a concern with the paths the objects had traveled throughout their long lives. But the objects from distant places were presented and thought of as documents of their own national cultures rather than as participants in the larger circulation and economy of things, and their personal history and the histories of their intersections with other objects and people were mostly ignored. As a result, the way we see these objects nowadays in museum displays is as so many tips of icebergs, with most of their histories submerged, away from viewers' eyes. In short, the effects of their portability were left out of the museological equation.

One attempt was made to counter the essentializing thrust of the museum display at the turn of the nineteenth century. In 1887, the anthropologist Franz Boas confronted his colleague, the curator Otis T. Mason, at the Museum of Natural History in New York with respect to his display strategies. The objects were classified and exhibited according to physical resemblance rather than to their place in specific cultures and contexts. By contrast, Boas's answer was the vitrine: glassed-in displays complete with figures and landscapes that re-created life situations like so many small theater sets or tableaux vivants in which objects (or animals) were shown in their habitats, the way they lived.[17] The confrontation amounted to a severe jolt; Boas won the debate, and thereafter museums of anthropology and natural history across the world followed suit and established vitrines as the default mode of display—or, in other words, sowed the seeds of cultural anthropology. Many of Boas's ideas owed to the art world he knew in his native Germany and, in turn, influenced that world through figures such as Aby Warburg, with whom Boas interacted in the 1890s.[18] Nowadays, contexts are again part of the art museum display as it emerges out of the modernist tradition of paintings and objects floating in isolation against plain white or gray walls. But another Boas may be necessary to extend the context to the biography of the objects and of those—people and things—they touched along the way.

But the museum mentality extended beyond the museums' walls and was inevitably translated into art-history scholarship, which evolved alongside and in synergy with the museum. While this was very much the case in the early days of the discipline and is certainly no longer so to the same degree, old sins do have long shadows, and once a certain type of blindness is embedded in a field—no matter how good the reason—it becomes hard to dislodge. And no network theory arose to do for art history what Bruno Latour's did for sociology and history of science.[19]

The focus on genius artists—a strategy that supports museum treasures—shaped much of the discourse at its inception and set off an inescapable pattern shoring up stability over mobility. The task was to identify an oeuvre and attribute it, thus placing the artists rather than the history of the work at the center of the art historian's interest. The fact that the discipline was much marked by books such as Jacob Burckhardt's *Civilization of the Renaissance* (1860), in which he attributed paradigmatic work to titanic figures (*Gewaltmenschen*) in politics as well as in the arts, added much fuel to this fire. In a circular move, this view, which had great influence on Friedrich Nietzsche (Burckhardt's friend and student), came to affect contemporary art and architecture deeply through the philosopher's hugely influential writings.[20] Such biases were far less at work in scholarship on medieval and Islamic art, where the minor arts played an important role and where major artists were not identified, as they had been for the periods starting with the Renaissance.

If not outright portability, at least dialogues between high and minor arts were much more readily envisaged there.[21] Perhaps the nomadic nature of the cultures (especially the Islamic ones) invited or, at least, permitted such an approach. Likewise, scholarship on American art—another culture that was paradigmatically on the move—has been quicker to revise old strategies and to question the effects of mobility on art objects.[22] But for the so-called European center, an age-old hierarchy of the arts had precluded such expansive readings. As to the portability of objects, their biographies, which also means letting go of the maker and allowing a history of serendipitous encounters by the object as result of the vicissitudes of the road, did not even come into question as an alternative to the biographies of major artists. The Pergamon Altar's effect on the Berlin audiences in the 1880s did not reflect on the artists who created it in the second century BCE. But the significant impact the altar had on the development of an entirely new aesthetic after its rediscovery is nevertheless an important part of the history of this object. Studying only its makers and the original artistic intention would completely miss this chapter in its life and, with it, a better understanding of nineteenth-century art. Luxury textiles and ceramics—those most portable of all artistic objects—and architecture are not normally discussed in the same studies. But the arrival in Italy of eastern fabrics and vessels, with their characteristic designs and ubiquitously present in rich merchants' environments, even on their bodies as vestments, helped create a sensibility for pattern and its deployment that showed up on their palace facades as incised ornamental decoration (*sgraffito*).[23]

The nationalist strain was easily absorbed into art history as part of the concept of regional school—whether of painting or architecture—that was finely graded enough to permit designations as precise as "Florentine painting" or "Roman Baroque." An ethnic art history started with Giorgio Vasari in the Renaissance—very much for political reasons that had to do with Medici claims to Tuscan supremacy—but it certainly gained momentum in the nineteenth century with historians such as Hippolyte Taine in France and Karl Schnaase in Germany: art and artists were seen as products of a place (milieu), of a time, and of an ethnic make-up.[24] However much this model may have been revised in the course of the following century, the concept of national art and of regional schools shaped art history from Heinrich Wölfflin and Bernard Berenson to the very division of academic teaching and the structuring of learning into chairs of a particular geographic (read, national) region. A transnational focus did emerge at times—Josef Strzygowski's

FIGURE 4.2: Giorgio Vasari, detail of sgrafitto façade, Palazzo dei Cavalieri di Santo Stefano, Pisa. Photograph by the author.

treatment of Eastern Europe and the *Völkerwanderung* being one such case in turn of the century Vienna.[25] But isolated efforts such as his had to work too hard against the grain, and it was too much of an oddity, in any event, as well as short-lived to make much of a difference.

III

But what might this so long considered peripheral history of an object's life that has to do with its portability as opposed to its appearance—its materials, making, owning, transporting, collecting, rediscovering—offer the discipline? Perhaps most important, it would offer the opportunity to think in terms of territory rather than nation or state, to write the history of or reevaluate much larger and interconnected geographic units. One such example, which I will discuss at greater length below, may be the Eastern European territories that extend from the Adriatic and Ionian seas east and north, connecting the Mediterranean world with the Russian steppes and the Polish and Lithuanian frontier:

"The stream that runs through the city of Sarajevo ... flows into the river of Saray"; this river in turn meets waters arriving from Herzegovina and Croatia before it flows over mountainous terrain into the Sava which "meets the Danube right beside Belgrade." The Danube itself in all its majesty eventually runs into the Black Sea, and "it is clearer than sunlight"; the Black Sea meets the Mediterranean in Istanbul and the Mediterranean, in turn, flows through the straits of Gibraltar into the Surrounding Sea which meets the larger Ocean "by the order of the Creator of both worlds." These are the words of Evliya Çelebi (1611–after 1683), the Ottoman traveler whose ten hefty volumes may well be the most monumental example of travel writing in any language.[26]

Indeed, as recounted by Cemal Kafadar, for this seventeenth-century author the rivers seem to have been a system of capillaries, forever in movement, flowing gently one into the next, filling out the seas, allowing them to flow farther, into one another, connecting the world—of the Ottomans and of the Europeans and farther, beyond the known boundaries, the mysterious oceans that hug the globe. For Claudio Magris, writing some four hundred years later, the Danube leaves behind "a Nilotic slime in which pullulate germs still confused and indistinct," a lively melting pot of races and cultures, a fertile mud in which flourished a Carpatho-Balkan community that resulted from an ancient but still extant underground stream—that of the Byzantine Turkish Mongols seeking the Lands of Rum—and that bathed the shores of the Danubian principates.[27] These two testimonies are remarkable for zeroing in on rivers as the cultural infrastructure of the Mediterranean world, as the carriers of people, things, and ideas that fused in myriad ways once they reached the larger pool of the inland sea, of the Mediterranean. In their own ways, Çelebi and Magris reveal an act of attention that is eloquently represented by the exaggerated emphasis on the rivers as blue highways linking various seas into a network on this fifteenth-century map.

Scholarship, however, has generally neglected this secondary system of contact. Instead, the Mediterranean has claimed a central place in recent work, especially among historians, although art historians have also joined the trend. But the original Braudelian idea of a shore and a hinterland and the ties between them has been somewhat moved to the sidelines, so appealing has the work on the cultures bordering the sea become.[28] Yet the liquid network of rivers—those natural highways—that extends inland and ties the golden fabled shores with the mountains and the peoples living in their shadow or along the paths of the rivers' passage is as interesting as it is understudied. Among them, the king of the rivers has to be the Danube, running a parallel course to the Mediterranean and cutting

FIGURE 4.3: Map of the Mediterranean, detail of world map. Niccolo de' Conti (?), Genoa, 1457 (reproduction, 1912).

across Europe from west to east, only to come to rest in the Black Sea, thus pouring itself into the system of communicating vessels of the Mediterranean—the old Roman *mare nostrum* itself, the Sea of Marmara, the Black Sea, and, the last ripple within this body of water that separates and unites three continents, the Sea of Azov. But the Danube is not alone in so swelling the Mediterranean world with the cultures along its shores. The Sava, the Adige, the Pruth, the Dniester, and the Dnieper, not to mention the Don (which flows into the Sea of Azov), connect the traditional Mediterranean cultures—the Italian, the Ottoman, the Greek/Byzantine, the Spanish—with the world of the Balkans and beyond: Albania, Slovenia, Croatia, and Hungary, with Serbia, Bulgaria, and Romania, but also, to the north and northeast, Poland, Ukraine, and Russia.

These were territories of transit as much as the home of their own indigenous populations. Alongside the caravan routes that crossed the Anatolian plateau and linked Tabriz and Baghdad with Bursa and Izmir on the east-west axis, and, on a north-south axis, Antalya with the Black Sea, the rivers also carried craftsmen and slaves, merchants and armies, silks and spices, furs and wheat, gold and silver, and, most of all salt, together with books and luxury objects, jewelry and painted panels, tiles and marble, in all directions moving toward the center—the sites of Mediterranean political power, Madrid, Rome, Constantinople—and radiating from it. Florentine silk merchants bought their raw materials from Asterabad (on the Caspian), and in the Middle Ages the city of Ancona had noteworthy colonies on the Black Sea and the Sea of Azov, as did the Genovese.[29] It is also no coincidence that the famous Battle of Mohacs (two of them, in fact, in 1526 and 1687) was fought on the shores of the Danube, along which the Ottomans penetrated into the heart of Europe and dreamed of extending their empire.

Starting from this perspective of powerful riverine ties between the sea and the hinterland, a framework could be developed for investigating the mediating role of the Balkans between east and west and their northern neighbors, as well as the region's contribution to the larger Mediterranean cultural melting pot in the early modern period.[30] It could be argued that the penetration of Islamic cultures into Europe occurred over a broader terrain than is generally acknowledged and that the eastern frontier extending away from the Mediterranean deep into the interior played a determinant role in negotiating the dialogue between Western Europe and Persia, Armenia, Georgia, and Ottoman Turkey. On the cusp between cultures and religions—mostly Eastern Orthodox (except for Hungary, Dalmatia, and Poland) and mostly of Slavic language (except for Romania and Hungary)—these principalities, kingdoms, and fiefdoms came to embody hybridity, to act as a form of buffer or cultural switching system that assimilated, translated, and linked the cultures of Central Asia with the Western European ones. Some became satellites of the Ottoman Empire, and others retained political, if not cultural, independence, but all testify to the seeping of a complex culture inland from the Mediterranean seas along riverine routes.

In this territory, art, architecture, ornament, literary texts, crafted small objects, fragments, materials, ideas, and scientific instruments circulated across caravanserais and *hans*, along river and transhumance routes, carried by merchants and armies, ambassadors and concubines, slaves and craftsmen. Along with the small objects, concepts for settlements, building types, and practices crossed this territory. These were multiuse building types such as caravanserais and hans; infrastructure such as bridges, fortifications, roads, and *lazzaretti* (quarantine spaces in ports); and domestic architecture typologies, domed structures, materials, artisanal practices, *Kleinarchitektur*, and portable architectural objects. Spolia, cloth and silks, goldsmithry, sculpture, leather, gems, books, and other luxury items were transported along the same routes, allowing ornamental forms and formal ideas to circulate and creating a taste for a hybrid aesthetic. Most of these artworks found their ultimate destinations in Venice, Rome, Vienna, or Lvov. But along the way, in the passage from one settlement to another, from one culture to another, they left traces: muqarnas in Romanian churches of the sixteenth century (Curtea de Arges); Mongol costumes in Poland; churches referencing Pisa in Dalmatia and Sicily; mosques transformed

FIGURE 4.4: Curtea de Argeș. Photograph by the author.

into Genovese churches in Crimea, only to be turned back into mosques in later years.

Such a study of art objects from the perspective of their portability would then be a study of interstices, of the in-between, not of departures and arrivals only. From a territorial perspective, this would be a transnational study that ignores boundaries and borders, then and now;[31] that draws attention to networks, routes, and territorial extension of ideas, to shipwrecks and markets, to forms and materials embedded in objects that cut across the cultural sky like fiery comets. It would have to envisage material shifts or translations: the effects of textile patterns on architecture; the dialogue between pottery techniques and sgraffito facades; the consequences of serendipitous encounters of artists and objects; the reevaluation of exile and its consequences.[32] It would also mean, for example, examining the geography of building types—where certain types of buildings occur—or approaches to ornament or to seismic resistance in structures and lay them over the known movement of migrants, goods, and armies across continents, rather as historians have done with patterns of disease and land cultivation.[33]

None of this can be undertaken by one scholar alone, and this is precisely the disciplinary consequence of such an approach. Expertise from many sources needs to be invoked to begin to chart the intersections among objects, geographies, and cultures. To be sure, the topic of dialogues across cultures has been present in the field, particularly with respect to Venice and its relationship to the East. But the mechanics of portability—of what moved where, when, and how—and what practices this engendered has not.[34] Such a perspective does not mean interdisciplinarity so much as it means cutting across historical and national boundaries, as well as problematizing mobility and its attendant portability, the quality of objects to be mobile because they are portable. It also means acceptance of and curiosity for what may seem to be oddball projects coming from the contemporary arts, such as Francesco Careri's *Walkscapes: Walking as an Aesthetic Practice.*

Resisting the power of statehood is never easy, as James C. Scott has argued with reference to migrants as alternative populations.[35] In the case of the history of art and architecture, resisting the power of academic structures is likewise difficult. Yet from this world of migrant objects and unexpected encounters, a history of art could yet emerge that follows serendipitous paths instead of being teleological or otherwise driven by strong narratives and nationally compartmentalized thinking.

NOTES

1. On the history of the obelisks, see Platner and Ashby, *A Topographical Dictionary of Ancient Rome.*
2. On the artist's mobility in the Renaissance, see Kim, *The Traveling Artist in the Italian Renaissance.*
3. For a discussion of this theme in Benjamin's *Berlinerchronik* and a wide-ranging overview of the question of space (and of the "spatial turn") in historical scholarship, see Schlögel, *Im Raume lesen wir die Zeit.*
4. Bilsel, *Antiquity on Display.*
5. On the topic of portability of architecture, see Payne, "Portable Ruins."
6. On the transport of marble columns for the Suleymaniye, see Necipoğlu, "Connectivity, Mobility and Mediterranean 'Portable Archaeology,'" chap. 10.
7. Condorelli, "Domenico Fancelli."
8. See Conforti, "Il Castrum Doloris (1689–1698) per san Francesco Saverio al Bom Jesu di Goa di Giovanbattista Foggini." See also the other essays in this section of the volume, all pertaining to architecture's behavior as object.
9. For an in-depth study of this crisis, see Payne, *From Ornament to Object.*
10. See Sahler, "Architektur als Objekt der Verehrung."
11. In art history, an example of recent cultural geography is Kaufman, *Toward a Geography of Art.* For the spatial turn, see Withers, "Place and the Spatial Turn in Geography and History."
12. Of course, the phenomenon of a nationalist literature and art go back in time to the Renaissance, if not earlier. Yet in the nineteenth century such readings received

their most extreme formulations and had their most effect: Casanova, *The World Republic of Letters*.

13 The historic monument and its various definitions were analyzed in a trailblazing essay by Riegl, "Der moderne Denkmalkultus, sein Wesen, seine Entstehung."
14 See, e.g., the origin of the museum of Lenoir, which later became the Museé Cluny: Bann, "Historical Text and Historical Object."
15 Some of the few interested in charting broader movements, such as the Austrian art historian Josef Strzygowski—though admittedly mostly at a formal level—are being rediscovered now in light of the global turn that has gripped the discipline: see Burioni, "Globalgeschichte der Renaissance circa 1935," 80–84; Marchand, *German Orientalism in the Age of Empire*, chap. 9.
16 For style as an organizational coordinate to order systematically and quickly the shipments of archaeologists to their museums in the nineteenth century, see Marchand, *Down from Olympus*.
17 Jacknis, "The Ethnographic Object and the Object of Ethnology in the Early Career of Franz Boas," 185–87.
18 Michaud, *Aby Warburg et l'image en mouvement*, 175.
19 Latour, "The Berlin Key"; Latour, *The Pasteurization of France*; Latour, *Reassembling the Social*.
20 August Buck, ed., *Renaissance und Renaissancismus von Jacob Burckhardt bis Thomas Mann* (Tübingen: Max Niemeyer, 1990).
21 See, e.g., Flood, *Objects of Translation*; Hoffman, "Pathways of Portability."
22 Roberts, *Transporting Visions*.
23 On the exchanges between architecture and textile as well as ceramics, see Payne, "Renaissance *Sgraffito* Façades and the Circulation of Objects in the Mediterranean."
24 Taine, *Philosophie de l'art*.
25 See Marchand, "The View from the Land," chap. 1; Wood, *The Vienna School Reader*.
26 Kafadar, "An Ottoman Gentleman's Encounter with Latinity," 59.
27 Magris quotes the Romanian historian Nicolae Iorga: Magris, *Danube*, 363.
28 Classic studies of the Mediterranean remain Braudel, *La Méditerranée et le monde méditerranéen à l'époque de Philippe II*; Goitein, *A Mediterranean Society*; Pirenne, *Mohammed et Charlemagne*. Recent scholarship, particularly in history, has returned to these themes: see, e.g., Abulafia, *The Mediterranean in History*; Harris, *Rethinking the Mediterranean*; Horden and Purcell, *The Corrupting Sea*; Piterberg et al., *Braudel Revisited*.
29 See esp. the activity of Tommaso Spinelli in Florence: Jacks, *The Spinelli of Florence*, 83. On Ancona's colonies along the Black Sea and Sea of Azov (threatened after 1375, the fall of the Armenian empire to the Mamluks), see Ashtor, "Il commercio levantino di Ancona nel basso Medioevo," 216.
30 This is the basis of a project I am currently heading under the title "From Riverbed to Seashore: Art on the Move in Eastern Europe and the Mediterranean in the Early Modern Period." The project is part of Connecting Art Histories, funded by the Getty Foundation.

31 For an example focusing on the littoral as an alternative geographic element that unites what borders try to separate, see Payne, *Dalmatia and the Mediterranean*.

32 For a recent foray into the world of exiles, see the conference "Images and Words in Exile: Avignon and Italy in the First Half of the 14th Century," Kunsthistorisches Institut in Florenz/Max Planck Institute Florence, April 2011.

33 For a global view in history, see most recently *Worlds Together, Worlds Apart*. For the circulation of techniques in response to seismic conditions, see EUROCOR, the project funded by the European Research Council and headed by Marco Rosario Nobile at the University of Palermo, 2011–15.

34 See, e.g., the work of Ennio Concina and Deborah Howard and exhibitions such as *Venice and the Islamic World*.

35 Scott, *The Art of not Being Governed*; Scott, *Seeing like a State*.

BIBLIOGRAPHY

Abulafia, David, ed. *The Mediterranean in History*. Los Angeles: J. Paul Getty Museum, 2003.

Ashtor, Eliyahu. "Il commercio levantino di Ancona nel basso Medioevo." In *Studies on Levantine Trade in the Middle Ages*. London: Variorum Reprints, 1978.

Bann, Stephen. "Historical Text and Historical Object: The Poetics of the Musée Cluny." *History and Theory* 17, no. 3 (1978): 251–66.

Bilsel, Cen. *Antiquity on Display: Regimes of the Authentic in Berlin's Pergamon Museum*. Oxford: Oxford University Press, 2012.

Braudel, Fernand. *La Méditerranée et le Monde Méditerranéen à l'époque de Philippe II*. Paris: Armand Colin, 1949.

Burioni, Matteo. "Globalgeschichte der Renaissance circa 1935." In *Was war Renaissance? Bilder einer Erzählform von Vasari bis Panofsky*, ed. Hans Christian Hönes et al., 80–84. Passau: Dietmar Klinger, 2013.

Careri, Francesco. *Walkscapes: El andar como práctica estética= Walking as an Aesthetic Practice*, Barcelona: Gili, 2002.

Casanova, Pascale. *The World Republic of Letters*. Cambridge, MA: Harvard University Press, 2007.

Condorelli, Adele. "Domenico Fancelli." In *Dizionario biografico degli italiani*, Gen. Ed. Alberto Ghisalberti, vol. 44, Rome: Istituto dell'Enciclopedia italiana, 1994.

Conforti, Claudia. "Il Castrum Doloris (1689–1698) per san Francesco Saverio al Bom Jesu di Goa di Giovanbattista Foggini." In *Architektur als Objekt/Architecture as Object*, ed. Alina Payne and George Satzinger. Nuremberg: Deutsches Nationalmuseum, 2014.

Flood, Finbarr Barry. *Objects of Translation*. Princeton, NJ: Princeton University Press, 2009.

Goitein, S. D. *A Mediterranean Society: The Jewish Communities of the Arab World as Portrayed in the Documents of the Cairo Geniza*. Berkeley: University of California Press, 1967–93.

Harris, W. V., ed. *Rethinking the Mediterranean*. Oxford: Oxford University Press, 2005.

Hoffman, Eva. "Pathways of Portability: Islamic and Christian Interchange from the Tenth to the Twelfth Century." *Art History* 24, no. 1 (2001): 17–50.

Horden, Peregrine, and Nicholas Purcell. *The Corrupting Sea: A Study of Mediterranean History*. Oxford: Oxford University Press, 2000.

Jacknis, Ira. "The Ethnographic Object and the Object of Ethnology in the Early Career of Franz Boas." In *Volksgeist as Method and Ethic: Essays on Boasian Ethnography and the German Anthropological Tradition*, ed. George W. Stocking Jr., 185–214. Madison: University of Wisconsin Press, 1996.

Jacks, Philip. *The Spinelli of Florence: Fortunes of a Renaissance Merchant Family*. University Park: Pennsylvania State University Press, 2001.

Kafadar, Cemal. "An Ottoman Gentleman's Encounter with Latinity: Evliya Celebi in Dalmatia." In *Dalmatia and the Mediterranean: Portable Archaeology and the Poetics of Influence*, ed. Alina Payne, 59–78. Leiden: Brill, 2014.

Kaufman, Thomas Da Costa. *Toward a Geography of Art*. Chicago: University of Chicago Press, 2004.

Kim, David. *The Traveling Artist in the Italian Renaissance: Geography, Mobility and Style*. New Haven, CT: Yale University Press, 2015.

Latour, Bruno. "The Berlin Key or How to Do Words with Things." In *Matter, Materiality, and Modern Culture*, ed. Paul M. Graves-Brown, 10–21. London: Routledge, 2000.

———. *The Pasteurization of France*. Cambridge, MA: Harvard University Press, 1988.

———. *Reassembling the Social: An Introduction to Actor-Network Theory*. Oxford: Oxford University Press, 2005.

Magris, Claudio. *Danube*. London: Collins Harvill, 1989.

Marchand, Susanne. *Down from Olympus: Archaeology and Philhellenism in Germany, 1750–1970*. Princeton, NJ: Princeton University Press, 1996.

Marchand, Susanne. *German Orientalism in the Age of Empire*. New York: Cambridge University Press, 2009.

———. "The View from the Land: Austrian Art Historians and the Interpretation of Croatian Art." In *Dalmatia and the Mediterranean: Portable Archaeology and the Poetics of Influence*, ed. Alina Payne, 21–58. Leiden: Brill, 2014.

Michaud, Philippe-Alain. *Aby Warburg et l'image en mouvement*. Paris: Macula, 1998.

Necipoğlu, Gülru. "Connectivity, Mobility and Mediterranean 'Portable Archaeology': Pashas from the Dalmatian Hinterland as Cultural Mediators." In *Croatia and the Mediterranean: Portable Archaeology and the Poetics of Influence*, ed. Alina Payne, 311–81. Leiden: Brill, 2014.

Payne, Alina, ed. *Dalmatia and the Mediterranean. Portable Archaeology and the Poetics of Influence*. Leiden: Brill, 2014.

———. *From Ornament to Object: Genealogies of Architectural Modernism*. New Haven, CT: Yale University Press, 2012.

———. "Portable Ruins: The Pergamon Altar, Heinrich Wölfflin and German Art History at the *fin de siècle*." RES: *Journal of Aesthetics and Anthropology* 54–55 (Spring–Autumn 2008): 168–89.

———. "Renaissance *Sgraffito* Façades and the Circulation of Objects in the Mediterranean." In *Synergies: Creating Art in Joined Cultures*, ed. Manuela DeGiorgi, Annette Hoffmann, and Nicola Suthor, 229–241. Berlin: Fink, 2013.

Pirenne, Henri. *Mohammed et Charlemagne*. London: G. Allen and Unwin, 1956.

Piterberg, Gabriel, Teofilo F. Ruiz, and Geoffroy Symcox, eds. *Braudel Revisited: The Mediterranean World, 1600–1800*. Toronto: Toronto University Press, 2010.

Platner, Samuel Ball, and Thomas Ashby. *A Topographical Dictionary of Ancient Rome*. Oxford: Oxford University Press, 2002.

Riegl, Alois. "Der moderne Denkmalkultus, sein Wesen, seine Entstehung." In *Gesammelte Aufsätze*, ed. Artur Rosenauer, 139–84. Vienna: Wiener Universitätsverlag, 1996.

Roberts, Jennifer L. *Transporting Visions: The Movement of Images in Early America*. Berkeley: University of California Press, 2014.

Sahler, Hildegard. "Architektur als Objekt der Verehrung. Entstehung und Wirkung der Großreliquien in Loreto, Assisi und Jerusalem." In *Architektur als Objekt/Architecture as Object*, ed. Alina Payne and Georg Satzinger. Nuremberg: Deutsches Nationalmuseum, 2014.

Schlögel, Karl. *Im Raume lesen wir die Zeit. Über Zivilisationsgeschichte und Geopolitik*. Frankfurt: Fischer, 2011.

Scott, James C. *The Art of not Being Governed: An Anarchist History of Upland Southeast Asia*. New Haven, CT: Yale University Press, 2009.

———. *Seeing like a State: How Certain Schemes to Improve the Human Condition Have Failed*. New Haven, CT: Yale University Press, 1998.

Taine, Hippolyte. *Philosophie de l'art*. Paris: G. Baillière, 1865.

Venice and the Islamic World, 828–1797. New York: Metropolitan Museum of Art, 2007.

Withers, Charles W. J. "Place and the Spatial Turn in Geography and History." *Journal of the History of Ideas* 70, no. 4 (October 2009): 637–58.

Worlds Together, Worlds Apart: A History of the World from the Beginnings of Humankind to the Present, 4th ed. New York: W. W. Norton, 2013.

Wood, Christopher. *The Vienna School Reader: Politics and Art Historical Method in the 1930s*. New York: Zone, 2000.

Chapter 5

Genealogies of Whitewash: "Muhammedan Churches," Reformation Polemics, and the Aesthetics of Modernism

FINBARR BARRY FLOOD

In 1928, in the course of repairs to the Friday Mosque of Damascus after a fire that had taken place in 1893, it was noticed that thick plaster on some of the walls of the court of the mosque covered an area of glass mosaic (see figure 5.1). The realization led the French Orientalist Eustache de Lorey to oversee its removal. The results were spectacular. From under the plaster, a 115 foot (35 meter) long panel of gold-ground mosaic emerged, the largest panel of wall mosaic to have survived from antiquity (see figure 5.2).[1] Against a scintillating gold ground, an elegant pastoral scene appeared, in which pearl-strung pavilions and multistoried buildings were disposed in a landscape punctuated by carefully tended trees (see figure 5.3). The mosaics, which were frequently praised in medieval sources, formed part of the original decoration of the mosque when it was completed in AD 715 as the Friday Mosque of the administrative capital of the Umayyads (r. 661–750), the first Islamic dynasty.

Both at the time of the discovery and subsequently, few paused to consider when and in what circumstances these remarkable mosaics had been plastered over and whitewashed. Yet the case of the Damascus mosaics was not unique. Until the late nineteenth century or early twentieth century, the Umayyad mosaics in the interior of the Dome of the Rock in Jerusalem, built in 692, and some or all of those in the adjoining Aqsa Mosque were also wholly or partially obscured by plaster or whitewash. The eventual concealment of the Umayyad mosaics is especially ironic in light of the status that they have assumed as evidence for the adoption of aniconism as a core aesthetic value of early Islamic sacred space; the fact that mosaics in both Damascus and Jerusalem were devoid of anthropomorphic or zoomorphic figures, consisting of architecture, trees, vegetation, and vessels, renders the reasons for their later whitening even more curious.

The date at which these masterpieces of early Islamic art were whitewashed is uncertain, although circumstantial evidence suggests that they were obscured in the sixteenth or early seventeenth century. Although it is tempting to see the whitewashing of the Damascus and Jerusalem mosaics as occurring simultaneously, part of a common programmatic reaction against the Umayyad ornaments in the shrines of both cities, the available evidence would not appear to support this scenario. The Damascus mosaics were certainly visible in the fourteenth century, when their content and renown was discussed by a number of Mamluk chroniclers.[2] References to the mosaics in sixteenth-century texts appropriate and recycle these fourteenth-century descriptions rather than adding to them, which suggests that they may no longer have been visible by the late 1500s. An extensive eyewitness account of the restoration of the Damascus mosque following a disastrous fire in 1479 tell us that the ceiling of the western portico—that is, the area that houses the mosaic panel uncovered in 1928—was burned in the fire but makes no mention of any mosaics. Noting this peculiarity, Doris Behrens-Abouseif remarks, "This raises the question as to whether the walls at that time were coated with plaster, which would have preserved the mosaics underneath."[3] If this is the case, then the mosaics in Damascus may have been whitewashed even before the Ottoman conquest of Syria and Egypt 1516–17.

If we can be more certain about when the Damascus mosaics were recovered than when they were covered in plaster, in Jerusalem the situation is reversed. Based on accounts of the Dome of the Rock by historians and travelers, the mosaics may have disappeared before 1634.[4] Writing between 1724 and 1744, the Franciscan friar Eleazar Horn gives a description of the interior of the Dome of the Rock culled from textual sources and contemporary eyewitness accounts in which he reports a process of selective whitewashing, stating, "The walls in the upper parts are adorned with mosaics; those that represented the figures of Angels etc. the Moslems caused to be whitened with lime, but those showing flowers were left intact." He adds that this was undertaken some years previously at the behest of a qadi, or judge.[5] I have been unable to determine either the exact date or the circumstances in which the mosaics of the Dome of the Rock were uncovered again, but some or all were visible four decades later, in the 1860s, when Melchior de Vogüé studied the monument and photographs of its interior were taken.[6]

FIGURE 5.1: Felix Bonfils, western portico wall of the Friday Mosque of Damascus around 1860, with its wall mosaics plastered and whitewashed. Myron Bement Smith Collection, Freer Gallery of Art and Arthur M. Sackler Gallery Archives, Smithsonian Institution, Washington, DC, FSA_A.04_02.6.1.11.

What is especially interesting about the whitewashing of the Umayyad mosaics in Damascus and Jerusalem during the sixteenth and seventeenth centuries is the temporal coincidence with the events of the Protestant Reformation in Europe. Even as these events were transforming the appearance of northern European churches, rewriting sacred space by means of hammers and whitewash, the glittering ornaments in a number of key late antique mosques and churches were being obscured by similar means in the Ottoman lands of the eastern Mediterranean. In fact, in later centuries the whitewashed interiors of the early Islamic shrines of Palestine and Syria struck a chord with European Protestants who visited the Umayyad monuments of Syria. The English physician Robert Richardson, who visited the Dome of the Rock around 1817–18 (at which time the mosaics were evidently still whitewashed), noted, "The inside of the wall is white, without any ornament, and I confess I am one who think ornaments misplaced in a house of prayer, or any thing to distract the mind when it comes there to hold converse with its God."[7]

FIGURE 5.2: Western portico wall of the Friday Mosque of Damascus with the original eighth-century mosaics revealed. Photograph, Manar al-Athar Photo Archive, MAA21827_052_IMG_2381.

FIGURE 5.3: Friday Mosque of Damascus, detail of the eighth-century mosaics in the western portico of the courtyard. Photograph, Manar al-Athar Photo Archive, MAA21841_066_IMG_2213A.

Such perceptions of a resonance between the aesthetics of reformed Christian churches and the altered, whitewashed interiors of certain mosques and shrines may not be entirely serendipitous. During the Protestant Reformations of the sixteenth century, Catholic iconophiles consistently accused Protestant reformists of transforming churches into mosques through their instrumentalization of iconoclasm and whitewash. I return to this theme later.

Richardson was probably unaware of the fact that the whitewashed interior he so admired was itself the result of a dramatic aesthetic transformation, but the likely reasons for it undoubtedly would have struck a chord as deep as its transcendental resonances. From as early as a year or two after the completion of the Damascus mosque in 715, objections were raised to the ostentation of its ornamentation and the expense that it had incurred. These anxieties about the ornaments of the mosque came to the fore in Damascus just before 720, in the wake of a failed attempt to capture Constantinople. The pious caliph 'Umar ibn 'Abd al-'Aziz, or 'Umar II (r. 717–20), is even reported to have gone as far as to temporarily cover its mosaics with white canvas or drapes and melt its golden lamps to remonetize their metal components.[8] Conversely, despite its ultimate failure, that campaign came close to succeeding and seems to have galvanized a sense among some Byzantine Christians that the proliferation of image veneration in Byzantium was responsible for the rise and military prowess of Islam.[9]

Debates about the appropriate ornamentation of sacred space that swirled in eighth-century Damascus were perpetuated in medieval Islamic juridical texts concerning the mosque, in which they assumed a paradigmatic role. The jurists adopted a variety of attitudes to the ornamentation of mosques—some even going as far as to prohibit the presence of Qur'anic inscriptions. Assuming a dialectical tension between unadorned piety and the elaboration of the mosque, objections to the aniconic ornament of the mosque are threefold: that the gold, marble, and mosaics attracted the gaze of the worshipers and distracted them from prayer; that gold should be used to mediate exchange rather than fetishized in its own right; and that the monies expended on the ornamentation of the mosque would have been better served in service of the *umma*, the transnational Muslim community.

The relationship of juridical norms to social practice was erratic, but it is clear that at certain times and in certain places anxieties about fancy ornaments in mosques, even aniconic ornaments, led to their destruction or their occlusion by plaster or whitewash.[10] It seems likely that the plastering of the mosaics in Damascus (see figure 5.1) and the whitewashing of those in Jerusalem represents a moment in the early modern period in which those who objected to glittering ornaments in mosques gained the upper hand.

Pious objectors not only contrasted the elaboration of the mosque with the simple piety of the Prophet Muhammad's time but worried that the use of fancy ornaments would lead to confusion, creating mosques that resembled churches and synagogues and undermining the articulation of a distinct Muslim identity. This concern with identity assumes a particular irony in light of the fact that it was the whitewashing of mosque ornaments that enabled a perceived homology with Christian sacred space on the part of post-Reformation visitors to the Middle East. This homology was, of course, itself enabled by the tumultuous events of the sixteenth century and the dramatic rearticulation or rewriting of sacred space that it produced in European Christendom. Just as in the Islamic world the application of whitewash could be represented as a reversion to a purer, prelapsarian practice, so Protestant revolutionaries frequently portrayed their actions as a reversion, a practical reform of corrupted sacred space.

There are, in fact, striking similarities between the precise nature of Islamic and Protestant objections to ornament and the remedial actions that they inspired. These commonalities reflect a shared debt to late antique discourses on ornament, images, and bodies, highlighting a relationship that is genealogical rather than truly serendipitous and in which concerns about aesthetics, economics, and ethics intersected within the "economy of piety."[11]

In a volume concerned with remapping cognitive frontiers, it may seem somewhat paradoxical to address the hoary topics of aniconism and iconoclasm, especially given the long-established clichés about Islam on this score. However, the past few decades have seen an exponential rise in articles and monographs on the topic of iconoclasm in general, and its role in the events of the Protestant Reformation in particular. What is especially striking to me, as an Islamicist, is the fact that Islam is largely, if not entirely, absent from this spate of publications on images, iconoclasm, and the Reformation.[12] One searches in vain in the indexes of these publications for "Islam," "Ottomans," or "Turks." In other words, for all their merits, they have added little or nothing to our understanding of Reformation image polemics as cross-culturally inflected. Yet as I will demonstrate, the experience and representation of Islam are deeply implicated in Reformation debates about aniconism, images, and the aesthetics of sacred space.

At a time in which the role and very visibility of Islam in European public life is again in contention, it is worth drawing attention to aspects of a historical entanglement that are both occluded in most modern scholarship and riddled with contradictions and paradoxes that are quite familiar from current discourses on Islam and the nature of European identity. Those contradictions were typified by the discursive representations of Islam and Muslims in the recent controversy over the Danish caricatures of the Prophet Muhammad, which reminded us that it is not only images and objects that circulate, remapping space and time in ways that alter, confound, consolidate, or undermine cultural or geographic imaginaries and the reified or stratified identities that underwrite them. No less important are the discursive formations that enable or impede the circulation and reception of artifacts, concepts, and practices, formations that condition both inter- and intracultural perceptions and representations of sacred space. When it comes to the polemics of aniconism, both images and discourses concerning their ontological status and epistemological value can be and have been mobilized in service of European identities defined relationally. In fact, from the perspective of the *longue durée*, one of the most striking features of this mobilization has been the inconstancy and instability of Islam's perceived aniconism and iconoclasm, despite the historical centrality of both to etic representations of Muslims. As the material presented here suggests, there is in fact a demonstrable correlation between historical moments of European angst about either Muslims or images (or both) and the production, modification, or reinvestment of discourses on Islamic aniconism and iconoclasm.[13]

If I offer here a very schematic reconstruction of one moment in a diachronic history that often appears agonistic, it is largely because of the importance that this moment has assumed in narratives of Europe's march toward modernity. This importance may, in part, explain the failure to interrogate the ways in which the experience of Islam was relevant to the Reformation and its discursive frameworks. In narratives of the emergence of European modernity, there is universal agreement that events of the sixteenth century mark a significant watershed. Depending on the narrative, the resulting break with an archaic medieval past was marked by the flourishing of humanism, a new spirit of scientific inquiry related (at least in part) to the experience of new worlds, major artistic innovations that promoted the autonomy of the image, a reformulation of the role of religion in public life that enabled the eventual emergence of a public sphere, and even a fundamental shift in the semiotic regimes of European cultures that rewrote the relationship between images, words, and their referents as arbitrary rather than essential or necessary.[14] This is a history from which Islamic cultures are generally excluded, reflecting a general agreement that they have not benefited from the same historical trajectory, now universalized as a transcendental necessity. The omission is all the more striking when one considers that many of these Reformation-era developments were promoted by a formative iconoclasm that was both figurative and literal; histories of image breaking are the one domain in which Islamic cultures are traditionally depicted as avant-garde.

When it comes to what traditionally has been called the Renaissance, recent scholarship has done much to redress the balance, pointing, for example, to the deep engagements between the Ottomans and the humanistic culture of peninsular Italy.[15] By contrast, the continued marginalization of the experience of Islam from accounts of what—from a European perspective, at least—was a foundational development of the sixteenth century is, I suspect, closely related to the central role that the events of the Reformation have assumed in narrative accounts of the emergence of European modernity, a phenomenon often seen as both historically unique and sui generis. Yet if the Reformation marks a crucial stage in the emergence of European modernity, the experience of Muslims (directly or in the form of rhetorical representations) as proponents of a particular belief system, mercantile allies or adversaries, military opponents, polemical figures, and even pietistic models was deeply implicated in that process.

A point of entry into this neglected history is provided by a remarkable sermon delivered on October 2, 1586, almost seventy years after the first shots of the Reformation are traditionally believed to have been fired. The preacher was the Anglican clergyman Meredith Hanmer (d. 1604), and the venue was the Collegiate Church of St. Katharine, next to the Tower of London. The occasion of the sermon was unique in the history of the Anglican church: it commemorated the baptism into Anglicanism of a Muslim Turk from Euboea, in Greece, whose name is given as Chinano and who had recently been rescued by Sir Francis Drake from decades of enslavement on a Spanish galley in the Caribbean. In Hanmer's sermon, Chinano's conversion to Anglicanism is said to have been prompted by an intense dislike of two essential Spanish characteristics: cruelty and "Idolatry in worshipping of images." Appropriately, Hanmer's sermon discussed the possibility of converting the Turks, emphasizing that the Turks scorned the pope and reviled unreformed churches for their idols and images, citing (if a little vaguely) a Turkish embassy that refused the invitation to convert to unreformed Christianity, since this was "the religion of idle persons, of faint, and weake people, and of Idolaters, worshipping of Images."[16] According to Hanmer, image worship had been a stumbling block to the earlier conversion of the Saracen Arabs in Spain. With its abolition in Protestantism, he expressed a common Protestant hope that heathens, Jews, Turks, and Saracens would soon be converted. Aniconism was thus presented as a virtue that not only excluded Catholics, but (rhetorically, at least) had the potential to bring Muslims into constellation with, and perhaps even transform them into, Protestant Christians.[17]

The hope that the common rejection of idolatry might draw together Arabs, Jews, Turks, and Protestants was something of a commonplace in Reformist polemics. In *A Treatise Declaring and Showing That Images Are not to Be Suffered in Churches* (1535), for example, the Strasbourg-born Martin Bucer denounced images as providing ammunition to Jewish and Muslim critics of Christianity while impeding their conversion. Similarly, in 1543, the French ecumenist Guillaume Postel (d. 1581) outlined twenty-eight points of resemblance between Islamic and Protestant beliefs and practices, the fourteenth of which was a rejection of images in places of worship.[18]

On occasion, Protestant aspirations for Muslim conversion even found a counterpart in the aspirations for Protestant-Muslim convergence that inform Ottoman realpolitik, which equally engage the question of the image. A letter addressed by sultan Selim II, successor of Suleiman the Magnificent, to the Lutheran law school or sect (*Lūtharān mezheb*) in 1574, when the Ottomans were contesting the western Mediterranean with the Hapsburgs, makes much of the common rejection of idolatry while mistakenly assuming that Protestants rejected the divinity of Jesus, as Muslims do:

> As you, for your part, do not worship idols, you have banished the idols (*būt*) and pictures (*ṣūrat*) and bells (*nāqūs*) from churches, and declared your faith by stating that God Almighty is One and Holy Jesus is His Prophet and Servant, and now, with heart and soul, are seeking and desirous of the true faith; but the faithless one they call Pāpā (i.e., the Pope) does not recognize his Creator as One, ascribing divinity to Holy Jesus (upon him be peace!), and worshipping idols and pictures which he has made with his own hands, thus casting doubt upon the Oneness of God and instigating how many servants of God to that path of error.[19]

The letter seems to have formed part of an Ottoman strategy to inspire a common anti-Hapsburg front consisting of Ottoman Muslims in North Africa; Moriscos (Spanish Muslims converted to Catholicism) in Spain, who had rebelled in 1568; and Dutch Protestants, who had led an iconoclastic revolt against Spanish rule in the Netherlands in 1566.[20] A letter reportedly written from the Moriscos to the Turkish bey of Algiers in 1568 and intercepted and translated by the Castillian rulers puts particular emphasis on Christian attempts to force the converted Muslims into image worship, one reason that crucifixes, paintings, and sculptures in the churches of Al-Andalus were specifically targeted by the Moriscos during their revolt.[21]

Sultan Selim's emphasis on a common rejection of the signs of idolatry finds a counterpart in the diplomatic protocols used by Elizabeth I of England in a letter written to his successor, Murad III, in 1579, in which she begins by styling herself as the defender of the Christian faith "against all kinde of idolatries," and ends by invoking the blessings of God, "a most severe revenger of all idolatrie," and false gods, upon the Ottoman sultan.[22] The exchanges between the Ottoman court and that of Elizabeth I reflect a common recognition of each as the enemy of idolatry, an understanding that was both economically and strategically beneficial. The emphasis on bells (literally, the *nāqūs* or *semantron* used by eastern Christians) in Selim's letter to the European Protestants, for example, assumes a special irony in light of the brisk sixteenth-century trade in bell metals—metals derived from the broken bells, images, and ornaments of Catholic churches and abbeys—between England and Ottoman Turkey, where the metals were used for Ottoman munitions, including those used against the Hapsburgs.[23]

The invocation of Protestant aniconism in an imperial Ottoman communiqué and an Anglican conversion sermon crafted within a decade or so of each other provides a dramatic illustration of the way in which Islam's relation to the image featured in both inter- and intra-sectarian polemical exchanges of the sixteenth century. Despite its palpable presence in these exchanges, as noted earlier, Islam is entirely absent from the spate of publications on images, iconoclasm, and the Reformation that have proliferated over the past three decades. Yet representations of Islam are inextricably linked to Reformation debates about aniconism, images, and idolatry, often in ways that appear contradictory or paradoxical to modern observers.

The function of Islam in these polemical exchanges is characterized by a dialectic of alterity and identity in which even perceived commonalities could be qualified to assert difference in similarity. The idea of a common bond between the aniconic worship of English Protestants and that of Ottoman Muslims did not, for example, find universal or unqualified appeal among many Reformers, for whom the use of images in secular contexts was a matter of indifference. By contrast, the inveterate opposition of the Turks to figurative imagery is a common trope. If, for example, bell metals could travel freely between Protestant Europe and the Ottoman sultan, other commodities proved more problematic, at least according to European observers. Writing about the reception of European clocks bearing figurative imagery, Salomon Schweigger, a member of the Hapsburg Embassy in Turkey between 1578 and 1581, reports, "They like the small striking clocks which are brought from Germany; but if they show engraved figures, the Turks have them removed and replaced by flowers."[24] In light of such generalized qualms about images even outside the realm of worship, Reformists such as the English Calvinist Bishop Gervase Babington (d. 1610) saw Turkish opposition to pictorial representation in all contexts as excessively superstitious.[25] In other words, while Protestant Reformers might invoke a shared belief in the necessity of aniconic worship, this was as the product of a rational approach to the question of religion not shared by the Turks, who were creatures of superstitious impulses that informed their suspicion of images in general, even outside the context of worship.

The endeavor to assert difference in commonality, to both reconfigure and reassert boundaries of belief and practice, is in fact illustrated by Hanmer's sermon of 1586, with which I began. While acknowledging the utility of aniconism to Protestant efforts to convert the Turks, Hanmer goes on to offer a genealogy of Muslim worship that locates its origins in worship of the pagan goddess Aphrodite/Venus at Mecca. This is a claim first made by John of Damascus in the eighth century, rare in Christian anti-Muslim polemics of the post-Crusade period, which tend to depict Muslims as heretics rather than pagans. Developing his theme, Hanmer distinguishes between the rejection of images by both Muslims and Protestants and Muslim practices that he sees as having more in common with those of unreformed Catholicism. For example, Hanmer asserts that Catholic devotion to pilgrimages, relics, and tombs is "Turkish and Mahometicall" by virtue of its resemblance to the veneration afforded the holy places of Arabia by Muslims and the "idolatrous priestes of Mahomet." The ambiguities revealed here—the notion that, in its rejection of images, Islam has something in common with the reformed church, while the veneration of holy places by Muslims evokes a simultaneous association with idolatrous Catholic practices—is central to understanding how, in the polemics of the sixteenth and early seventeenth centuries, the specter of Islam could be invoked by and against both Catholics and Protestants respectively.

Although 1517, the year in which Martin Luther pasted his ninety-five theses to the door of Wittenberg's Schlosskirche, is conventionally given as the start of the Reformation, the question of the image that was so central to these exchanges was in contention long before 1517. The issue had been rendered pressing by the experience of a newly resurgent Islam on the eastern borders of the European principates. It is worth remembering that the early events of the Reformation took place against a burgeoning Ottoman power that rapidly expanded westward during the reign of sultan Suleiman the Magnificent (r. 1520–66), whose reign saw the fall of Belgrade in 1521, the defeat of the Hungarians at Mohacs in 1526, the sack of Buda and the consequent occupation of Hungary, and the siege of Vienna in 1529.

Christian doubts about image worship preceded this zenith of Ottoman expansion, being first raised as part of the mood of introspection that followed the fall of Constantinople to the Ottomans in 1453. A treatise on the Turks published in 1481 by George of Hungary, who had been an Ottoman prisoner between 1438 and 1458, emphasizes the Turks' lack of ostentation in religious matters and their rejection of images, sculptures, and representations of all sorts. George goes on to elaborate contemporary perceptions of the relation between the aniconism of Islam, its potential appeal to Christians, and the successes of the Ottomans: "When simple folk understand that the Turks hate idols, reject every representation and image as they do hell-fire, profess and preach so constantly the cult of a single God, then their last suspicions about the Turks disappear. But certain men of letters have also said that the endurance of this sect in relation to other sects and heresies derives from the fact that they detest idols and worship a single God."[26]

George rejects the (evidently widespread) idea that Islam is Christianity's bad conscience in respect of images, asserting that the sin of idolatry is less serious than that of the Turks, who worship God falsely by rejecting his holy mysteries. Nevertheless, the idea was clearly being mooted decades before the traditional date for the start of the Reformation. Just as some Byzantine Christians of the eighth century had seen Arab victories against Byzantium as a sign of divine disfavor, so some German and Swiss Christians of the sixteenth century contrasted the aniconic worship of Islam with the image-rich culture of contemporary Christianity, concluding that Christian iconolatry was a sin that had led God to favor the Ottoman Turks and use them as an instrument of punishment against idolatrous Christians.

Luther initially opposed resisting the Turks on the grounds that they were God's chosen instruments of punishment for the vices of Christians, which needed to be addressed before the Turks could be defeated.[27] The theme was elaborated by Luther's follower Philipp Melanchthon (d. 1560), who proposed a causal chronology that related the corruption of Christianity through the worship of images and the promulgation of the doctrine of transubstantiation (the doctrine that the eucharistic gifts are literally transformed into the body and blood of Christ) and the rise of the Turks, noting (erroneously) that the idolatrous doctrine of transubstantiation was promoted by the Fourth Lateran Council of 1215, while Othman, the founder of the Ottoman dynasty, ascended the throne in 1250. He wrote, "The power of the Turks came to increase so that the world would be chastised because of the idols, the adoration of the saints, and the profanation of the Supper of the Lord."[28] Linkage between Christian idolatry and Turkish scourge is also made by the Lutheran authors of the Türkenbüchlein, the anti-Ottoman polemical pamphlets and tracts that proliferated in sixteenth-century Germany.[29]

The aniconic worship of the Turks provided a convenient stick with which to chastise Catholic iconolatry, but it could also be deployed against fellow

Reformists. An ironic passage in Luther's *Vom Kriege wider die Türken* (On War against the Turk), published in 1529, three years after the fall of Buda to the Ottomans and the same year that Suleiman the Magnificent laid siege to Vienna, cites the strict aniconism of Islam as a pious virtue that contrasts with the hypocrisy and inconsistency of Protestant iconoclasts, chief among them Andreas Karlstadt, with whom Luther had clashed a few years earlier on the subject of images and iconoclasm: "It is part of the Turks' holiness, also, that they tolerate no images or pictures and are even holier than our destroyers of images. For our destroyers tolerate, and are glad to have, images on gulden, groschen, rings, and ornaments; but the Turk tolerates none of them and stamps nothing but letters on his coins."[30]

That the aniconism of Islam could be deployed to polemical effect against both Catholics and Karlstadt, mobilized variously as virtue or vice, serves as a reminder that representations of Islam's relation to the image in premodern and early modern Christian texts consistently articulate intra-Christian anxieties about images and their status in worship, anxieties amplified by the experience of an expansionist Muslim polity.

While Reformists might acknowledge the virtue of aniconic worship in Islam, Catholics could equally invoke the specter of its correlate, Islamic iconoclasm, in their denunciations of the material changes through which Protestant aniconism was enacted. The Catholic author of one of the Türkenbüchlein genre, published in 1527 in response to the fall of Hungary, asserted, "The Turk tears down churches and destroys monasteries—so does Luther. The Turk turns convents into horse-stables and makes cannon out of church bells—so does Luther."[31]

Writing in 1573, the English Catholic John Fowler noted that, although the Turkish military victories were physically remote from England, through the actions of the Protestant Reformists, "Turkish fashions and persecutions" were brought into the heart of Christendom itself.[32] The metaphorical remapping of the boundaries of Christian practice implied here sometimes found more literal expression in imperial realpolitik: in 1566, for example, the French ambassador to the Ottoman court proposed to assume control over Moldovia and Wallachia (in what is today Romania) in a rear-guard action that would extend Valois influence to the east of its Hapsburg rival by settling the area with hundreds of French Huguenots, whose aniconism meant that they would be easily assimilated and become Turks.[33] In this way the perceived confessional proximity of French Protestants to Islam might mediate a reconfiguration of political geography designed to cement an anti-Hapsburg bond between the Sublime Porte and the Catholic king of France.

Like the sermon of 1586 commemorating the conversion of a Turk seized from a Spanish galley in the Caribbean, these kinds of projects provide a dramatic illustration of the way in which the European kingdoms, including the Ottoman sultanate, were remaking and remapping (quite literally in terms of contemporary cartography) the boundaries between Africa, Asia, the Americas, and Europe during the sixteenth century and early seventeenth century. Yet the omission of Islam from narratives of the Reformation and the reform of the image in particular finds interesting parallels in accounts of contemporary European expansion, which tend to marginalize or neglect the extent to which the experience of Islam shaped the responses of European Christians to the new worlds to which they laid claim. This was not merely a question of providing a functional paradigm of alterity vis-à-vis religious belief and practice. In some cases, it manifested a deeper resonance in which the very protocols of conquest employed against and modes of taxation imposed on the subjugated *Indios* of the New World were adapted from those previously employed against Christians in the Arab principalities of Al-Andalus—protocols that had been adopted by Christians during and after the *reconquista*. This debt to Islamic practice was readily apparent to at least some sixteenth-century Spaniards, who questioned whether it was appropriate for a Christian empire to "mimic Muhammad" in its protocols and rationalizations of New World conquest.[34]

The kinds of geographic and temporal displacements attested by such adaptations are integral to understanding the representation and role of Islam in the image polemics of the Reformation. While in earlier centuries the trope of the Muslim as idolater facilitated the distinction of Christian icons from idols, the exploration of new worlds enabled the charge of idolatry to be displaced onto new pagans at the very moment that it was being leveled at Catholics by Protestant Reformers.[35] It is not by coincidence that New World spectacles of destruction involving ritual paraphernalia and "horrible idols" (*simulacros horrendos*) such as that described and depicted by Diego Muñoz Camargo in his *Descripción de la ciudad y provincia de Tlaxcala* (1584) (see figure 5.4) echo those illustrated in the paintings and prints then circulating in Europe depicting the destruction of idolatrous Catholic artifacts and images and the whitewashing of churches (see figure 5.5). These events were occurring even as the Aztec temples of Mexico, identified as mosques by the first Spaniards to encounter them, were being cleansed of their idols, whitewashed, and dedicated to the Virgin following a formula established earlier for the conversion of both Muslim believers and sacred space in medieval Iberia.[36] The fall of Granada in 1492 and the subsequent conversion or extermination of Iberian Muslims facilitated this displacement, but even as political Islam waned in the West, it waxed in the East with the

FIGURE 5.4: Franciscan friars burning the clothes, books, and paraphernalia of the Aztec priests. Diego Muñoz Camargo, *Historia de Tlaxcala*, 1584. © Glasgow University Library/Bridgeman Art Library, Ms. Hunter 242, fol. 242r.

FIGURE 5.5: A scene of iconoclasm at Zurich in 1524 by Heinrich Thomann (1544–1618). In Heinrich Bullinger, *Reformationschronik*, 1564, Zentralbibliothek Zürich, ms. B 316, fol. 134r.

victories of the Ottomans and the concurrent rise of the Safavids and Mughal empires beyond.

In the contemporary rhetoric of the Catholic Counter-Reformation, both space and time were relevant to the cultural and political boundaries being refigured by Turk and Protestant. In *That One Should not Remove Images of Saints from the Churches* (1522), a treatise published in response to the influential tract *On the Removal of Images*, written by the arch-iconoclast Andreas Karlstadt, the German Catholic Hieronymous Emser situated the iconoclasm of the Reformists within a long tradition of attacks on the church led by heretics, Jews, Turks, and Arabs (Saracens), following a line of thought first used by supporters of images during the period of Byzantine iconoclasm. Conflating Arabs and Turks under the sign of iconoclasm, Emser reinvests an old notion that Jewish aniconism informed Islamic iconoclasm, explaining how "the Jews first attached themselves to Mohammed, the Lawgiver to the Turks, and attempted to destroy Christian images."[37]

As Emser suggests, for many defenders of images against Protestant critics, their rejection indicated not only a conceptual or genealogical link with the aniconism of earlier Jewish and Muslim opponents of Christianity but also actual affinities with the religious ideas of the contemporary other par excellence: the Ottoman Turks. The theme was amplified in the rhetoric of the Catholic Counter-Reformation. Writing in 1567, the English Catholic priest Nicholas Sander provides a genealogy of iconoclasm that originates in the persecutors of the Old Testament and proceeds through Julian the Apostate, the heretical followers of Arius, Byzantine iconoclasts, Jews, devil worshipers, and the Saracens, "who now worship Mahomet," to Reformist iconoclasts such as Wycliff, Huss, Luther, and Calvin.[38] Just as Jews and Muslims were mutually implicated in both iconoclasm and idolatry in earlier Christian polemical writings, so now in the sixteenth century a constellation of Arabs, Jews, Turks, and Protestants was implicated in the heresy of iconoclasm. As late as the 1670s, European tracts penned in defense of image veneration were addressed to "Jews and heretics and Muslims who say we adore idols."[39]

Jews, Turks, and Protestants alike thus appear as reiterations of the originary iconoclasts, those who tortured the body of the living Christ when it hung on the cross. The theme resonated as far away as Mexico, or "New Spain," where Moors or Saracens (i.e., Arabs) and Turks were often conflated in theatrical spectacles of defeat and victory.[40] An extraordinary image of the Mass of St. Gregory executed in the indigenous medium of rare bird feathers as a gift for the pope in 1539 (see figure 5.6) shows a turbaned Turk and a Protestant working in concert to torment the suffering Christ (see figures 5.7 and 5.8),

FIGURE 5.6: Mass of St. Gregory, feather painting (68 cm × 56 cm), Mexico, 1539, Musée des Jacobins, Auch. Photograph by Benoît Touchard. © RMN-Grand Palais/Art Resource, New York.

FIGURE 5.7: Detail of Mass of St. Gregory, feather painting.

FIGURE 5.8: Detail of Mass of St. Gregory, feather painting.

FIGURE 5.9: Iconoclasts attacking an image of the *Adoration of the Magi*, oil on wood panel (104 cm × 140 cm), Flanders, late sixteenth or early seventeenth century. Douai, Musée de la Chartreuse, inv. 1598. Photograph by Daniel Lefebvre.

recalling earlier Byzantine visual polemics in which the centurion torturers of Christ were equated with Christian iconoclasts.[41]

Among the Old World variants on this theme is a large-scale oil painting on wood produced in Flanders toward the end of the sixteenth century (see figure 5.9). In it, we see a large painting of the adoration of the Magi. To the right of the painting is a bearded and turbaned figure lunging at the painted throat of the Virgin with a sharp pike. Behind him, a figure in contemporary European dress wields an ax against the painting, restrained by the hand of a tonsured cleric.[42] The painting entails a Gestalt, a meta-commentary on both images and iconoclasm, in which the painting of the painted image of the Virgin appears, at first glance, as a depiction of her living body, so that the casual viewer registers the attack on the painting as an attack on the Virgin rather than on her representation. The attack represents a coordinated effort of destruction by the Turk and the figure of a Protestant Reformist, but its iconography lends it a strongly intertextual dimension. For example, the garb of the Turk and the lance that he wields recall the centurion that tortured Christ on the cross, collapsing the distinction between Roman and Muslim attacks on Christianity, on the one hand, and images and incarnated flesh, on the other.

The iconography of the painting was adopted from a depiction of an infamous purported attack on a statue of the Virgin in the nearby convent of Notre Dame de Cambron (Belgium) by a converted Jew in 1322, during which the image was stabbed with a pike multiple times and is said to have bled (see figure 5.10).[43] Here, the theme is reworked in light of the events of the Reformation, including the well-documented outbreak of Protestant iconoclasm that took place in the Low Countries in 1566.[44] The complex iconography of the painting reflects not just a temporal collapse but also the reinvestment of a late medieval anti-Semitic trope of Jewish attacks on Christian images to address the perceived threats posed by the combined forces of Ottoman Islam and Reformed Christianity.

At the end of the sixteenth century and beginning of the seventeenth century, the kinds of polemical accusations visualized in this painting were canonized through the coining of hyphenated neologisms, such as Calvino-Turk, Luthero-Turk, and Turko-Papist, to name the supposed Islamic affinities of Calvinism, Lutheranism, and Catholicism respectively. In an influential anti-Protestant tract published posthumously in Antwerp in 1597 (and again in 1603), the English Jesuit William Rainolds initiated this phenomenon by coining the hybrid term "Calvino-Turcismus" (see figure 5.11) to naturalize and popularize the idea that the theology of Calvinism and Ottoman Islam were imbricated and mutually implicating. Rainold's tract found an immediate response in the Anglican

Matthew Sutcliffe's *De Turcopapismo* (first published in 1599 and again in 1604), which put into circulation a corresponding neologism (see figure 5.12).[45] In *De Turcopapismo*, papists and Turks are described as brothers, the pope and Muhammad compared, and Muslims in general and Muhammad in particular are described as partaking of the heresies of Arian and Marcion—early church heresies centered on whether or not Christ had a divine nature and that, not coincidentally, had found their epicenters in lands now under Muslim control. Enabled by print technology (a key point), this rapid-fire exchange set the pattern for a subsequent pattern of attack and response that popularized hybrid terms implicating Islam in Christian schism.

Forged as part of an aggressive intra-Christian dialogue, these etic representations of Islam served to construct boundaries that were no longer reducible to the gulf between Christian and Muslim. The polemical force of medieval representations of Islam often derived from the mapping of practices associated with pagans, those irredeemably outside the fold, onto those of Muslims. In Reformation-era debates about images, by contrast, the polemical value of Islam derived from its ability to be mapped onto the practices of fellow Christians in a complex dialectic of alterity and identity that depended on the perception of Muslims as heretics and, thus, not entirely other.

In *Calvino-Turcismus*, Rainolds depicts both Calvinism and Islam as modes of Christian heresy, detailing a number of parallels between the beliefs of Muslims and of Protestants, suggesting that Calvinist doctrines concerning the Trinity may have been inspired by the Qur'an and comparing Reformist rejection of religious images as idols to critiques leveled by Muslim Turks against Christian iconolatry.[46] In a particularly dramatic passage, the assault by followers of Jean Calvin and Huldrych Zwingli on religious images and church interiors in Geneva and Zurich (see figure 5.5) is compared with the destruction of the altars and divine images by Ottoman iconoclasts in the churches of Buda, the Hungarian capital, after it fell to Suleiman the Magnificent in 1526. A similar accusation had appeared in an anti-Protestant tract published in Antwerp in 1566, which compared the assault of Reformists on the materiality of Christian worship to the iconoclasm of the Turks after the fall of Constantinople in 1453.[47] By analogy, Rainolds accuses Protestant Reformists of effecting through iconoclasm the de facto transformation of Catholic sanctuaries into "Muhammedan Churches" (Ecclesias Mahumetanis).[48] The phrase establishes a homology (if not a genealogical relation) between the image-free, whitewashed spaces of Reformed Christianity (see figure 5.13) and the iconoclasm and whitewashing through which Christian cathedrals and churches were converted for use as Ottoman mosques (see figure 5.14). It also recalls eyewitness accounts of

FIGURE 5.10: Detail of an engraving of a medieval twelve-image panel painting narrating the Miracle of Notre-Dame de Cambron, ca. 1890, J. van Péteghem, Brussels.

FIGURE 5.11: Frontispiece in William Rainolds, *Calvinoturcismus* (Cologne, 1603).

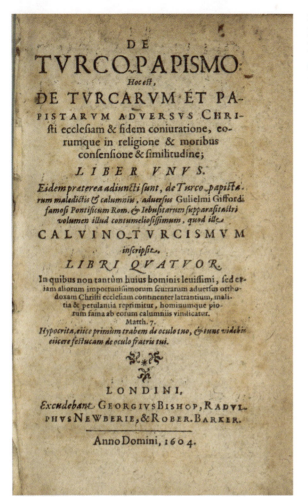

FIGURE 5.12: Frontispiece in Matthew Sutcliffe, *De Turcopapismo* (London, 1604).

the fall of Constantinople 150 years earlier, which describe the transformation of Hagia Sophia into the "House of Muhammad" through the removal of its images. The accusation appears to have been common; in 1595, a Spanish raiding party referred to a Catholic church in Cornwall converted to Protestant worship as a "mosque" (even as the Aztec temples of Mexico were being referred to in similar terms), refraining from sacking it only because of its former Catholic associations.[49] A century later, the English Presbyterian Joseph Pitts, who had been enslaved in North Africa between 1678 and 1693, noted that Muslims favored Protestants over Catholics on account of a common preference for aniconic simplicity in their places of worship: "But they have nothing of any *fine Ornaments* in these their *Geameas* or *Mosques*, neither any *Pictures*,

FIGURE 5.13: Pietr Jansz Saenredam (1597–1665), St. Catherine's Church, (116.8 cm × 95.9 cm), Utrecht, 1636. Upton House UPT.P.128 © NTPL/Christopher Hurst.

FIGURE 5.14: Whitewashed interior of the Selimiye Mosque, the former Cathedral of St. Sophia, Lefkoşa/Nicosia, begun in 1209 and transformed into an Ottoman mosque in 1570. Photograph courtesy of Nicholas Kaye.

Images or any thing of *that* Nature; but the walls are *naked white*, for they utterly abhor *Images*, or any thing *like* them. They blame the Papists for having so many *Trumperies* in their *Churches*, and have a greater respect for *Protestants*, because they have not the like."[50]

What is particularly interesting about these polemical exchanges is not only the role that the destruction or negation of the image plays within them. Rather, it is the intertwining of aesthetics and ethics in the mutual appeal ascribed to the religious forms and practices of Islam or Reformed Christianity and the complex relationship between mosques and the spaces of Reformed worship that arises from it. A practical expression of these aesthetic intersections flourished in Transylvania, an Ottoman protectorate known for sheltering heterodox Christians, where large quantities of imported aniconic Turkish rugs (including prayer rugs) were hung on the whitewashed walls of churches converted to Protestant use during the sixteenth and seventeenth centuries.[51]

Following David Freedberg's landmark study of 1991, there has been much discussion of the "power of images" in recent years.[52] However, neither the currency of this idea nor its own familiarity with the aesthetics of modernism should blind us to the "power of aniconism," its profound aesthetic and moral appeal, especially when posed as an alternative to the corruptions of an established order. Zwingli's celebration of the churches of Zurich as "positively luminous" and "beautifully white" in their transformed state after 1524 may have cut little ice with a contemporary Catholic observer,[53] but it offered the possibility of seeing in the whitewashed churches not merely a negation of the image but the positive assertion of an alternative aesthetic with moral overtones (see figure 5.13). The power of aniconism was doubled by its ability to index the transformation of Catholic space, both by the absence of images (whose defacement or destruction often left telltale traces) and the application of whitewash and words.[54] Just as the reforms could be presented as a reversion to an originary Christianity corrupted through time, the new aesthetic could be seen as the restoration of a primal or prelapsarian aesthetic obscured through the proliferation of images.[55] However, the resonances of the new Christian aesthetic with that described in mosques by fourteenth-and fifteenth-century travelers to the Middle East (who often referred to mosques as "Saracen churches") and the common use of iconoclasm in the transformation of pre-existing churches were no less clear to contemporary observers, whether glossed in positive or negative terms.[56]

In these polemical exchanges, we witness the intertwining of aesthetics and ethics in the perception of a relationship between mosques and the spaces of Reformed worship. Calls for Protestant-Ottoman collaboration, such as that found in sultan Selim's letter of 1574 or appeals for Muslim conversion such as that heard in Hanmer's sermon of 1586, assert the common appeal of image-free practices and spaces of worship, couching in aesthetical-ethical terms a rapprochement that might even culminate in identity. However, this was a double-edged sword, not only because it risked providing ammunition to Catholic polemicists seeking to smear Reformists with the charge of being crypto-Muslims, but also because it acknowledged the potential appeal of Islamic doctrines and aesthetic forms. In 1542, the German Lutheran Heinrich Knaust published the pamphlet *On the Lowly Origin, Shameful Life, and Ignominious Death of the Turkish Idol Mahomet*, which, he explained, was addressed to those Christians who might fall into Ottoman hands and be tempted to apostatize, "led astray by the false glitter of the Turkish religion," a theme common to other Türkenbüchlein of the period.[57] Similarly, Luther's writings on the Turks acknowledge the rational appeal of a religion that lacks the ineffable mysteries of Christianity (a point of attraction for contemporary anti-Trinitarian Christians) and that is marked by the devotion to prayer of the Muslim Turks, their piety and rejection of extravagance and ostentation in both dress and the ornamentation of their buildings. In his 1530 introduction to an edition of a late-fifteenth-century tract on the religion and customs of the Turks, for example, Luther praises the author for presenting both negative and positive aspects of Islamic beliefs, customs, and practices, contrasting the discipline and simplicity of Ottoman religious ceremonies and worship with the empty ceremonies of the papists, which appear as profanely elaborated displays, "mere shadows," by comparison with the disciplined sobriety of the Turks. "This is the reason," Luther explains, "why so many persons easily depart from the faith in Christ for Muhammadanism and adhere to it so tenaciously. I sincerely believe that no papist, monk, cleric, or their equal in faith would be able to remain in their faith if they should spend three days among the Turks."[58]

Ultimately, however, it is this very clarity, simplicity, and rationalism that enables Luther, like Hanmer, to reprise the theme of Muslim idolatry, despite the aniconic nature of Islamic worship. Although Luther acknowledges this as a virtue, in its radical monotheism and its rejection of all expressions of anthropomorphism it is an empty kind of monotheism that appeals to natural reason, a kind of lowest common denominator that excludes the ineffable mystery of the Incarnation and the dogmas of Christ's divinity that lie at the heart of Christianity. In doing so, Luther argues, Islam reiterates the absence at the heart of idolatry. Luther's follower Melanchthon asserts that in the absence of belief in the divinity of Christ, the God of the Muslims is an idol. Similarly, in a volume on the Turks co-written with Matthias Erb in 1567, the Zurich Reformer

Heinrich Bullinger (d. 1575) explains, "Although the Turks do not represent God by images, and although they do not have and do not worship other types of images, their heart is, all the same, full of horrible idols and false beliefs, and they will not be received by God and his saints."[59]

In this way, the Reformists squared the circle, reconciling apparently incommensurate notions of Islamic worship as both aniconic and idolatrous that had circulated for several centuries before the Reformation. However, doing so required a shift in emphasis from the materiality of idolatry, a central feature of Protestant critiques of Catholic beliefs and practices, to its semiotic implications—that is, from the crafted image as an inert form erroneously invested with sacred presence to the mental image as an illusory immaterial presence lacking any referent in an external reality. Perhaps the clearest exposition of this is in Calvin's *Institutes of the Christian Religions* (2:6.4), in which he argues that, through their rejection of the divinity of Christ, the Turks substitute an idol (*idolum*) for the true God, despite their vociferous assertions that God is the Creator of heaven and earth. Elsewhere, Calvin explains that, once the name of God is separated from Christ, it becomes an empty idea so that in semiotic terms the void at the heart of Islam is a signifier with no signified.[60]

The shift from a material to a semiotic explanation of idolatry in the work of Calvin and others is in keeping with the promotion of a theory of semiosis that has come to be seen as a hallmark of early modernity, a theory in which signs (whether images or words) are distinct from and only contingently related to their referents.[61] This was one reason, of course, that Protestants rejected the Catholic doctrine of transubstantiation, the ritual transformation of bread and wine into the actual body and blood of Christ. Despite attempts to depict Muslims as wedded to superstitious forms of reference that conflated images with their referents or failed to distinguish fact from fiction, it is worth emphasizing that for a significant number of Protestant intellectuals, Islam offered a more rational alternative to the doctrines in contention between Christians, an appeal that in some cases led to a mobility not only between theological concepts but also between faiths and polities. One might mention, for example, the infamous Adam Neuser, who began as the anti-Trinitarian pastor of a parish church in Heidelberg, fled to Ottoman Transylvania, and ended his life living at the court of the Ottoman sultan Selim II, after having apparently converted to Islam; Rainold's *Calvino-Turcismus* invoked Neuser as an example of the slippery theological slope that led from Christian heresy to Islamic conversion.[62] The biography of Neuser might in fact be considered paradigmatic of the complex entanglements among empires, faiths, and individuals in the sixteenth century, as demonstrated in recent work on Ottoman self-narratives of religious conversion by Tijana Krstić, who argues the need to acknowledge "Ottoman participation in the age of 'confessionalization.'"[63]

The point I am making is not merely the perceived mutability of religious identity in intra-Christian polemics of the sixteenth century, or even the acknowledged appeal of Islam in a push and pull that threatened the sacralized authority, aesthetic values, and ethical legitimacy of Christianity, reformed or not. Instead, I would lay stress on the constellation of imperial expansionism, diplomatic realpolitik, subaltern aspirations, and theological anxieties that shaped perceptions of Islam in sixteenth-century Europe and the shifts that these occasioned in contemporary cultural and geographic imaginaries. Contemporary Christian discourses on images and Islam offer especially suggestive evidence of the ways in which this constellation was implicated in and by the events of the sixteenth century, providing a cogent reminder that if the Reformation marked a milestone in the emergence of European modernity, as is often claimed, the phenomenon was far from sui generis. In fact, what is particularly striking about this neglected history is that it was not confined to the realm of polemics. Catholic suggestions that Protestants were converting churches into mosques find a counterpart in the hope of many Reformists that the whitewashed spaces of reformed worship might facilitate the movement of Muslims toward a purified Christianity, a hope reflected not only in positive Ottoman perceptions of image-free Protestant churches, but also in Protestant concerns that the lack of ostentation in Ottoman sacred space and practice might attract Christian converts.

As a coda, one might consider the aesthetics of whitewash itself, returning to the Syrian mosques and shrines with which I began. For several hundred years, the splendid Umayyad mosaics lay hidden, occluded from the view of those worshiping within the Umayyad mosques and shrines of both Damascus and Jerusalem (see figures 5.1 and 5.2). Although their plain white appearance was radically at odds with that envisaged by their original patrons, it enabled modes of reception that they never could have imagined. Serendipitously, perhaps, the whitewashing of the Umayyad mosques and shrines seems to have occurred at almost exactly the same time that the Protestant Reformation was radically transforming the interior appearance of Christian sacred space in Europe, at a time that Catholics were accusing Protestant Reformists of achieving through iconoclasm the de facto transformation of Catholic sanctuaries into Muhammedan Churches, even as Protestants sometimes expressed the hope that the banishment of the image from reformed churches would facilitate a rapprochement with Muslims drawn to the image-free worship of reformed

Christianity. The affinities between the aesthetics of whitewash and its moral resonances in both Islamic and Protestant spaces of worship (see figures 5.13–5.14) were sometimes recognized by European Christians, as Robert Richardson's admiring appraisal of the whitewashed interior of the Dome of the Rock in 1817–18 suggests.

Richardson's perception of a link between ornament, prayer, and distraction is perfectly in keeping with the sensibilities of those who whitewashed the glittering mosaics that lay beneath the blank surface visible to him and may reflexively invoke contemporary comparisons between Protestantism and Islam.[64] It highlights the fact that both in its theorization of materiality and consumption and its practical effects, the iconomy of theological Islam reiterates early Christian and Jewish critiques of materiality and anticipates the Protestant Reformists of the sixteenth century who (often drawing on the same late antique sources) rejected excessive expenditure on and ostentation in architecture, ornamentation (of bodies and buildings), food, and language to assert the primacy of interior adornments over an investment in worldly embellishments.[65] Considering the legacy of this Protestant tradition, the anthropologist Webb Keane notes that, "to the extent that their worries about fleshly language articulate with their worries about other aspects of the 'external' world like showy clothing, the forms of etiquette, liturgical rites, architectural ornament, or religious icons, they are part of a more general representational economy."[66] In "its celebration of function over appearance, its rejection of surfaces not just as superfluous but as immoral," Keane sees a continuity of aesthetic tradition between the plain white churches and unadorned speech of nineteenth-century Protestantism and the high modernism of the twentieth century, emblematized by common suspicion not just of ostentation but also of semiotic mediation *tout court* in favor of a representational economy characterized by unmediated transparency.[67]

In fact, one might go further, sketching an aesthetic genealogy from the rejection of ornamented bodies and spaces in early patristic literature through concerns with ornament and the related promotion of whitewash by Protestant reformers (who often drew directly on such literature), among them Zwingli, who wrote around 1520, "In Zurich we have churches which are positively luminous; the walls are beautifully white," and Le Corbusier, whose enthusiasm for whitewash was elaborated in his 1937 book *Quand les cathédrales étaient blanches* (*When the Cathedrals Were White*), and who famously exclaimed, "Whitewash is extremely moral."[68] Between the two lies Adolf Loos's (in)famous 1908 essay "Ornament and Crime," arguing an inverse correlation between ornamental elaboration and civilizational development. Loos's prescriptive aesthetics of modernism not only inspired Le Corbusier, but also echoed Zwingli's celebration of whitewash as embodying a positive aesthetic rather than negation four centuries earlier. Externalizing the interior aesthetic of the Protestant church, Loos transposed its radiant transcendental blankness onto the urban landscapes of modernity: "We have gone beyond ornament, we have achieved plain, undecorated simplicity. Behold, the time is at hand, fulfillment awaits us. Soon the streets of the cities will shine like white walls! Like Zion, the Holy City, Heaven's capital. Then fulfillment will be ours."[69]

The promotion of correct aesthetic form in certain strands of theological Islam anticipates not only Zwingli's, Loos's, and Le Corbusier's enthusiasm for whitewashed walls, but also a rhetoric of whitewashing as an act of restitution or restoration common to late antique Christianity and its legacy to both Protestant and modernist aesthetics.[70] It comes as little surprise, therefore, that just as the whitewashed interior of the Dome of the Rock struck a chord with the young Protestant Robert Richardson when he visited in 1818, the whitewashed aesthetic of Islamic vernacular architecture and mosques resonated deeply with Le Corbusier, who was to insist that "whitewash exists wherever peoples have preserved intact the balanced structure of a harmonious culture." Writing about his encounter with the Ottoman mosques of Istanbul during a visit in 1911, he enthuses about their brilliant white domed exteriors and the blue-glazed tiles of interiors also "clothed in a majestic coat of whitewash."[71] These resonances between the aesthetics of the classical Islamic mosque architecture and Le Corbusier's conception of modernism did not go unremarked. Writing in 1931, Hubert Lyautey, the French governor-general of Morocco whose modernization programs did much to transform the appearance of many Moroccan cities, explained that "Islam gave me a taste for great white walls and I could almost claim to be one of the forerunners of Le Corbusier."[72]

While the intricate gilded ornament rejected by modernist aestheticians and purveyors of religious purity alike instantiates and performs its own intrusive materiality, whitewash, by contrast, appears as a type of cladding or clothing that effaces itself while acting (however paradoxically) as an index of beauty, morality, purity, and truth.[73] More significant, the liberating universalism of whitewash is closely related to questions of temporality, to a paradoxical interplay between the historical and the transhistorical that manifests itself in the rhetoric of restitution. Following a similar logic, Islamic and Protestant reformists could represent the inscription of blankness or whiteness on existing sacred space as a reformation of sacred space that reinstituted a pristine state corrupted through innovation and ostentation. In certain modernist perceptions, as in earlier theological discourses, the white surface is no less imagined as a kind of restoration or restitution of a formal purity subverted by the proliferation of a representational excess manifest in images and ornament. While lavishing fulsome praise on the whitewashed aesthetic of Ottoman mosques, for example, Le Corbusier went on to denounce the painted decorations recently introduced to their interiors, "the ignominy of repugnant and revolting painted ornamentation," which he attributed to contemporary campaigns of modernization. Paradoxically, for Le Corbusier (who here echoes Loos), the purity, simplicity and inherent modernity of this historical aesthetic was being eroded and masked by the application of surface ornament introduced by the "Young Turks . . . ashamed of the simplicity of their fathers." In other words, a true aesthetic of modernity was being effaced by early twentieth-century campaigns of modernization. By contrast, those places "where the twentieth century had not yet arrived" remained bastions of a whitewashed aesthetic soon to be driven out by mass-produced paper, porcelain, and metal ornaments. This attack on "the morality of centuries of tradition" by the virus of industrialization was especially acute in Republican Turkey, where the modernization program of Mustafa Kemal (Ataturk), according to Le Corbusier, had especially pernicious effects on the culture of whitewash. Writing in 1925, he lamented, "No more whitewash in Turkey for a long time to come!"

Paradoxically, it was as a restoration of the morality of an aesthetic tradition not bounded by stylistic nationalism that the whitewash promoted by European modernism promised to reinvigorate the authentic and anticipatory aesthetic modernity of the East.[74] However, even as Le Corbusier was preaching the gospel of radiant blankness, an alternative European vision of both aesthetics and history was stripping the dusty white plaster from the shimmering gold mosaics in the early Islamic mosques and shrines of Damascus and Jerusalem (see figure 5.2 and figure 5.3).

NOTES

Elements and earlier versions of this chapter were presented in the workshop "1500–1600. Entre Islam et Nouveaux Mondes: les réformes dans un contexte global," organized by Alexander Nagel as part of the program *Histoire sociale de l'art, histoire artistique du social*, Institut National de l'Histoire de l'Art, Paris, 2010; as the Trehan Lecture at Bard Graduate Center in New York in 2010; to the Transcultural Visuality Learning Group of Heidelberg University; at the workshop on color at Bilgi University, Istanbul, in 2011; and at the American University in Cairo in 2014. I thank Gülru Necipoğlu for her insightful comments on an earlier draft and Sana Mirza and Jennifer E. Berry at the Freer Gallery of Arthur M. Sackler Gallery, Washington, DC, for help with obtaining images.

1. De Lorey, "Les Mosaïques de la Mosquée des Omayyades à Damas."
2. The mosaics make an appearance in the works of Damascene writers such as Shaikh al-Rabwa al-Dimashqi (d. 1327) and Ibn Shakir al-Kutubi (d. 1361).
3. Behrens-Abouseif, "The Fire of 884/1479 at the Umayyad Mosque in Damascus and an Account of Its Restoration," 283.
4. The mosaics are mentioned in accounts written before 1495, but in his account of the Dome of the Rock, written between 1616 and 1634, the Franciscan missionary Francesco Quaresmio cites earlier accounts of the mosaics, explaining that in his day the interior walls of the building were whitewashed, leaving only ornaments and arabesques. "In praesentia melius diceretur deforis quidem in superiori parte ornamentis et floribus damasceno artificio exornatum esse, et intus totum album, ut qui diligenter interius viderunt testati sunt, et credo, quia communiter sunt albae turcarum mesquitae": Quaresmio, *Historica theologica et moralis Terræ Sanctæ elucidatio*, 87.
5. Horn, *Ichnographiae monumentorum Terrae Sanctae*, 204–5. This may suggest that the whitewashing was undertaken during the restorations to the Dome of the Rock and Aqsa Mosque in 1721–22, which were verified by the qadi of Jerusalem: Göyünç, "The Procurement of Labor and Materials in the Ottoman Empire," 328–29. As to the reason for the whitening of the Dome of the Rock mosaics, Horn's reference to concerns with the figures of angels is intriguing, since no such subjects are immediately evident in the mosaics. The identification recalls reports that seventh-century mosaics covering the exterior before being replaced with Ottoman tiles in the sixteenth century bore numerous winged motifs, presumably similar to those found today on the mosaics on the interior drum of the dome. The exterior winged motifs are identified as cherubim by Felix Fabri, a Swiss pilgrim who wrote in the 1480s; this may be an error, since Fabri was forced to view the building from a distance, but it may also preserve a germ of truth. It has, for example, been suggested that the winged motifs here and in other Umayyad contexts were intended as aniconic evocations of the cherubim that guarded the Holy of Holies in the Jewish Temple that formerly stood on the site: Raby, "In Vitro Veritas: Glass Pilgrim Vessels from 7th-Century Jerusalem," 129–30; Flood, "The Qur'an," 272–73. One intriguing possibility is that the identification of the wing motifs in the Dome of the Rock as angels was made on the basis of their perceived resemblance to images of angels depicted in the mosaics in another celebrated monument under Ottoman control: the church of Hagia Sophia in Constantinople/Istanbul. After the conversion of the church into a mosque following the Ottoman conquest of Constantinople in 1453, the figural mosaics immediately within the view of the worshippers were plastered over. However, the images of the winged seraphim in the pendentives of the Hagia Sophia dome remained visible even after more of the remaining Byzantine mosaics were plastered or whitewashed as part of a major restoration undertaken at the behest of the Ottoman sultan Ahmed I (r. 1603–17), and were identified by later viewers as angels: Necipoğlu, "The Life of an Imperial Monument," 211–19.
6. Melchior de Vogüé, *Le Temple de Jérusalem*.

7 Richardson, *Travels along the Mediterranean and Parts Adjacent*, 296.
8 For an interesting account of these events and their implications for early Islamic aesthetics, see Alami, *Art and Architecture in the Islamic Tradition*, 159–88. See also Flood, "Bodies, Books and Buildings"; Flood, *Islam and Image*, chap. 3.
9 Flood, "Faith, Religion and the Material Culture of Early Islam," 255.
10 Flood, "Bodies, Books and Buildings"; Flood, *Islam and Image*.
11 Wandel, *Voracious Idols and Violent Hands*, 97–98, 100. See also Flood, "Bodies, Books and Buildings."
12 See, e.g., Koerner, *The Reformation of the Image*. A notable exception is Michalski, *The Reformation and the Visual Arts*, which includes a two-page appendix drawing attention to the ways in which the Ottoman Turks were implicated in the polemical exchanges between Catholics and Reformists over the question of the image. See also Kaufmann, *"Türkenbüchlein,"* 44–46.
13 A full discussion of the historiography of the "image problem" in relation to the representation of Islam can be found in chapter 1 of Flood, *Islam and Image*. See also Flood, "Inciting Modernity?"
14 Among many others Cottin, "L'Iconoclasme des réformateurs comme modèle de nouvelles formes esthétiques"; Hofmann, "Die Geburt der Moderne aus dem Geist der Religion; Greene, "Language, Signs and Magic."
15 See, e.g., Necipoğlu, "Suleyman the Magnificent and the Representation of Power in the Context of Ottoman-Hapsburg-Papal Rivalry"; Necipoğlu, "Visual Cosmopolitanism and Creative Translation."
16 Hanmer, *The baptizing of a Turke*, n.p.
17 For a sixteenth-century German pamphlet intended to prepare Turks for baptism and a remarkable early seventeenth-century painting depicting the baptism of the son of an Ottoman pasha, see Deutsches Historisches Museum. *The Luther Effect: Protestantism—500 Years in the World*, Nos. 26 & 27.
18 Bucer, *A Treatise Declaring and Showing That Images Are not to Be Suffered in Churches*, 41–42, adapted for modern orthography; Segesvary, *L'Islam et la réforme*, 100, n. 44.
19 Amended slightly from Skilliter, *William Harborne and the Trade with Turkey*, 37, using the Ottoman text of Bey, *Mecmua-i münşeat üs-selāṭīn*, 2:543.
20 Hess, "The Moriscos," 17–20. On the relationship between Moriscos and Protestants, including conversion, see Cardaillac, *Morisques et chrétiens*, 125–53.
21 Pereda, *Las imágenes de la discordia*, 351–53.
22 Skilliter, *William Harborne and the Trade with Turkey*, 69, 71; Burton, "Anglo-Ottoman Relations and the Image of the Turk in Tamburlaine," 136. William III of England (d. 1702) uses the same phrase later in a letter to the Mughal Emperor Aurangzeb: British Library, Add. MS 31302.
23 Burton, "Anglo-Ottoman Relations and the Image of the Turk in Tamburlaine."
24 Cited in Kurz, *European Clocks and Watches in the Near East*, 46.
25 Spraggon, *Puritan Iconoclasm during the English Civil War*, 16. For the ways in which the notion of a common Christian front against the Turks prevailed in

Europe for most of the sixteenth and seventeenth centuries, see Baumer, "England, the Turk, and the Common Corps of Christendom."

26 Translated from de Hungaria, *Tractatus*, in de Hungaria, *Des Turcs*, 83–84, 89–90, 105–6, 142.
27 Grislis, "Luther and the Turks," 281; Henrich and Boyce, "Martin Luther," 253.
28 Pannier, "Calvin et les Turcs," 284; Köhler, *Melanchthon und der Islam*, 70.
29 Bohnstedt, "The Infidel Scourge of God," 29. See also Kaufmann, *"Türkenbüchlein."*
30 Luther, "Vom Kriege wider die Türken," 107–48. The translation is from Schultz, *Luther's Works*, 46:183.
31 Cited in Bohnstedt, "The Infidel Scourge of God," 24.
32 Highley, *Catholics Writing the Nation in Early Modern Britain and Ireland*, 60.
33 Vaughan, *Europe and the Turk*, 177. Pope Pius II had invited Mehmed II, the conqueror of Constantinople, to convert to Catholicism in return for recognizing Ottoman rule in the former Byzantine domains, an idea already raised by the humanist scholar Erasmus (d. 1536).
34 Seed, *Ceremonies of Possession in Europe's Conquest of the New World*, 92–93.
35 On Protestant perceptions of analogies between African fetishes and Catholic images, see Pietz, "The Problem of the Fetish II," 39–40. See also Eire, "The Reformation Critique of the Image," 52.
36 Eire, "The Reformation Critique of the Image," 52; Remensnyder, "The Colonization of Sacred Architecture," 195–206, app.; Remensnyder, *La Conquistadora*.
37 Mangrum and Scavizzi, *A Reformation Debate*, 12–14. For Byzantine antecedents, see Sahas, *Icon and Logos*, 21.
38 Sander, *A Treatise of the Images of Christ*, 36–37.
39 Bugge, "Effigiem Christi, qui transis, semper honora," 135.
40 On the Iberian roots of these spectacles of Moors or Turks being defeated, see Harris, *Aztecs, Moors, and Christians*, 180–81.
41 The theme of the Turkish threat or its defeat by the Catholic Hapsburgs seems to have been a constant refrain in the visual culture of New Spain in the sixteenth century, finding expression in both public theatrical performances and at least one other feathered object, a shield made for Phillip II, which depicted a series of historical Iberian victories over both Arab and Turkish forces: Gruzinski, *What Time Is It There?* 10–11, 137; Feliciano, "Picturing the Ottoman Threat in Sixteenth-Century New Spain," 244–45, 256–59.
42 Dupeux et al., *Bildersturm*, no. 1510.
43 Lejeune, "Notre-Dame de Cambron et sa légende"; Zafran, "An Alleged Case of Image Desecration by the Jews and Its Representation in Art."
44 For this reason, Norbert Schnitzler's insistence on the Jewish identity of the iconoclast in both paintings is too reductive: Schnitzler, "Anti-Semitism, Image Desecration, and the Problem of 'Jewish Execution,'" 359–60; Schnitzler, "Der Vorwurf des 'Judaisierens' in den Bilderkontroversen des späten Mittelaters und der frühen Neuzeit," 333–58.
45 Rainold, *Calvino-Turcismus*; Sutcliffe, *De Turco-papismo*, 1:3, 20–21. Mout, "Calvinoturcisme in de zeventiende eeuw." I thank Patricia Spyer for help with the Dutch.

46 Rainold, *Calvino-Turcismus*, 7–13, 339, 840, 1010–11. The key section on images occurs on pages 339–52.
47 Highley, *Catholics Writing the Nation in Early Modern Britain and Ireland*, 62.
48 Rainold, *Calvino-Turcismus*, 345. Conversely, writing in 1541, Luther lamented the fall of Buda and the conversion of churches (identified as houses of idolatry by the Turks) for Muslim worship: Ehmann, *Luther, Türken und Islam*, 411. For Ottoman iconoclasm in Hungary, see Török, "Bilderstürme durch die Türken in Ungarn."
49 Doukas, *Decline and Fall of Byzantium to the Ottoman Turks*, 231–32; Jackson, "cristen, ketzer, heiden, jüden," 22.
50 Auchterlonie, *Encountering Islam*, 148.
51 Ionescu, *Antique Ottoman Rugs in Transylvania*, 37.
52 Freedberg, *The Power of Images*.
53 Dillenberger, *Images and Relics*, 178.
54 Garside, *Zwingli and the Arts*, 160.
55 Decades before the Reformation, the Florentine artist Lorenzo Ghiberti (d. 1455) had explained that when Christianity became the state religion in the fourth century AD, drawings, pictures, and statues were destroyed; art came to an end; and the temples were made white: Buddensieg, "Gregory the Great, the Destroyer of Pagan Idols," 44.
56 For examples of such earlier descriptions of mosques, see Bonnardot and Longnon, *Le Saint Voyage de Jherusalem du Seigneur d'Anglure*, 59–60; Fabri, *The Wanderings of Felix Fabri*, 303–4; von Harff, *The Pilgrimage of Arnold von Harff*, 117, 209.
57 Bohnstedt, "The Infidel Scourge of God," 22.
58 Henrich and Boyce, "Martin Luther," 259–60; Francisco, *Martin Luther and Islam*, 160–61. See also Vitkus, *Turning Turk*, 51–52.
59 Calvin, *Ioannis Calvini Opera quae supersunt omnia*, 23:680. See also Segesvary, *L'Islam et la réforme*, 13; Slomp, "Calvin and the Turks," 130–32.
60 Calvin, *Ioannis Calvini Opera quae supersunt omnia*, 47:115.
61 Greene, "Language, Signs and Magic"; Dekoninck, "De la violence de l'image à l'image violentée," 57–67; Dekoninck, "Des idoles de bois aux idoles de l'esprit," 203–16; Squire, *Image and Text in Graeco-Roman Antiquity*, 15–89.
62 Rainold, *Calvino-Turcismus*, 13; *Four Treatises Concerning the Doctrine, Discipline and Worship of the Mahometans*, 212–18; Slomp, "Calvin and the Turks," 134–35.
63 Krstić, "Illuminated by the Light of Islam and the Glory of the Ottoman Sultanate," esp. 48–49; Krstić, *Contested Conversions to Islam*.
64 This was recognized by certain Protestant commentators in the eighteenth and nineteenth centuries for whom the textual basis of Islam and its rejection of idolatry was worthy of praise, even if its contemporary expression was characterized by stasis and stagnation: Almond, "Western Images of Islam," 419–20.
65 See, e.g., Pauck, *Melanchton and Bucer*, 354–56.
66 Keane, "Sincerity, 'Modernity,' and the Protestants," 66.
67 Keane, "Signs are not the Garb of Meaning," 184. See also Keane, "The Hazards of New Clothes," 2, 4.

68 Garside, *Zwingli and the Arts*, 160; Le Corbusier, *Quand les cathédrales étaient blanches*, translated into English as Le Corbusier, *When the Cathedrals Were White*; Le Corbusier, *L'Art décoratif d'aujourd'hui*, 193, translated into English as Le Corbusier, *The Decorative Art of Today*, 192. On the convoluted aesthetic entanglements of modernism and late antique anti-ornamental discourses, see Flood, "God's Wonder."

69 Loos, *Ornament and Crime*, 168.

70 In the period before Christianity developed a richly figural tradition, the early church fathers sometimes presented it as restoring an aniconic natural religion that had been occluded by the representational excesses of Greco-Roman polytheism: Finney, *The Invisible God*, 47. Variants of the idea survived into the early modern period, evident, for example, in Ghiberti's assertion that with the triumph of Christianity art came to an end and the temples were made white: see n. 54.

71 Le Corbusier, *L'Art décoratif d'aujourd'hui*, 187–95; *The Decorative Art of Today*, 185–92; Le Corbusier, *Journey to the East*, 102–3.

72 Lyautey, cited in Çelik, "Le Corbusier, Orientalism, Colonialism," 66.

73 George, *Whitewash and the New Aesthetic of the Protestant Reformation*, esp. 30–33, 200–201; Wigley, *White Walls, Designer Dresses*. In a passage that could have been written about the aesthetics of the Reformation rather than those of modernism, Wigley writes, "The whitewash is not simply what is left behind after the removal of decoration. It is the active mechanism of erasure. Rather than a clean surface, it is a cleaning agent, cleaning the image of the body in order to liberate the eye": Wigley, *White Walls, Designer Dresses*, 8.

74 Çelik, "Le Corbusier," 65; Le Corbusier, *L'Art décoratif d'aujourd'hui*, 187–95; *The Decorative Art of Today*, 185–92; Le Corbusier, *Journey to the East*, 94, 102–3, 129. For Le Corbusier's engagement with Turkish Architecture, see Kortan, *Turkish Architecture and Urbanism through the Eyes of Le Corbusier*. On modernism's self-representation as a balm for the wounds that it inflicted on traditional forms and practices, see Isenstadt and Rizvi, "Introduction," 20.

BIBLIOGRAPHY

Alami, Mohammed Hamdouni. *Art and Architecture in the Islamic Tradition: Aesthetics, Politics and Desire in Early Islam*. London: I. B. Tauris, 2011.

Almond, Philip. "Western Images of Islam, 1700–1900." *Australian Journal of Politics and History* 49, no. 3 (2003): 412–24.

Auchterlonie, Paul. *Encountering Islam: Joseph Pitts: An English Slave in 17th-Century Algiers and Mecca*. London: Arabian, 2012.

Baumer, Franklin L. "England, the Turk, and the Common Corps of Christendom." *American Historical Review* 50, no. 1 (1944): 26–48.

Behrens-Abouseif, Doris. "The Fire of 884/1479 at the Umayyad Mosque in Damascus and an Account of Its Restoration." *Mamluk Studies* 8, no. 1 (2004): 279–97.

Bey, Feridun. *Mecmua-i münşeat-üs-selāṭīn*, 2 vols. Istanbul: n.p. 1275/1858.

Bohnstedt, John W. "The Infidel Scourge of God: The Turkish Menace as Seen by German Pamphleteers of the Reformation Era." *Transactions of the American Philosophical Society* 58, no. 9 (1968): 1–58.

Bonnardot, François, and Auguste Longnon. *Le Saint Voyage de Jherusalem du Seigneur d'Anglure*. Paris: Le Puy, 1878.

Bucer, Martin. *A Treatise Declaring and Showing That Images Are not to Be Suffered in Churches*. London: W. Marshall, 1535.

Buddensieg, Tilmann. "Gregory the Great, the Destroyer of Pagan Idols: The History of a Medieval Legend Concerning the Decline of Ancient Art and Literature." *Journal of the Warburg and Courtauld Institutes* 28 (1965): 44–65.

Bugge, Ragne. "Effigiem Christi, qui transis, semper honora: Verses Condemning the Cult of Sacred Images in Art and Literature." *Institutum Romanum Norvegiae Acta ad Archaeologiam et Artium Historiam Pertinentia* 6 (1975): 127–39.

Burton, Jonathan. "Anglo-Ottoman Relations and the Image of the Turk in Tamburlaine." *Journal of Medieval and Early Modern Studies* 30, no. 1 (2000): 125–56.

Calvin, Jean. *Ioannis Calvini Opera quae supersunt omnia*, 59 vols. Brunsvigae: Schwetschke, 1863–1900.

Cardaillac, Louis. *Morisques et chrétiens: Un affrontement polémique (1492–1640)*. Paris: Klincksieck, 1977.

Çelik, Zeynep. "Le Corbusier, Orientalism, Colonialism." *Assemblage* 17 (1992): 58–77.

Cottin, Jérôme. "L'Iconoclasme des réformateurs comme modèle de nouvelles formes esthétiques." In *Les Protestants et la creation artistique et littéraire (Des Réformateurs aux Romantiques)*, ed. Alain Joblin and Jacques Sys, 11–24. Arras: Artois Presses Université, 2008.

de Hungaria, Georgius. *Des Turcs: Traité sur les moeurs, les coutumes et la perfidie des Turcs*, trans. Joël Schnapp. Toulouse: Anacharsis, 2003.

———. *Tractatus de moribus condicionibus et nequicia Turcorum*. Urach: Conrad Fyner, 1481.

Dekoninck, Ralph. "Des idoles de bois aux idoles de l'esprit: Les métamorphoses de l'idolâtrie dans l'imaginaire modern." *Revue théologique de Louvain* 35 (2004): 203–16.

———. "De la violence de l'image à l'image violentée: L'Iconoclasme protestant comme rupture fondatrice de notre conception moderne de l'image et de l'art." *Ateliers* 28 (2001): 57–67.

de Lorey, Eustache. "Les mosaïques de la Mosquée des Omayyades à Damas." *Syria* 12 (1931): 326–349.

Deutsches Historisches Museum. *The Luther Effect: Protestantism—500 Years in the World*. Berlin: Hirmer, 2017.

de Vogüé, Charles-Jean Melchior. *Le Temple de Jérusalem, monographie du Haram-ech-Chérif, suivie d'un Essai sur la topographie de la Ville-saint*. Paris: Liège, 1864.

Dillenberger, John. *Images and Relics: Theological Perceptions and Visual Images in Sixteenth-Century Europe*. New York: Oxford University Press, 1999.

Doukas. *Decline and Fall of Byzantium to the Ottoman Turks*, trans. Harry J. Magoulias. Detroit: Wayne State University Press, 1975.

Dupeux, Cecile, Peter Jezler, and Gabriele Keck, eds. *Bildersturm: Wahnsinn oder Gottes Wille? Katalog zur Ausstellung Bernisches Historiches Museum, Musée de l'Oeuvre Notre-Dame, Strassburg*. Zurich: NZZ Verlag, 2001.

Ehmann, Johannes. *Luther, Türken und Islam: Eine Untersuchung zum Türken-und Islambild Martin Luthers (1515–1546)*. Gütersloh, Germany: Gütersloher Verlagshaus, 2008.

Eire, Carlos M. N. "The Reformation Critique of the Image." In *Bilder und Bildersturm im Spätmittelalter und in der frühen Neuzeit*, ed. Bob Scribner, 51–68. Wiesbaden: Harrassowitz, 1990.

Fabri, Felix. *The Wanderings of Felix Fabri*. New York: AMS Press, 1971 [1892–93].

Feliciano, María Judith. "Picturing the Ottoman Threat in Sixteenth-Century New Spain." In *The Turk and Islam in the Western Eye, 1450–1750: Visual Imagery before Orientalism*, ed. James G. Harper, 243–65. Burlington, VT: Ashgate, 2011.

Finney, Paul Corby. *The Invisible God: The Earliest Christians on Art*. New York: Oxford University Press, 1994.

Flood, Finbarr Barry. "Bodies, Books and Buildings: Economies of Ornament in Juridical Islam." In *Clothing Sacred Scripture*, ed. David Ganz and Barbara Schellewald, *Manuscripta Biblica*, forthcoming.

———. "Faith, Religion, and the Material Culture of Early Islam." In *Byzantium and Islam: Age of Transition*, ed. Helen Evans, 244–57. New York: Metropolitan Museum of Art, 2012.

———. "'God's Wonder': Marble as Medium and the Natural Image in Mosques and Modernism." *West 86th 23*, no. 2 (2017): 168–219.

———. "Inciting Modernity? Images, Alterities and the Contexts of 'Cartoon Wars.'" In *Images That Move*, ed. Patricia Spyer and Mary Margaret Steedly, 41–72. Santa Fe: School for Advanced Research Press, 2013.

———. *Islam and Image: Polemics, Theology and Modernity*. London: Reaktion Books, forthcoming.

———. "The Qur'an." In *Byzantium and Islam: Age of Transition*, ed. Helen Evans, 265–84. New York: Metropolitan Museum of Art, 2012.

Four Treatises Concerning the Doctrine, Discipline and Worship of the Mahometans. London: J. Darby for B. Lintott, and E. Sanger, 1712.

Francisco, Adam S. *Martin Luther and Islam: A Study in Sixteenth-Century Polemics and Apologetics*. The History of Christian-Muslim Relations. Leiden: Brill, 2007.

Freedberg, David. *The Power of Images: Studies in the History and Theory of Response*. Chicago: University of Chicago Press, 1989.

Garside, Charles, Jr. *Zwingli and the Arts*. New Haven, CT: Yale University Press, 1966.

George, Victoria Ann. *Whitewash and the New Aesthetic of the Protestant Reformation*. London: Pindar, 2012.

Göyünç, Nejat. "The Procurement of Labor and Materials in the Ottoman Empire (16th and 18th Centuries)." In *Économies et sociétés dans l'Empire ottoman (fin du XVIIIe–début du XXe siècle)*, ed. Jean-Louis Bacqué-Grammont and Paul Dumont, 327–33. Paris: Centre National de la Recherche Scientifique, 1983.

Greene, T.M. "Language, Signs and Magic." In *Envisioning Magic: A Princeton Seminar and Symposium*, ed. P. Schäfer and H.G. Kippenberg, 255–72. Leiden: Brill, 1997.

Grislis, Egil. "Luther and the Turks." *Muslim World* 64, no. 3 (1974): 180–93.

Gruzinski, Serge. *What Time Is It There? America and Islam at the Dawn of Modern Times*. Malden, MA: Polity, 2010.

Hanmer, Meredith. *The baptizing of a Turke: A Sermon preached at the Hospitall of Saint Katherin adjoining unto her Majesties Tower the 2. of October 1586. at the baptizing of one Chinano a Turke, borne at Nigropontus*. London: Robert Wald-grave, 1586.

Harris, Max. *Aztecs, Moors, and Christians*. Austin: University of Texas Press, 2000.

Henrich, Sarah, and James L. Boyce. "Martin Luther—Translations of Two Prefaces on Islam: Preface to the Libellus de ritu et moribus Turcarum (1530), and Preface to Bibliander's Edition of the Qur'ān (1543)." *Word and World* 16, no. 2 (1996): 250–66.

Hess, Andrew C. "The Moriscos: An Ottoman Fifth Column in Sixteenth-Century Spain." *American Historical Review* 74, no. 1 (1968): 17–20.

Highley, Christopher. *Catholics Writing the Nation in Early Modern Britain and Ireland*. Oxford: Oxford University Press, 2008.

Hofmann, Werner. "Die Geburt der Moderne aus dem Geist der Religion." In *Luther und die Folgen für die Kunst*, ed. Werner Hofmann, 23–71. Munich: Prestel-Verlag, 1993.

Hom, Elzear. *Ichnographiae monumentorum Terrae Sanctae (1724–1744)*. Jerusalem: Franciscan Press, 1962.

Ionescu, Stefano. *Antique Ottoman Rugs in Transylvania*. Rome: Stefano Ionescu, 2005.

Isenstadt, Sandy, and Kishwar Rizvi. "Introduction: Modern Architecture and the Middle East: The Burden of Representation." In *Modernism and the Middle East: Architecture and Politics in the Twentieth Century*, ed. Sandy Isenstadt and Kishwar Rizvi, 3–36. Seattle: University of Washington Press, 2008.

Jackson, Timothy R. " 'cristen, ketzer, heiden, jüden': Questions of Identity in the Middle Ages." In *Encounters with Islam in German Literature and Culture*, ed. James Hodkinson and Jeffrey Morrison, 19–35. Rochester, NY: Camden House, 2009.

Kaufmann, Thomas. *"Türkenbüchlein": Zur christlichen Wahrnehmung "türkischer Religion" in Spätmittelalter und Reformation*. Göttingen, Germany: Vandenhoeck and Ruprecht, 2008.

Keane, Webb. "Signs Are Not the Garb of Meaning: On the Social Analysis of Material Things." In *Materiality*, ed. Daniel Miller, 186–87. Durham: Duke University Press, 2005.

———. "The Hazards of New Clothes: What Signs Make Possible." In *The Art of Clothing: A Pacific Experience*, ed. Susanne Küchler and Graeme Were, 1–16. London: University College London Press, 2005.

———. "Sincerity, 'Modernity,' and the Protestants." *Cultural Anthropology* 17, no. 1 (2002): 65–92.

Koerner, Joseph L. *The Reformation of the Image*. Chicago: University of Chicago Press, 2004.

Köhler, Manfred. *Melanchthon und der Islam: Ein Beitrag zur Klärung des Verhältnisses zwischen Christentum und Fremdreligionen in der Reformationszeit*. Leipzig: L. Klotz, 1938.

Kortan, Enis. *Turkish Architecture and Urbanism through the Eyes of Le Corbusier*. Istanbul: Boyut Kitaplari, 2005.

Krstić, Tijana. *Contested Conversions to Islam: Narratives of Religious Change in the Early Modern Ottoman Empire*. Stanford, CA: Stanford University Press, 2011.

———. "Illuminated by the Light of Islam and the Glory of the Ottoman Sultanate: Self-Narratives of Conversion to Islam in the Age of Confessionalization." *Comparative Studies in Society and History* 51, no. 1 (2009): 35–63.

Kurz, Otto. *European Clocks and Watches in the Near East*. London: Warburg Institute, 1975.

Le Corbusier (Charles-Édouard Jeanneret-Gris). *L'Art décoratif d'aujourd'hui*. Paris: G. Crès et Cie, 1925.

———. *The Decorative Art of Today*, trans. James Dunnett. Cambridge, MA: MIT Press, 1987.

———. *Journey to the East*, trans. Ivan Žaknić. Cambridge, MA: MIT Press, 2007.

———. *Quand les cathédrales étaient blanches*. Paris: Gonthier, 1965 [1937].

———. *When the Cathedrals Were White: A Journey to the Country of Timid People*, trans. Francis E. Hyslop Jr. New York: Reynal and Hitchcock, 1947.

Lejeune, Théophile. "Notre-Dame de Cambron et sa légende." *Revue de l'art Chretien* (1863): 457–81.

Loos, Adolf. *Ornament and Crime: Selected Essays*. Riverside, CA: Ariadne, 1998.

Luther, Martin. "Vom Kriege wider die Türken." In *D. Martin Luthers Werke: Kritische Gesammtausgabe*, vol. 30, part II. Weimar, Germany: Hermann Böhlaus Nachfolger, 1967.

Mangrum, Bryan D., and Giuseppe Scavizzi. *A Reformation Debate: Karlstadt, Emser, and Eck on Sacred Images, Three Treatises in Translation*. Toronto: Centre for Reformation and Renaissance Studies, Victoria University, 1991.

Michalski, Sergiusz. *The Reformation and the Visual Arts: The Protestant Image Question in Western and Eastern Europe*. London: Taylor and Francis, 1998.

Mout, M.E.H. Nicolette. "Calvinoturcisme in de zeventiende eeuw." *Tijdschrift voor Geschiedenis* 91 (1978): 576–607.

Necipoğlu, Gülru. "The Life of an Imperial Monument: Hagia Sophia after Byzantium." In *Hagia Sophia: From the Age of Justinian to the Present*, ed. Robert Mark and Ahmet Cakmak, 195–225. Cambridge: Cambridge University Press, 1992.

———. "Suleyman the Magnificent and the Representation of Power in the Context of Ottoman-Hapsburg-Papal Rivalry." *Art Bulletin* 71 (1989): 401–27.

———. "Visual Cosmopolitanism and Creative Translation: Artistic Conversations with Renaissance Italy in Mehmed II's Constantinople." *Muqarnas* 29 (2012): 1–81.

Pannier, Jacques. "Calvin et les Turcs." *Revue Historique* 180 (1937): 268–86.

Pauck, Wilhelm. *Melanchton and Bucer*. Philadelphia: Westminster, 1969.

Pereda, Felipe. *Las imágenes de la discordia: Política y poética de la imagen sagrada en la España del cuatrocientos*. Madrid: Marcial Pons Historia, 2007.
Pietz, William. "The Problem of the Fetish II: The Origin of the Fetish." RES: *Anthropology and Aesthetics* 13 (1987): 23–45.
Quaresmio, Francesco. *Historica theologica et moralis Terræ Sanctæ elucidatio: A Cypriano de Tarvisio recognitia*. Venice: Antonellianis, 1880–81.
Raby, Julian. "In Vitro Veritas: Glass Pilgrim Vessels from 7th-Century Jerusalem." In *Bayt al-Maqdis: Jerusalem and Early Islam*, Oxford Studies in Islamic Art 9.2., ed. Jeremy Johns, 113–90. Oxford: Oxford University Press, 1999.
Rainold, William. *Calvino-Turcismus*. Antwerp: Beller, 1597.
Remensnyder, Amy G. "The Colonization of Sacred Architecture: The Virgin Mary, Mosques, and Temples in Medieval Spain and Early Sixteenth-century Mexico." In *Monks and Nuns, Saints and Outcasts: Religion in Medieval Society, Essays in Honor of Lester K. Little*, ed. Sharon Farmer and Barbara H. Rosenwein, 189–219. Ithaca, NY: Cornell University Press, 2000.
———. *La Conquistadora: The Virgin Mary at War and Peace in the Old and New Worlds*. Oxford: Oxford University Press, 2014.
Richardson, Robert. *Travels along the Mediterranean and Parts Adjacent, in Company with the Earl of Belmore, 1816–1818*. London: T. Cadell, 1822.
Sahas, Daniel J. *Icon and Logos: Sources in Eighth-Century Iconoclasm*. Toronto: University of Toronto Press, 1986.
Sander, Nicholas. *A Treatise of the Images of Christ, 1567*. Ilkley, UK: Scolar, 1976.
Schnitzler, Norbert. "Anti-Semitism, Image Desecration, and the Problem of 'Jewish Execution.'" In *History and Images: Towards a New Iconology*, ed. Axel Bolvig and Phillip Lindley, 357–78. Turnhout, Belgium: Brepols, 2003.
———. "Der Vorwurf des 'Judaisierens' in den Bilderkontroversen des späten Mittelaters und der frühen Neuzeit." In *Macht und Ohnmacht der Bilder: Reformatorischer Bildersturm im Kontext der europäischen Geschichte*, ed. Peter Blickle, André Holenstein, and Heinrich Richard Schmidt, 333–58. Munich: Oldenbourg, 2002.
Schultz, Robert C., ed. *Luther's Works*, vol. 46. Philadelphia: Fortress, 1967.
Seed, Patricia. *Ceremonies of Possession in Europe's Conquest of the New World*. Cambridge: Cambridge University Press, 1995.
Segesvary, Victor. *L'Islam et la réforme. Etude sur l'attitude des réformateurs zurichois envers l'Islam, 1510–1550*. San Francisco: International Scholars, 1998.
Skilliter, Susan A. *William Harborne and the Trade with Turkey, 1578–1582*. London: British Academy, 1977.
Slomp, Jan. "Calvin and the Turks." In *Christian-Muslim Encounters*, ed. Yvonne Yazbeck Haddad and Wadi Zaidan Haddad, 126–42. Gainesville: University Press of Florida, 1995.
Spraggon, Julie. *Puritan Iconoclasm during the English Civil War*. New York: Boydell, 2003.
Squire, Michael. *Image and Text in Graeco-Roman Antiquity*. Cambridge: Cambridge University Press, 2009.

Sutcliffe, Matthew. *De Turco-papismo*. London: George Bishop, 1604.

Török, Gyöngyi. "Bilderstürme durch die Türken in Ungarn." In *L'Art et les révolutions, Section 4: Les iconoclasmes, Actes du XXVIIe Congrès International d'Histoire de l'Art, Strasbourg, 1–7 septembre 1989*, ed. Sergiusz Michalski, 261–74. Strasbourg: Société Alsacienne pour le Développement de l'Histoire de l'Art, 1992.

Vaughan, Dorothy M. *Europe and the Turk: A Pattern of Alliances, 1350–1700*. Liverpool: Liverpool University Press, 1954.

Vitkus, Daniel. *Turning Turk: English Theater and the Multicultural Mediterranean, 1570–1630*. New York: Palgrave Macmillan, 2003.

von Harff, Arnold. *The Pilgrimage of Arnold von Harff*, trans. Malcolm Letts. Millwood, NY: Kraus Reprint, 1990 [1946].

Wandel, Lee Palmer. *Voracious Idols and Violent Hands: Iconoclasm in Reformation Zurich, Strasbourg, and Basel*. Cambridge: Cambridge University Press, 1994.

Wigley, Mark. *White Walls, Designer Dresses: The Fashioning of Modern Architecture*. Cambridge, MA: MIT Press, 2001.

Zafran, Eric M. "An Alleged Case of Image Desecration by the Jews and Its Representation in Art: The Virgin of Cambron." *Journal of Jewish Art* 2 (1975): 62–71.

Chapter 6

Mobility and Material Culture: A Case Study

DIANA SORENSEN

Cultural encounters involve crossings and mixings; when objects move across frontiers, they can be studied as tangible engagements between regions that are not entirely determined by a single state power. The study of material culture on the move offers interdisciplinary networks of understanding through which we can discern connections that tend to go unnoticed in stationary, nation-based organizations of knowledge. To try out these ideas in a hands-on way, I will work within the paradigm of the case study, and pay attention to its very specific workings, while drawing generalizations and theoretical insights from singular, historically framed trans-local networks. The knowledge produced by a case study operates within the analogical intelligibility of the example: a case study is not a generalizable, scientific model, but even as it exhibits its singularity in its story, it makes intelligible other, analogous examples or ensembles.[1] Based on a similarity of relations, analogy helps us discern what a singular case can teach us about what can be applicable to other cases.[2] The challenge is to find the right balance between the theoretical or generalizable, on the one hand, and the specificity of each case, on the other.

Now to the case study: it traces the interaction between mobility and art collecting in the late nineteenth century and early twentieth century. By studying the circulation of objects of value, we can look into conditions of possibility derived from diverse historical junctures, together with matters of value, aesthetics, and taste—all within the framework provided by individual and collective agency. Our point of departure is Bernard Berenson, Harvard Class of 1887, who bequeathed to the university Villa I Tatti, his villa in Florence, which is now the Harvard University Center for Italian Renaissance Studies. The brilliant son of poor Lithuanian Jewish parents, Berenson became a rich and famous connoisseur of Italian Renaissance painting. He led a peripatetic life that had his Florentine villa as its base. Villa I Tatti became a cosmopolitan crossroads for the cultured and moneyed elite of the time: the long list of his guests includes such figures as Edith Wharton, Roger Fry, King Gustaf Adolf VI of Sweden, William and Henry James, Vanessa Bell, Bertrand Russell, Benedetto Croce, Isabella Stewart Gardner, and many others. Purchased in 1907, Villa I Tatti over the years became the repository of Berenson's vast library and art collection. When he died in 1959, it was bequeathed to Harvard as an institute that would house fifteen fellows at the earlier stage of their careers. Its library holdings include a broad representation of Renaissance humanistic learning: musicology, history of art and architecture, literature, history, and history of science.

Berenson's work as collector and as connoisseur provides a rich case study for reflecting on the complex intersections of art, value, and society in the final decades of the nineteenth century and the early twentieth century. The map that would chart Bernard Berenson's world, while certainly not planetary, cannot be contained by the nation-state; nor would it fit neatly in the rubric of European studies, because it extends beyond the West to Asia. In the imbrication of multiple, sometimes overlapping territories and their uneven historical interactions we can discern a meaningful balance between the causality of historical context and individual agency. This will yield a dynamic geography constituted by interactions that produce a diverse regime of explanation.

The dynamic geography I consider includes the eastern United States (from Boston to Washington, DC), the Italian Peninsula, and the great manor houses of the British Isles. In each place, very specific local circumstances enabled the circulation of artworks that were being found, identified, authenticated, restored, bought, sold, copied, taxed, shipped, and smuggled between the 1890s and the end of World War II. Market forces helped regulate the logic of circulation, which depended on the ability to pay and the production of desire, on the existence of goods and the need to sell.

A bit of historical context is in order. In the United States, the extraordinary purchasing power of the tycoons who came on the scene in the 1870s and 1880s was the result of the expansion of the industrial capitalist system in the decades that followed the Civil War. The period's name (the "Gilded Age") comes from the title of the novel published in 1874 by Mark Twain and Charles Dudley Warner. We are all familiar with the less lofty phrase "robber barons" to refer to millionaires such as J. P. Morgan, the Rockefellers, Andrew Carnegie, Henry Clay Frick, Benjamin Altman, Cornelius Vanderbilt, Peter Widener, Edward Henry Harriman, Leland Stanford, and Collis Porter Huntington, who were buying (among many other things) early Renaissance Italian art. Their resounding economic success was based on such developments as the unprecedented growth of the great American city, the revolution in transportation and communications brought on by the railway system, the development of industry and the corporation, and the professionalization of management. Adding to these powerful forces were the mechanization of labor and the resulting increased productivity, as well as the drive west with the end of Native American resistance. It was a uniquely transformative era—urban in nature[3]—that produced great wealth and possibilities of consumption.

As we move closer to the question of things and mobility, we alight on the great mansions that were built for Morgan, Frick, Widener, Isabella Stewart Gardner, and Altman. An unsurprising correlation existed between great, recently acquired wealth and the construction of an elite culture that bespoke class privilege, refinement, and the prestige of the past. The echoes of the Medici can be discerned as art was summoned to rise above the materiality of wealth. But while the Medici commissioned artworks to decorate their palaces and chapels, the late nineteenth-century millionaires bought old artworks: culture had to be sought in the sacred fountains of the distant past and from overseas, in what Alan Trachtenberg has called a "privileged domain of refinement."[4]

The paradigm of circulation calls for an understanding of the conditions that enable or hinder flows and portability. While in the United States we have wealth, grand homes in need of decoration, and the desire for distinction, in most of Europe we have great artistic collections of earlier times and dwindling wealth and power. For my purposes as I deal with Berenson and his world of objects in motion, the two main European areas to consider are the United Kingdom and Italy, where most of the artworks of the early Italian Renaissance were located.

In the United Kingdom, to account for the British aristocracy's great collections of Italian Renaissance art, we need to invoke the mobility of a particular kind of tourism that defined the place of Italy in the European imaginary of the seventeenth and eighteenth centuries. What went on to be called the Grand Tour was a cultural pilgrimage to the springs of antiquity in Rome (Greece remaining inaccessible under Ottoman rule), broadened over time to include Florence, Venice, Naples and Pompeii, Genoa, Milan, Siena, Pisa, and Bologna. The Italian Peninsula provided a mixture of spiritual and sensory experiences that defined an aristocratic education that was rich in literature and the arts, ancient and modern history, music and theater, local customs and folklore.

Until the Napoleonic adventures shifted attention to Africa and the Middle East, and before the advent of mass tourism in the mid-nineteenth century, the Grand Tour was a formative cultural destination, a cosmopolitan experience leading to what one scholar has called a "wandering academy" that studied landscape, religious and secular traditions, architectural design, and art. Supplementing the notion of the Grand Tour as a mobile education, we must note that traveling to acquire knowledge of the arts was recommended not simply as part of the essential *bildung*, but also as a compensatory exercise: as a remedy for the absence of a strong British school of painting. In a series of books published in the early eighteenth century, Jonathan Richardson bemoaned the lack of interest in painting among the English: "'Tis remarkable that in a Countrey as ours, Rich, and abounding with Gentlemen of a Just, and Delicate Taste, in Musick, Poetry, and all kinds of Literature; Such fine Writers! Such Solid Reasoners! Such Able Statesmen! . . . and yet so few, so very few Lovers and Connoisseurs in Painting!"[5] In the spirit of the civilizing impulse of the eighteenth century, Englishmen were exhorted to develop a taste for art to counterbalance less desirable inclinations to "Profuse Gluttony" and "Exorbitant Drunkenness."[6] What Richardson decried and the ways it was remedied is, itself, part of an open, layered system of explanation that one could liken to a palimpsest.

If, as we have seen, the poverty of the British art scene called for procuring paintings from other regions, one could have expected the collections to include Italian, as well as French, Spanish, Dutch, and Flemish, artworks. Italy did have the added prestige of antiquity, an imperial past, and the glories of the Renaissance. But the desirability of its artworks was enhanced by another order of causality: the economic one. Long periods of economic decline in the very areas that held the richest stock of paintings (Venice, Florence, and Rome) led to a willingness to sell, despite arbitrary and sporadic export restrictions that often were avoided. An English buyer would find little internal competition for Italian masterpieces—certainly not the case in the Low Countries or in France, which had vigorous art markets in Amsterdam, Antwerp, and Paris.

In the 1880s—the very same decade that witnessed the rapid ascent of the American millionaires—British art collections came on the market at an unprecedented rate. This is a turning point in the history of British patrician wealth and power, as has been meticulously argued by David Cannadine.[7] The causes, complex and diverse, include the worldwide collapse in agricultural prices, which led to the fall of estate rentals and land prices, and the Third Reform Act of 1884–85, which extended suffrage and shifted political power away from a reduced circle of grandees. Instead, in America, fabulous wealth was being generated in business, industry, and finance, not in land holdings. This is a far-reaching transformation that affected a way of life and values—the future was elsewhere, all signs seemed to portend. As Cannadine notes, "The whole territorial basis of patrician wealth was undermined."[8] The prestige derived from owning works of art from the past was, if anything, enhanced: not only were they scarce and hard to obtain, but, more significantly, they were the emblems of the transfer of distinction and refinement from the European aristocracy to the new American elites.[9]

The third point on our map is Italy, where the artworks whose movement we are tracing were commissioned and created in the thirteenth, fourteenth, and fifteenth centuries. Although some of them were owned by the nobility, there was an abundance of neglected riches in the many churches, convents, and monasteries that were scattered all over the peninsula. A determining factor was Italian unification in 1861; in its drive toward the invention of a national tradition and the inventory of treasures, the central government began to focus on national patrimony. Giovanni Morelli (1816–91), the Swiss-educated art theorist who was to establish the anatomy of connoisseurship, returned to his homeland to work on the administration of the nation's fine arts and to begin the important task of inventorying what lay in dusty storage near and far. Morelli's work reveals the extremely close connection between nation building and artistic patrimony: the effort to attribute, inventory, and keep the collections on native soil was integral to his patriotic labors. His itinerant practice was based on visiting religious institutions, notebook in hand, finding paintings, altarpieces, and praedellae. In 1861, he was elected to the first Italian Parliament; in the very same year he became the president of the government commission to record all works of art in public institutions in Umbria and the Marches. Morelli's official sixty-eight-day trip with his assistant Giovanni Cavalcaselle has become emblematic of the role played by looking and attributing in the construction of Italian patrimony. In fact, Berenson and his wife, Mary, literally followed in Morelli's footsteps, and we cannot think of Berensonian connoisseurship without Morelli's foundational work. Yet while Morelli represents the conjunction between national interests and the consolidation of a certain science of connoisseurship, Berenson, instead, helped engineer the greatest transfer of artworks out of Italy and to the United States. Berenson's time in Italy in the 1890s and into the first half of the twentieth century has an inaugural quality. It established a taste for early Renaissance art, and in the process of discussing attending matters of form, style, authenticity, and provenance, he participated in the formation of a particular form of art-history criticism: connoisseurship.

No doubt, Berenson was not the first English-speaking buyer and writer to develop a passion for Italian paintings of the thirteenth and fourteenth centuries, called gold background paintings or Italian primitives. But he succeeded in managing dispersed spatialities and standards of taste where others had failed. Until Berenson came on the scene, and except for the masterpieces of Michelangelo, Leonardo da Vinci, and Raphael, American collectors tended to be drawn to French, Dutch, and Flemish art. In Berenson's youth, there were few Italian paintings of importance in America. There are more now than anywhere else outside Italy. What made Berenson succeed? How did he establish himself as a connoisseur of authority that guided the collecting urges of the Gilded Age? We might think about this question through the lens provided by an earlier story of failure: that of James Jackson Jarves, who in the 1850s had been a pioneer in the acquisition of early Renaissance paintings, or Italian primitives. Jarves realized during his pre–Civil War European travels that the supply of pictures in Italy was "as plentiful as its beggars," and he proceeded to amass a collection that included works by Cimabue, Taddeo Gaddi, Gentile da Fabriano, and others. Yet when he returned to the United States in the 1860s, Jarves was met by an unresponsive audience: in Civil War America it was impossible to generate interest in these artworks. Berenson, instead, operated in a scene that offered the material conditions for taste making and buying. Affluence and travel made for more sophisticated understandings not only of art, but of the art market itself. Berenson's canny use of writing made him not an amateur, like Jarves, but an authority on Italian painters, and he became the quintessential connoisseur, making more of aesthetics than of profit. Although Jarves wrote a few essays about these gold-backed paintings, and even tried to set up a museum of his own on Broadway, he was in many ways untimely—or, perhaps, ahead of the times—and unable to successfully manipulate the relationships among value, aesthetics, and the market. Berenson, by contrast, benefited from the emergence of great collectors such as Morgan, Altman, Widener, and Gardner in the later decades of the nineteenth century, which were marked by the post–Civil War economic boom.

Collecting, of course, involves the serial gathering of objects. In the case of art collecting, the guiding role of the connoisseur establishes value: we cannot separate the emergence of the connoisseur from the practices of collecting that were integral to the Gilded Age. Those new mansions needed to be decorated, but it was the culture of collecting that lent decorating a different status. For Carlo Ginzburg, the *differentia specifica* of the human species is not the use of tools, but the habit of collecting. As we collect, hoard, and arrange, Ginzburg notes, the objects we gather acquire the function of signifying, of establishing communication between us and what is distant in space and time. What things could signify more powerfully than Renaissance masterpieces relocated in America?

Collecting in the Gilded Age was bound up with the specific qualities of its spaces and of its temporality. A sense of belatedness led to the compensatory move of acquisition and accumulation, as if a gaping emptiness required filling. Unlike category-based types of collecting (such as stamp collecting), the principle of organization that ordered the artworks purchased by collectors such as Gardner and Widener was broadly historical: focused on Old Masters, it was not limited to Italy or painting as an art form, for it also included sculpture, rare books, and diverse objets d'art. The key values were authenticity, rarity, and quality, all of which could be delivered by the connoisseur. Despite the connoisseur's crucial expertise, it was the collector herself or himself who organized the narrative of the collection, making the individual subject as possessor the principle of intelligibility of the assemblage. In serial accumulation one can detect signifying processes that transform the objects in their relationship to space, time, meaning, and exchange value.

In the case of early Renaissance artworks, the move out of religious institutions and into the newly erected mansions of the American millionaires reconfigured the devotional by giving it a decorative function. The narrative of the collection was thus superimposed over the life of the work of art, the history of its commission, and the history of its religious function. The domestic interior became a space for self-presentation; filling up walls and display spaces with collected objects secularized them, allowing them to operate in relationships of contiguity with paintings and objects that might never have been exhibited together. The context of origin gave way to the collector's *dispositio*. Arrangement and manipulation were aesthetic practices bearing the collector's personal signature. An owner and collector tends to establish a fetishistic relationship with her collection. As Jean Baudrillard and Susan Stewart (following Freud) have suggested, the fetishism of collecting resides in the "systematic quality of the objects" rather than in the objects themselves.[10] Each one substitutes for a lack, in an open seriality constructed by a chain of acquisitions.

Few collectors exemplify the complex relationship between object and owner more vividly than Isabella Stewart Gardner, whose private collection was one of America's greatest in 1900. A major portion of it was purchased with Berenson's guidance; the correspondence between them reveals the intense emotions that were set in motion as she undertook her serial purchasing. Berenson's and Gardner's transatlantic exchanges can be read as the backdrop for understanding the more personal aspect of the networks of mobility in our case study: the transactions combine libidinal investments through business and aesthetics. Whatever the roots of the fetishistic attachments at work in her desire for works of art, Gardner played the game of collecting with passionate seriousness. Possession of ever rarer and more coveted paintings was activated by a peculiar marriage of quality and quantity: each unique object acquired became subordinated to the drive for seriality. As Baudrillard observed with regard to collecting, "An object acquires its exceptional value *by dint of being absent*."[11] No sooner had Gardner obtained the most celebrated of all Titians, *The Rape of Europa*, than she coveted that rarest of finds: a Giorgione. Moreover, as Gardner and Berenson discuss money—which they do in practically every letter—they allow us to reflect on the crucial question of value, both in the art market and beyond. Obtaining the best was crucial, but it had to be at a low cost. Her thrill was enhanced by obtaining highly coveted paintings; inciting jealousy only intensified the thrill of ownership. When she obtained the Titian, she was especially gratified to hear that the Berlin Museum had wanted to get it. Berenson was careful to subordinate value to the aesthetic experience while offering the information needed to assess provenance, authenticity, and, yes, cost. The correspondence stages the wiles of seduction mobilized by art collecting: a libidinal investment is at work in both their pens, which flow with rapturous prose dealing with books and art. Berenson calls her an "enchantress," a role she performs in her letters. Even the artworks are eroticized: unpacking her *Phillip IV* by Velázquez in 1897, she exclaims, "His Majesty is here! . . . He is glorious. I am quite quivering and feverish over him."[12]

As noted earlier, Berenson's published books validated his standing in the art market. Although writing came to him with difficulty, and he often spent long spells in bed with nervous exhaustion and digestive problems, he produced a body of work that made him an authority on Italian painters, starting, in 1907, with *The North Italian Painters of the Renaissance*, and publishing successively on Sienese, Venetian, and Florentine art. By organizing his work around regions, he mapped an archive that ensured coverage. There were books on general questions related to his own practice, such as *The Study and Criticism of Italian Art* and *Aesthetics and History in the Visual Arts*. Urged by the ambitious dealer Sir Joseph Duveen, he wrote a book about Widener's collection in Philadelphia, increasing the prestige of purchases he had helped set up. A number of his writings for *Art in America* dealt with recent private acquisitions, such as an essay he contributed to the October 1920 issue on the *Christ between Saint Peter and Saint James* acquired by Carl Hamilton from Duveen in 1919. In it, Berenson discussed his claim that it was an early Cimabue, not a Margaritone d'Arezzo.[13] That attribution change multiplied the price by three. Perhaps the most influential tool he developed with his wife, Mary, was the lists of attributions that he produced and revised during his long life. A name change by Berenson could mean that a painting's value would rise or fall precipitously. An "Amico di

Sandro" was worth much less than a real Botticelli; a work from a workshop, less than one attributed to an old master.

Although Berenson insisted that connoisseurship had to be enjoyed "for no utilitarian or pretentious reason" but "for its own sake and because it exercises eyes, mind, and judgment,"[14] it did, as we can see, have a powerful material impact on the world of dealers, collectors, and museums. Yet it was not the path the discipline of art history was to take, and toward the end of his life Berenson would regret the material entanglements that had both enabled and constrained his dealings with art.

The multiple nature of the dynamic geographic connections traced in this case study suggests, I hope, the complex regimes of explanation that are invoked when objects of value are followed in their circulation. What is made legible is the scholarly footwork that is called for as we follow things on their circuitous ways across land and sea, propelled by a relationality of symbolic and material force fields in productive tension. It seems to me that in this tension lies the possibility for a new kind of knowledge, unfettered from the trammels of sedentarism.

NOTES

1 For more on this *problématique*, see Agamben, *The Signature of All Things*.
2 For an enlightening mathematical discussion of the concept of analogy in its intersections with generalization, specialization, and induction, see Pólya, *Induction and Analogy in Mathematics*, chap. 2.
3 The following figure gives us an idea of the magnitude of the urbanization of America at this time: 40 percent of the population of urban townships seemed to disappear at this time. It is interesting to note, as discussed later, that in the 1880s the British Isles and the European continent in general suffered greatly as the result of the worldwide collapse in agricultural prices: see Cannadine, *The Decline and Fall of the British Aristocracy*.
4 Trachtenberg, *The Incorporation of America*, 143.
5 Richardson, *Two Discourses*, quoted in Gibson-Wood, *Studies in the Theory of Connoisseurship from Vasari to Morelli*, 98. Richardson's advice deals with taste and its civilizing effects precisely in the century in which the notion of "civilization" is established, and it is important to note that the understanding of painting is considered a central component.
6 See Aglionby, *Painting Illustrated in Three Diallogues*, 17–19, quoted in Gibson-Wood, *Studies in the Theory of Connoisseurship from Vasari to Morelli*, 97.
7 Cannadine, *The Decline and Fall of the British Aristocracy*.
8 Cannadine, *The Decline and Fall of the British Aristocracy*, 27.
9 Berenson subscribed to the *Illustrated London News*. This publication includes a revealing inventory of the artistic and decorative objects found in great British manor

houses, a veritable guide of privileged lifestyles, elegant homes, and valuable objects on which collectors and dealers would want to keep an eye.

10 See Baudrillard, *Le système des objets*; Stewart, *On Longing*.
11 See Baudrillard, "The System of Collecting," 13.
12 In Hadley, *The Letters of Bernard Berenson and Isabella Stewart Gardner*, 65.
13 See Samuels, *Bernard Berenson*, 275. The painting now hangs at the National Gallery, to which it was bequeathed by Paul Mellon, and it is identified as the work of a follower of Cimabue. As Samuels notes, "The authorship of the painting has been the subject of considerable dispute."
14 In Berenson, "Nove pitture in cerca di un'attribuzione," 774.

BIBLIOGRAPHY

Agamben, Giorgio. *The Signature of All Things: On Method*. New York: Zone, 2009.
Aglionby, William. *Painting Illustrated in Three Diallogues*. London: John Gain, 1685.
Baudrillard, Jean. *Le Système des objets*. Paris: Gallimard, 1968.
———. "The System of Collecting." In *The Culture of Collecting*, ed. John Elsner and Roger Cardinal, 7–25. Cambridge, MA: Harvard University Press, 1994.
Berenson, Bernard. "Nove pitture in cerca di un'attribuzione." *Dedalo* 5 (1924–25): 601–42, 688–722, 745–75.
Cannadine, David. *The Decline and Fall of the British Aristocracy*. New York: Vintage, 1999.
Foucault, Michel. *The Archaeology of Knowledge*, trans. A. M. Sheridan Smith. New York: Pantheon, 1973.
Gibson-Wood, Carol. *Studies in the Theory of Connoisseurship from Vasari to Morelli*. New York: Garland, 1988.
Hadley, Rollin van N., ed. *The Letters of Bernard Berenson and Isabella Stewart Gardner*. Boston: Northeastern University Press, 1987.
Pólya, George. *Induction and Analogy in Mathematics*. Princeton, NJ: Princeton University Press, 1954.
Richardson, Jonathan. *Two Discourses: I. An Essay on the Whole Art of Criticism as It Relates to Painting, Shewing I. Of the Goodness of a Picture; II. Of the Hand of the Master; and III. Whether 'tis an Original, or a Copy; II. An Argument in behalf of the Science of a Connoisseur: Wherein Is Shewn the Dignity, Certainty, Pleasure and Advantage of It*. London: B. White & Son, 1719.
Samuels, Ernest. *Bernard Berenson: The Making of a Legend*. Cambridge, MA: Harvard University Press, 1987.
Stewart, Susan. *On Longing: Narratives of the Miniature, the Gigantic, the Souvenir, the Collection*. Durham, NC: Duke University Press, 1993.
Trachtenberg, Alan. *The Incorporation of America: Culture and Society in the Gilded Age*. New York: Hill and Wang, 2007.

PART III

Worlding, Rights, and Regimes of Representation

. . . . .

Chapter 7

World Literature and the Health Humanities:
Translingual Encounters with Brain Disorders

KAREN THORNBER

The geographic imaginaries of many humanistic disciplines remain relatively disciplined, presuming the boundedness of societies, nations, regions, and empires.[1] This tendency persists despite the fact that people and cultural products have always been spatially and linguistically mobile, crisscrossing the globe in multiple languages and forms along countless, often under-recognized trajectories. Expanding the study of cultural products in new directions by focusing on both relationality and networks of contact—especially along the world's many still neglected pathways of cultural movement and exchange—enables more innovative, less hierarchical approaches to scholarship. It also gives vital new perspectives on cultures of empire and conceptions of power, transoceanic formations and intra- and inter-regionalisms, resource conflicts and environmental crises, socioeconomic and environmental justice, and disease and public/global health.

To give one example, enhancing public health, global health, and health and well-being in general is one of the largest and most important challenges of the twenty-first century. Over the past hundred years, improvements in human health worldwide have been monumental, and there is much to celebrate. Yet significant challenges remain. Inequalities within and among communities remain entrenched. Health gains are often tenuous and can be rapidly unraveled by economic and social changes. According to the World Health Organization (WHO), children younger than fifteen account for nearly four in ten deaths in low-income countries, where people continue to die disproportionately of infectious diseases, including lower respiratory infections, HIV/AIDS, diarrheal conditions, malaria, and tuberculosis. Even when long-standing problems are largely resolved, new challenges frequently emerge to take their place.[2] Chronic conditions such as rheumatoid arthritis (rheumatoid disease), asthma, cancer, chronic obstructive pulmonary disease (COPD), diabetes, cardiovascular disease, HIV/AIDS, and inflammatory bowel disease are the leading cause of death in high-income countries and are on the rise worldwide.

So, too, are brain disorders. The recent deaths of the legendary boxer Muhammad Ali (1942–2016) from Parkinson's disease and winningest college basketball coach Pat Summitt (1952–2016) from early-onset Alzheimer's disease have drawn renewed attention to this public health crisis.[3] The number of dementia cases is rising rapidly as populations age globally; the World Health Organization (WHO) reports that 7.7 million cases of dementia are diagnosed annually, and nearly 48 million people worldwide live with dementia, with 75.6 million predicted by 2030 and 135.5 million by 2050.[4] The WHO estimates that the total global cost of dementia in 2010 was $604 billion, or a full 1 percent of the gross world product. A related public health priority is traumatic brain injury (TBI), the leading causes of which are falls, vehicle-related collisions, violence, sports injuries, and explosive blasts and other combat injuries. At particular risk are members of the armed forces, athletes, and the elderly, but TBI can happen to anyone.[5] Approximately ten million people are affected annually, with the WHO predicting that road accidents will follow only heart disease and depression as the leading contributor to the global burden of disease and disability.[6] Increasingly, those who do not live with brain disorders themselves are close to someone who does.

More is being done than ever before—by researchers in an array of fields—to develop prevention strategies, earlier diagnoses, effective treatments, and appropriate care for dementia, TBI, and a range of related brain disorders.[7] Creative writers, too, including J. Bernlef (1937–2012) from the Netherlands, Lisa Genova (1970–) from the United States, Alice Munro (1931–) from Canada, Ogawa Yōko (小川洋子, 1962–) from Japan, and Shin Kyung-sook (Sin Kyŏngsuk, 신경숙, 1963–) from Korea, have published a robust corpus of spatially and linguistically mobile literary works on these conditions, thereby increasing public awareness and helping change popular understandings throughout the world as their works are translated into dozens of languages.[8] Many of these creative texts depict people living with brain disorders in a far more "complex, empathic, and sensitive way than medical models can transmit."[9] While encouraging sensitivity and empathy toward individuals with brain disorders, literary works frequently reveal the arbitrariness of describing these conditions, pointing to just how readily, and often unintentionally, patients can be pigeonholed and misunderstood.

For their part, scholars and practitioners of the medical and, more recently, health humanities have used literature, together with a palette of artistic products, in an attempt to transform treatment of affected individuals in the clinical setting, in families, and in society more broadly.[10] In addition to analyzing the assumptions, methods, and models of medical education, research, and practice, the health humanities also are devoted to appreciating better the complexities and nuances of clinical and other encounters among patients, caregivers, and communities, the needs of both patients and health-care providers, and the interests and responsibilities of people and societies. In so doing, the health humanities have deepened understandings of the diverse lived experiences of suffering across time and space from multiple standpoints—those of patients, professional health-care providers (e.g., physicians, nurses, nurse practitioners, and social workers), nonprofessional caregivers (e.g., family members, friends, and neighbors who assume primary or secondary caregiver responsibilities), and the patient's other loved ones, as well as communities, societies, and humanity writ large.

To date, scholarship in the health humanities, and especially in the subfield of literature and medicine, has tended to focus on Anglo-American writings. For instance, far more attention has been given to North American writing on HIV/AIDS than to texts on this disease from other parts of the world, despite the fact that the HIV/AIDS population of Sub-Saharan Africa dwarfs that of North America.[11] Furthermore, the health humanities for the most part have not examined how these texts circulate, in the original and in translation, regionally and globally. In contrast, the field of world literature not only is less constrained geographically but also has devoted significant attention to creative mobility within and between languages.[12] Yet world literature so far has not given sustained consideration to the travel and transformation of texts engaging with many matters of urgent global concern, including health and well-being.[13] Thinking along the lines of a global world literature, and in this case doing more to integrate world literature and the health humanities, promises to provide vital insights into how discourse on disease, as well as illness, is created and translated within and across cultures.[14] And one of the most productive ways to integrate the health humanities with world literature is to analyze the global literature of major public health epidemics, including brain disorders.[15]

The spatial and linguistic mobility of the Japanese writer Ogawa Yōko's bestselling and globally translated *Hakase no aishita sūshiki* (博士の愛した数式, *The Equations the Professor Loved*, 2003) is particularly revealing.[16] This novel is narrated by a woman who looks back at her time caring for a mathematics professor in his sixties who, twenty years earlier, in 1975, sustained a traumatic brain injury in a traffic accident. The professor's memory of events before the accident is intact, but he has only eighty minutes of short-term memory.[17] Eventually, even these eighty minutes disappear as the professor loses his short-term memory altogether. The final few pages of *The Equations* cover the professor's last decade, which he spends in a long-term care facility, visited frequently by the narrator and her son.

Ogawa's novel probes the dynamic not of people refusing to listen to patients' stories of illness or of people sidestepping these stories, as is common in many works about illness, but of attempts to relate to an individual living with TBI whose combination of memory loss and intrinsic reticence concerning his personal life beyond mathematics and baseball prevents him from talking about his medical condition and his life more generally. *The Equations* speaks to the challenges and possibilities of understanding, communicating with, and caring for individuals physically or emotionally unable to speak about their experiences with illness.[18] Emphasized throughout the novel is the importance of being empathic and sensitive to the well-being of others, of consciously striving to do right by others even when conventional communication is impeded.

In *The Illness Narratives*, Arthur Kleinman asserts that patients order their experience of illness "as personal narratives" and that "to fully appreciate the sick person's and the family's experience, the clinician must first piece together the illness narrative as it emerges from the patient's and the family's complaints and explanatory models.... Time must be devoted in the [medical school] curriculum to teaching students how to interpret the illness narrative and assess the illness experience."[19] Building on Kleinman's scholarship, Rita Charon established the now flourishing field of narrative medicine, understood broadly as harnessing "narrative theories and practices to improve the care of the sick" and as "medicine practiced with the narrative skills of recognizing, absorbing, interpreting, and being moved by the stories of illness."[20] Sayantani DasGupta similarly argues that "Narrative Medicine is the clinical and scholarly movement to honor the central role of story in healthcare.... we [should] hold in equal stead multiple ways of knowing—the scientific and the storied."[21] But what happens when there is no illness narrative—or, rather, no narrative from the patient about illness; when the professor in Ogawa's novel is virtually silent about his own condition and experiences, even as he is loquacious regarding mathematics, baseball, and the well-being of his caregiver's son?[22]

The Equations is inconsistent regarding the professor's condition, providing conflicting information on the state of his overall memory, how his short-term memory functions, the condition of his mind and brain, and his lived experience; the professor's condition is interpreted in multiple ways, even by the same person. These differences bring renewed attention to the difficulties inherent in categorizing a disease and illness experience about which the affected individual says virtually nothing and to the randomness with which people and conditions are labeled. Compounding the inconsistencies within the text itself are the variations across the novel's many different translations. An unrelentingly mobile novel, *The Equations* has been translated into more than a dozen languages worldwide, including Catalan, Chinese, Dutch, English, French, German, Greek, Hebrew, Italian, Korean, Malay, Persian, Slovenian, Spanish, Swedish, and Vietnamese.[23] This range of translations, from other parts of East Asia to Southeast Asia, the Middle East, Europe, and North America, is a reminder of the spatial and linguistic mobility of literature on health and illness, whether from a non-Western language into a Western language (or vice versa), the most commonly studied vectors after translations between Western languages; from one non-Western language directly into another; or from a non-Western language into another non-Western language via a Western language.[24]

Just as important, the many differences in how the translations of *The Equations* describe the professor's overall memory, how his short-term memory functions, the condition of his mind and brain, and his lived experience cannot readily be attributed to cultural differences regarding treatment of TBI or brain disorders more generally. In other words, to give one example, the differences between the German and the Korean versions of Ogawa's novel do not stem from differences between German and Korean attitudes toward brain disorders. Instead, taken together, the differences among the translations of *The Equations* underscore the fundamental subjectivities and even capriciousness at play in labeling and describing people and conditions. The differences reinforce our continued lack of understanding about brain disorders and the experiences of those who live with them. Ogawa's novel suggests, and its many translations emphasize, that more caution is needed in speaking about these conditions and that more care must be given to grasping what patients most want and need from their caregivers and from society writ large.

The pages that follow analyze how seven translations of the Japanese-language version of *The Equations*—two Chinese in addition to English, French, German, Italian, and Korean—grapple with describing both the professor's medical condition and his experiences with this condition.[25] All versions agree that the professor's memory of events before his car accident in 1975 remains intact but that he has only eighty minutes of short-term memory, a condition brought on by a TBI suffered in the crash. Yet the translations vary in their interpretations of the implications of this condition; the fact that these divergences do not stem from cultural differences further highlights the arbitrariness of how conditions, and people, are categorized.

To begin with, there is the state of the professor's overall memory: given his eighty-minute short-term memory, does his overall memory simply have problems, is it actually impaired, or does it not work at all? The first thing the professor's sister-in-law tells the narrator as she (the narrator) is interviewing for the position of the professor's housekeeper is that "his memory is impaired" (記憶が不自由なのです).[26] Li Jianyun's Chinese version from 2005 similarly translates this as "his memory has defects/flaws" (他是記憶有缺陷).[27] But Wang Yunjie's Chinese version (published in Taiwan in 2004) leaves open the possibility that the professor's memory is not as severely affected, translating this sentence as "his memory has problems" (他的記憶有問題).[28] So, too, do the French and Italian versions, which read, respectively, "Il a des troubles de mémoire" (He has memory problems) and "Significa che ha problemi di memoria" (It means he has memory problems).[29] The English and German versions—"He has difficulties with his memory" and "Sein Gedächtnis lässt ihn im Stich" (His memory lets him down)[30]—are similar, although the German version presumes to know how the professor reacts to his memory loss. These translations all leave room for speculation as to the condition of the professor's memory. In contrast, the Korean translation declares emphatically yet erroneously (given that the professor retains his pre-1975 memories) that the professor's (overall) memory "does not work" (기억을 못하는 거죠).[31] So a memory that initially was described as "impaired" in the Japanese version ranges in the translations from one that merely has "problems" to one that "does not work" at all. Juxtaposing translations of *The Equations* makes it clear just how differently a limited short-term memory can be interpreted and the person with this memory can be imagined—as an individual hampered slightly by a memory that can be a bit problematic, or one whose memory cannot be trusted at all, as someone with a minor medical condition or a person with a significant handicap. These examples spotlight the indeterminacy of categorizing a medical condition the patient cannot or will not describe.

Second, there is the question of how the professor's short-term memory functions. The sister-in-law declares in the Japanese version:

> My brother-in-law's memory stopped accumulating things in 1975 [記憶の蓄積は、一九七五年で終わっております]. After that, even though he tries to keep on piling up new memories, they soon end up collapsing [新たな記憶を積み重ねようとしても、すぐに崩れてしまいます].

In short, he has a single eighty-minute videotape inside his head. When he records anything on it, previous memories are erased.³²

The sister-in-law's metaphors are conflicting. On the one hand, she speaks of the professor's efforts to accumulate new memories as "piling [them up]" (積み重ねる), only to have them quickly collapse. In other words, she depicts her brother-in-law's memories as building one atop the other, only to tumble down precipitously, over and over again, a jerky, jarring ride. But almost immediately thereafter she likens the professor's memory to an eighty-minute videotape that appears automatically and smoothly to record new memories over old memories. Ultimately, neither image fully captures the professor's reality for the previous seventeen years, given that he also retains his long-term (preaccident) memory. Because the professor is described as having both a long-term memory that is very much intact and an incessantly changing/collapsing eighty-minute tape/tower, it is no surprise that, as the narrator is wrapping up her interview with the professor's sister-in-law, she declares that her previous work experiences will be of little use to her here.

Translations of *The Equations* have tackled this passage in a variety of ways. They tend to follow the Japanese version in likening the professor's memory to a videotape that every eighty minutes records over the previous eighty minutes. And some, like the Korean version, maintain the idea of memories attempting to accumulate only to collapse at once (그방 무너져 내려요),³³ but the English and the German versions decline the opportunity to refer to both accumulating and collapsing edifices of memory. The English reads only, "Since then [the accident], he has been unable to remember anything new. His memory stops in 1975."³⁴ The German version likewise deletes references to collecting memories: "Vor siebzehn Jahren hat er sich bei einem Autounfall eine schwere Kopfverletzung zugezogen und leidet seitdem an Gedächtnisverlust. Seit 1975 funktioniert sein Kurzzeitgedächtnis nun schon nicht mehr" (Seventeen years ago he incurred a serious head injury in a car crash and since then has suffered from memory loss. His short-term memory hasn't worked since 1975).³⁵ By retaining the comparison to an eighty-minute videotape and glossing over the reference to an unsuccessful struggle to pile up memories, the English and German versions suggest that, however traumatic the accident, what is left of the professor's short-term memory works relatively smoothly, giving the impression of a man who is hampered but not imperiled.

Other versions of *The Equations* speak of the professor as attempting to accumulate memories but say only that he cannot do so or that these memories rapidly disappear, as opposed to the Japanese version's claim that they "quickly collapse." Wang's Chinese version, for instance, states that the professor's memory "lasts only until 1975 [記憶只到一九七五年為止]. After that, even though he wanted to accumulate new memories, this was a futile effort [即使想要累積新的記憶也徒勞無功]."³⁶ Li's Chinese version claims that before the accident there was a "stockpiling movement of the professor's memory storehouse" (记忆库的存储活动), but "after that, even though he wanted again to accumulate new memories, new memories immediately disappeared" (即使再想积累新的记忆、新的记忆也将马上消失)."³⁷ Li's translation draws more attention to the professor's loss than does Wang's, contrasting the "memory storehouse" of the past with the near blank slate of the present.

As with the two Chinese translations, the French translation states only that the memories the professor has attempted to accumulate after his accident are "erased immediately": "Il a beau tenter d'accumuler de nouveaux souvenirs, ils s'effacent aussitôt."³⁸ The verb "s'effacer" is echoed several lines later, when the professor's sister-in-law comments that if he records something on the eighty-minute videotape inside his head, "les souvenirs précédents s'effacent au fur et à mesure" (previous memories are erased gradually). The phrase "au fur et à mesure" (gradually) here sets up a contrast between what happens to the memories the professor "attempts to accumulate," which vanish instantly, and the memories on the eighty-minute videotape, which disappear gradually. Repeating "s'effacer" to describe two very different types of erasing of the same memories points again to diagnostic instability and especially the difficulties inherent in describing, much less understanding, the professor's condition.

For its part, the Italian translation paints a more tragic picture. New memories not only have no time to accumulate; they dramatically shatter: "La sua memoria si è fermata al 1975. Da quella data in poi, qualsiasi nuova informazione cerchi di memorizzare finisce per sbriciolarsi in mille pezzi" (His memory stops in 1975. From that date forward, whatever new information he tries to save ends up crumbling into a million pieces).³⁹ But just two sentences later, consistent with the other translations, the Italian version maintains the comparison to an eighty-minute videotape, asserting that on this videotape the professor's "previous memories are erased" (i ricordi precedent i si cancellano),⁴⁰ suggesting a much smoother process. The move from information shattering into a million pieces to memories merely being erased points to the ambiguities inherent both in medical conditions and in attempts to describe these conditions.

Translations of *The Equations* readily follow their Japanese source in likening the professor's eighty-minute short-term memory to an eighty-minute endlessly re-recording videotape. And some maintain the contradiction present in the Japanese version between a smoothly re-recording videotape, on the one hand, and memories disappearing, on the other. But precisely how these memories disappear is another matter entirely: do they just evaporate; do they collapse; do they crumble into a million pieces? In other words, which description most closely resembles the professor's actual experience? No one knows for certain, except, perhaps, the professor, who maintains his silence. These inconsistencies between translations, as well as within translations and the initial Japanese version itself, underscore diagnostic randomness; in each case, the sister-in-law tells the narrator what she believes to be the case, presenting the reader with many different impressions of the professor and life with very limited short-term memory.

Given the professor's difficulties with memory, how, then, can the condition of his mind, his brain, be described? Immediately after telling the narrator that the professor's memory is impaired, the professor's sister-in-law declares, as if to reassure her potential employee, "His mind hasn't gone soft" (惚けているのではありません).[41] The two Chinese versions of *The Equations* are less subtle, leaving open the possibility of a slightly more serious condition; they state only, "He's not senile" (没有癡呆; 不是癡呆), as do the English, German, and Korean versions, using the words "senile," "senil," and 노망, respectively. Taking a similar approach are the French (*gâteux*; doddering) and Italian (*demente*; demented, insane) versions.[42]

The different translations of *The Equations* agree that the professor's mind is not decrepit, but they follow this statement with diverging impressions on the condition of his brain. The Japanese version insists, "On the whole, his brain cells are completely healthy" (全体として脳細胞は健全に働いているのです). The Chinese, French, and Italian versions downgrade "completely healthy" to "healthy": "On the whole, his brain cells are in good health/function normally," while the Korean version omits the modifier "on the whole" (全体として), stating without caveat, "his brain cells are functioning healthfully" (뇌 세포는 건강하게 움직이고 있으니까요). Given that the Korean translation had just declared that the professor's memory "didn't work," this text accentuates even more than other versions of *The Equations* the disparity between the health of an individual's brain cells, at least in the mind of a nonspecialist, and the actual function of his or her memory. For their part, the English and German versions delete mention of brain cells altogether, following the assurance that the professor is not senile with "his brain works well" and "seine Geisteskraft ist unvermindert groß" (His mental vigor remains strong),[43] the latter especially an apparent contradiction with earlier declarations that the professor's memory is leaving him in the lurch. Internal contradictions in each version of *The Equations* are multiplied by the novel's multiple translations, as family members and translators alike struggle to shed light on a mind so far out of their reach. Paradoxically, at the same time that references to healthily functioning brain cells can provide deeper assurances of health, they also skirt the issue of whether the professor's mind/brain works well as a whole.

What then about the lived experience of the professor? What impact does the inscrutability of his condition have on those around him and on the quality of his care? Somewhat surprisingly, considering the sister-in-law's description, the professor bonds quickly with the narrator and her son, whom the professor has nicknamed Root. The professor listens carefully to Root, even correcting him gently when his table manners leave something to be desired and encouraging him to eat larger portions so he will grow stronger. Although the professor dislikes being disturbed while working, he emerges from his study the moment Root returns home, eager to converse with the boy. To be sure, as with most children, Root prefers playing baseball with his friends to studying mathematics, but the professor is a gifted and patient teacher, always full of praise for his young pupil, even when Root is making little progress on his homework. The two grow so close, in fact, that the narrator feels excluded when they are together, but she allows the relationship to blossom, recognizing how good it is for her son to have the professor in his life. Many of her conversations with the professor similarly revolve around mathematics, equations filling the air and the pages of *The Equations*; the narrator claims that she detested mathematics as a child, but, thanks to the professor, she has become fascinated with the subject and eventually sees prime numbers and equations everywhere around her.

But the relationship between the professor and the narrator is not without its challenges and pitfalls. Much is said between the two about numbers and baseball and so little is said about the professor himself. This is as the professor prefers it, yet there are consequences. Most important, the narrator learns very little about the accident's impact on the professor beyond what she is told during her interview with his sister-in-law.

Early in the novel, the narrator comments on the relative ease of her new position from the perspective of a housekeeper: the professor lives in a small cottage, never has visitors, and shows very little interest in food, leaving her ample time to clean. But she laments that she has great difficulty understanding how the professor's memory actually works and the effect his truncated memory has on him. She recalls his sister-in-law's comment that the professor's memory stopped in 1975 but regrets that she still does not comprehend, "for example, what yesterday meant to him, or whether he could think ahead to tomorrow, and the extent of the anguish [苦痛] brought about by his impairment/inconvenience [不自由さ]."[44] In contrast with the professor's sister-in-law, the narrator reveals her own attempts to understand not just the nature of the professor's memory loss but how he lives, and suffers, because of it.

Translations of *The Equations* replicate the narrator's uncertainty concerning the degree to which the professor suffers from his condition, but the varying ways these texts label the condition again reveal diagnostic instability, how differently the same symptoms can be interpreted. The narrator in the Japanese version echoes the professor's sister-in-law by depicting the professor as afflicted by an "impairment" or "inconvenience" (不自由さ). This sentiment is replicated in the Korean version and in Li's Chinese translation, where the terms 부자유 스러움이 and 不便 are used, respectively; it also is repeated in the German version, which speaks of the professor as suffering from *Einschränkung* (restrictions).[45] But the idea of impairment/inconvenience is adapted slightly in Wang's Chinese translation: 不知道這種記憶障礙會給他帶來多大的痛苦 (I didn't know how much suffering these kinds of memory impediments had brought him),[46] where the narrator speaks of "memory impediments" rather than of "impairments" or "inconveniences." In contrast, the French and Italian translations speak explicitly of the professor's "handicap," while the English states merely, "I had no idea . . . how much he suffered," refusing to attach any label to the professor's condition.[47] Ultimately, then, among these translations the professor is described as everything from suffering to handicapped and suffering, the different versions unclear both internally and among themselves whether his condition is a handicap, an impairment, a problem, or just something from which he suffers.

However, while the narrator speaks in this passage in the Japanese version of the professor's "impairment"/"inconvenience," later in the novel she wonders how much the professor understands of his "illness" (病気), a term that—unlike "impairments" or "inconveniences"—is closely replicated in the Chinese (自己生的病; 病況), French (*maladie*), Italian (*malattia*), and Korean (병) versions.[48] For its part, the English moves from refraining to label the professor's condition to speaking of his "memory problem," whereas the German moves from referring to "restrictions" on the professor's life to speaking only of the professor understanding how his memory is ordered (*sein Gedächtnis bestellt war*).[49]

The narrator strives to do right by the professor, who does not remember her from one day to the next or even at different points during the same day if she is away from him for more than eighty minutes. She comments that she is always afraid she will say the wrong thing, and she reveals that in retrospect she felt terrible suggesting that the professor should purchase a television to watch the Barcelona Olympics in 1992 when the last Olympics he remembered were the Munich games in 1972. But she also confesses that the professor himself did not appear bothered by such comments, noting, "When the conversation went off in a direction that he couldn't follow, he wouldn't get angry, or impatient, but instead would simply wait until it returned to something he could talk about."[50]

The narrator can only surmise what the professor is thinking and why he is so garrulous on some topics and so reticent on others. She guesses that it likely is not pride that prevents him from asking for help but, instead, aversion to troubling "people living in the world of normal memory" (ごく当たり前の記憶の世界に生きる人々).[51] This being the case, the narrator decides to say as little as possible to her charge. Noteworthy here is the separation the narrator makes not only between herself and the professor, but also between the professor and the world of "normal memory." Further isolating the professor from his surroundings, the English translation rewrites "people living in the world of normal memory"—repeated in the Chinese versions—as "those of us who lived in the normal world."[52] In other words, both the Japanese and the English versions of *The Equations* posit the professor as living in a world that is different from that of most individuals, but while in the Japanese text the professor is separated only from the world of "normal memory," the English version has him isolated from the "normal world" itself. So does the German translation, which speaks of the professor as separate from the "normalen Welt" (normal world).[53] Taking a middle ground, the Italian translation refers to the "normalissimo mondo della memoria" (normal world of memory),[54] leaving open the possibility that while the professor does not inhabit this "normal world" of memory, there are other "normal worlds" still open to him, as in fact is evidenced by how he has adapted to his new life. In contrast, the French translation omits the reference to "world" altogether, speaking of the professor as reluctant to disturb "ceux qui vivaient avec une mémoire tout à fait normale" (those who lived with a totally normal memory).[55] So does the Korean version, speaking only of "people who remember the past as a matter of course" (과거를 당연히 기억하고사는 사람),[56] paradoxically leaving more space for the professor in the "normal world." The differences among these translations again reveal the ease with which an individual can be included, and excluded, from the "world."

As the professor's housekeeper and caregiver, the narrator works diligently to spare him suffering. She makes clear that she and her son had promised themselves that they would do their best to avoid confusing the professor because "confusion of any kind caused the professor sadness" (どんな種類である混乱は、博士に悲しみをもたらした).[57] Yet the closer their bond grows, the easier it is to forget about the professor's physical condition and inadvertently inflict pain. On one occasion, the narrator stays with the professor overnight after he develops a high fever; the next morning she mistakenly speaks with him as she would with someone who has a longer short-term memory: forgetting for a moment that he will not remember who she is, she tells him that he should get more rest and that she will purchase new sheets and clothes to make him more comfortable. But the professor has no idea who she is and sheds quiet tears, in a voice she has never heard from him before, as he reads the most prominent of the many reminders pinned to his jacket: "My memory is only eighty minutes." The narrator is ashamed of her neglectfulness: "Every morning, when the Professor woke up and got dressed, he was sentenced [宣告] by a memo in his own hand to the illness he had contracted [博士は自分が罹っている病]. . . . I had not once thought about the reality for him of awakening every day alone on the bed to receive repeatedly this cruel sentence [こんな 残酷な宣告]."[58] Despite her deep affection for the professor and curiosity about his condition, she did not pause to consider the havoc it might (or must) wreak on his psyche.

Failure to pay closer attention to the professor—as opposed to his equations—also prevents the narrator from noticing changes in his physical condition. The professor becomes enamored of Root, watching out for him and thinking always of his best interests. When Root injures his hand, the professor not only comforts the narrator while her son is being treated; he also cares for Root after he returns home. The contrast between the professor's vigilance and the narrator's negligence comes to the fore in the novel's ninth chapter, when the professor experiences an unexpected medical emergency: "One day near the end of summer vacation the professor's tooth swelled up so much he could no longer hide it. . . . It seemed as though he'd been enduring this alone, saying not a word to anyone. Had he given himself one-tenth of the attention that he showed toward Root, things would never have gotten this bad. By the time I noticed, the left side of his face was so deformed with swelling [いびつに膨らみ] that he could barely open his mouth."[59]

The narrator chastises the professor for paying closer attention to her son than he does to himself. But she seems oblivious to her own inattentiveness: she never questions why it took the professor's being unable to open his mouth for her to notice that he needs to visit a dentist.

Even more significant, the narrator barely seems to notice that what remains of the professor's already damaged memory is beginning to fail him. At Root's eleventh birthday party, the professor forgets who she and Root are in far fewer than the usual eighty minutes. Yet the narrator appears to think nothing of this, claiming, "The fact that the professor had forgotten about us in under ten minutes was no reason to panic. We just started the party as planned. We'd already piled up plenty of experience [もう十分な訓練を積んでいた] dealing with the professor's memory. We coped by adapting to the circumstances, setting up rules and devising various means so as not to thoughtlessly hurt the professor."[60] The more the narrator has piled up experiences, the less the professor is able to pile up memories. Fearing that she and Root will offend her patient, the narrator consciously disregards a significant change in his health.

And so it is his sister-in-law who, two days later, moves him into a long-term care facility. When the narrator expresses surprise at the seeming suddenness of the move, the sister-in-law replies that this has actually been planned for some time, saying, "You must have been aware of what was happening." The narrator has no response. Similarly, when the sister-in-law tells her, "His eighty-minute tape is broken. My brother-in-law's memory does not go beyond 1975, not even for a minute," the narrator responds simply, "I'd be happy to go to the facility to look after him."[61] The narrator's desire to help the professor is clear. But the compromise to her empathy and sensitivity is striking, especially her obliviousness to the true nature of his condition and her utter lack of concern even when the details of her patient's condition are spelled out for her explicitly. She does not seem to care that the memory tape is broken and what this might mean for the professor's quality of life.

For the next decade, until the professor's death, the narrator and her son visit him regularly at his new residence, where they talk mathematics and toss baseballs. Even though the narrator admits that the professor's sister-in-law now is "the only person who shares memories with him,"[62] her description of visits to the professor gives no indication that he fails to recognize them. Condensing the final eleven years of the professor's life into the final few pages of *The Equations*, the narrator instead speaks of gentle games of catch between Root and the professor, records a conversation they had on prime numbers during their last visit, and shares the professor's delight at the news that Root is preparing for a career as a middle school teacher. As before, she sidesteps the deterioration of the professor's brain, focusing instead on his weakening physical body, as well as the apparent joy he derives from sharing math problems with her and her son.

On the final page of *The Equations*, Ogawa lists eight texts consulted while writing the novel, including one on the eccentric Hungarian mathematician Paul Erdős.[63] Notably absent is Sylvia Nasar's biography *A Beautiful Mind*, published in 1998 and translated into Japanese in 2002, and Ron Howard and Akiva Goldsman's Academy Award–winning film of the same title, on the American mathematician and Nobel Prize–winner John Nash, who lived with paranoid schizophrenia.[64] Also conspicuously absent is writing, both fiction and nonfiction, on brain disorders more generally. Ogawa and her narrator draw attention away from the professor's problems with memory and toward his continued fluency with mathematics. As its Japanese title suggests, *The Equations* highlights what the professor continues to cherish—mathematics, and especially equations, which are scattered throughout the Japanese narrative and duplicated in the many translations of this spatially and linguistically mobile text. In contrast, the novel's descriptions of the professor's overall memory, how his short-term memory functions, and the condition of his mind and brain, as well as his lived experience with a brain disorder, vary within and across versions, underscoring the arbitrariness with which labels are attached and conditions are understood, particularly diseases which for whatever reason prevent individuals from expressing their own explicit illness narratives.

In a recent article on his brief episode of anterograde amnesia, the American journalist Trip Gabriel asks, "Without our memories, who are we?"[65] Gabriel goes on to comment, "The ability of the mind to hold short-term recollections, and to retrieve longer-term memories and the feelings they evoke, is essential to being human." In contrast, *The Equations* depicts life continuing meaningfully and productively, albeit with great difficulty, after traumatic brain injury. Ogawa's novel and its many translations throughout the world highlight the pervasiveness of diagnostic instability and caution against both rushing to judgment and assuming to know fully the experiences and needs of another person. Unlike many translations of literature on illness, the translations of Ogawa's novel discussed in this chapter give insight not into the differences and tensions among the many cultures and linguistic communities in which *The Equations* now circulates. Instead, they provide greater awareness of what it means to care for people who cannot speak about their experiences, regardless of culture. The translations also give insight into the fundamental importance of learning to appreciate people's experiences, however they are communicated, and never forgetting not only how they have suffered but, even more important, their humanity.

NOTES

This work was supported in part by a grant from the Academy of Korean Studies (AKS-2011-R20).

1 Thornber, "Breaking Discipline, Integrating Literature."
2 Mathers and Bonita, "Current Global Health Status," 23.
3 Alzheimer's long was seen solely as an issue of aging and in many parts of the world continues to be perceived that way, but the Alzheimer's Association and other organizations make the case for Alzheimer's as a public health crisis: see http://www.alz.org/publichealth/what-you-need-to-know.asp. In 2012, the WHO declared dementia a "public health priority."

4 World Health Organization Dementia Fact Sheet, April 2016, http://www.who.int/mediacentre/factsheets/fs362/en.
5 Mayo Clinic, "Traumatic Brain Injury," May 15, 2014, http://www.mayoclinic.org/diseases-conditions/traumatic-brain-injury/basics/causes/con-20029302.
6 Humphreys et al., "The Costs of Traumatic Brain Injury," 281.
7 See Alzheimer's Association, www.alz.org/research.
8 The best known is the neuroscientist Lisa Genova's novel *Still Alice* (2007), which was on the *New York Times* bestseller list for more than a year and adapted for the stage in 2013 and into an Academy Award–winning film in 2014. The story of a renowned linguistics professor diagnosed with early-onset Alzheimer's disease, *Still Alice* has been translated into nearly forty languages in Asia, Europe, and the Middle East. Genova is also author of *Left Neglected*, about a professional woman who suffers from the neurological condition left neglect brought on by a car accident. Prominent, as well, is Ogawa's novel *Hakase no aishita sūshiki* (博士の愛した数式, *The Equations the Professor Loved*), the focus of the second half of this chapter. Alice Munro received the Nobel Prize in Literature in 2013; her short story "The Bear Came over the Mountain" (1999) features a couple of fifty years torn apart by the wife's Alzheimer's. Another runaway global best seller engaging with brain disorders is Shin's *Ŏmma rŭl put'akhae* (엄마를 부탁해, *Please Look After Mom*, 2009), about a family whose wife/mother develops dementia and is last seen on the Seoul subway; this novel has been adapted into a stage play and musical and has been translated into more than thirty languages. For its part, J. Bernlef's well-traveled short novel *Hersenschimmen* (Out of Mind, 1984) features a narrator with Alzheimer's.
9 Kaplan, "Do You Remember Me?" 295.
10 The medical humanities and health humanities have both clinical and scholarly components. In their most basic sense, the medical humanities "explain medicine to itself. To ourselves, to the world": Hunter, "What We Do," 377. See also Brody, "On Explaining Medicine to Itself," 5. Many take the field of medical humanities to concentrate on "the recording and interpretation of experiences of medical [care] and healthcare" both in and via the study of film, literature, music, the visual arts, philosophy, and other cultural discourse and production with the goal of nurturing "observation, empathy, and self-reflection" primarily in physicians but ultimately in society at large: Evans and Finlay, "Introduction," 77; Nora Tong, "A Dose of Humanities for Medical Students," March 11, 2013, http://www.scmp.com/lifestyle/family-education/article/1186397/dose-humanities-medical-students. As the name suggests, the health humanities tend to center more on human health than do the medical humanities, which often place more emphasis on the practice of medicine, but the line between the two is frequently blurred. The International Health Humanities Network (www.healthhumanities.org) is a global platform that provides ways for everyone, from humanities scholars and health-care providers to the wider public, to "explore, celebrate and develop new approaches in advancing health and well-being through the arts and humanities in hospitals, residential and community settings." For a compelling recent account of the therapeutic value of

the arts, see Carol Adams, "Jane Austen's Guide to Alzheimer's," *New York Times*, December 19, 2015, http://www.nytimes.com/2015/12/20/opinion/jane-austens-guide-to-alzheimers.html. Adams writes, "Early on in tending to my mother, who had Alzheimer's, I was sustained by other Austen novels, but during the middle stages of her disease it was all [the novel] *Emma* all the time. What started as entertainment soon became an important guide."

11 Aids.gov, "Global Statistics," November 25, 2015, https://www.aids.gov/hiv-aids-basics/hiv-aids-101/global-statistics.

12 World literature has been open to a greater variety of literatures than have been the health humanities, but the Eurocentrism of the field remains a significant hurdle. See, for instance: Thornber, "Comparative Literature, World Literature, and Asia"; Thornber, "The Many Scripts of the Chinese Scriptworld, the *Epic of King Gesar*, and World Literature"; Thornber, "Neglected Texts, Trajectories, and Communities: Reshaping World Literature and East Asia."

13 Many have critiqued the field of world literature for aiming at an impossible totality, depending too heavily on translations, eschewing close readings, and remaining persistently Eurocentric. Another criticism is that despite its emphasis on literature "for the world" and examining how creative works "reach out and away" from their points of origin, world literature has remained relatively silent on the relationship between world literature and many, although by no means all, urgent matters of global significance. After two generations of great concern with the tensions and problems of the Cold War, and the very real social problems of neocolonialism and neoliberal economic expansion worldwide, it is now appropriate for world literature to become more truly global in the sense of dealing more rigorously with a broader range of global issues. Moreover, to *world literature* we might add *global literature* or, more precisely, *global world literature*—that is, literature that addresses serious global problems, including disease—literature that has been taken up by the world. I understand *global literature* to be creative texts that engage with serious global problems—that is, problems that have global implications or counterparts globally, such as war, poverty, slavery, human rights violations, environmental degradation, and disease/illness. In short, the methodologies of world literature have the capacity to contribute to improving care and well-being, particularly as the field embraces more fully both a broader world geography and a greater variety of urgent matters of global significance. In other words, when the field opens itself to global world literature. For more on the explicit and implicit biases of world literature, as well as new possibilities for the field, see Thornber, "Empire of Texts in Motion"; Thornber, "Global World Literature and the Medical Humanities"; Thornber, "Why (not) World Literature?"

14 Regarding the difference between "illness" and "disease," as Arthur Kleinman argues, "Illness refers to how the sick person and members of the family or wider social network perceive, live with, and respond to symptoms of disability. . . . In the narrow biological terms of the biomedical model . . . , disease is reconfigured *only* as an alteration in biological structure or functioning": Kleinman, *The Illness Narratives*, 3, 6. Likewise, as Arthur Frank explains, "Disease can be reduced to

biochemistry, while illness involves a biography, a reflected consciousness, multiple relationships, and institutions.... The humanities become necessary resources as soon as people try to live illness as more than bare disease": Frank, "Being a Good Story," 14.

15 Other possibilities include the influenza epidemic of 1918–19, which was incubated on ships carrying soldiers from Europe into battlefields across the world and by some estimates caused thirty million deaths worldwide; the HIV/AIDS epidemic of the 1980s and 1990s that currently infects thirty-seven million people, the majority of whom live in low- and middle-income countries; and Hansen's disease (leprosy), which infected 10 million–12 million people worldwide as recently as the 1980s: Aids.gov, "Global HIV/AIDS Overviews," November 25, 2015, https://www.aids.gov/federal-resources/around-the-world/global-aids-overview; S. K. Nordeen, L. Lopez Bravo, and T. K. Sundaresan, "Estimated Number of Leprosy Cases in the World," *Bull World Health Organ* 70, no. 1 (1992): 7. Leprosy is one of the most stigmatized diseases in world history, with writings dating back thousands of years. There is also a body of literature engaging with the SARS and Ebola public health scares of the past few decades. It is well known that public health epidemics have had a great impact in redefining relationships among people, concepts, and medical knowledge transfer systems. These phenomena have been widely studied, albeit primarily by anthropologists and historians of medicine.

16 Within Japan, *The Equations* was one of the major Japanese publisher Shinchōsha's fastest selling paperbacks. The published English translation of *The Equations* is *The Housekeeper and the Professor*.

17 For instance, at 2 PM on Saturday, May 16, 1992, the professor could not remember anything that had occurred between 1975 and 12:40 PM on Saturday, May 16, 1992.

18 The narrator depicts the professor as extremely reticent about his condition; he tells her only that he has just eighty minutes of short-term memory.

19 Kleinman, *The Illness Narratives*, 49, 255.

20 Charon and DasGupta, "Editors' Preface," vii–xiii; Charon, *Narrative Medicine*.

21 For critiques of narrative medicine, see Downie, "Medical Humanities." Downie, among others, has pointed out that the term "narrative" conceals as much as it illuminates, given the brevity of many conversations between patients and physicians. Narrative medicine presumes the luxury of time, enjoyed by only a small subset of those suffering from disease. As the narrator of Charles Brock's recent novel *Alice and Oliver* laments as his wife's physician informs them of her diagnosis of acute myeloid leukemia, "Medical personnel, doctors and nurses alike, talked in this clipped manner: short sentences, quick back-and-forth exchanges.... Time was a premium.... In the medical realm ... doctors pretended it mattered if the patient understood, before continuing to the next thing": Brock, *Alice and Oliver*, 54.

22 Although everyone in the novel claims that the professor's pre-1975 memory is intact, the only evidence of this that the narrator shares with the reader is that the professor is still able to talk about and do mathematics.

23 In 2006, the novel was also adapted into a feature film of the same title that received a Japanese Academy Award.

24 See, e.g., the case of the Urdu-language publisher Mashal Books, which has translated numerous works of non-Western literature into Urdu via their English translations. Prominent among literary texts translated by Mashal are East Asian novels that grapple with illness and health, including Yi Ch'ŏngjun's (이청준) novel *Your Paradise* (Tangsindŭl ŭi ch'ŏn'guk, 당신들의 천국, 1976). For more on this phenomenon, see Thornber, "Mashal Books as Cultural Mediator"; Thornber, "Neglected Texts, Trajectories, and Communities."
25 I also refer briefly to the Hebrew translation: Ogawa Yōko, *Matnat ha-misparim*.
26 Ogawa Yōko, *Hakase no aishita sūshiki*, 8.
27 Ogawa Yōko, *Boshi de aiqing suanshi*, 8. I thank Miya Xie for proofreading my Chinese and Korean translations and Manuel Alamo for proofreading my Japanese and Korean translations.
28 Ogawa Yōko, *Boshi reai de suanshi*, 8.
29 Ogawa, *La formule préférée du professeur*, 14; Ogawa Yōko, *La formula del professore*, 13.
30 Ogawa, *The Housekeeper and the Professor*, 10; Ogawa Yōko, *Das Geheimnis der Eulerschen Formel*, 11.
31 Ogawa Yōko, *Paksa ga sarang han sushik*, 11.
32 Ogawa, *Hakase no aishita sūshiki*, 8–9.
33 Ogawa, *Paksa ga sarang han sushik*, 11.
34 Ogawa, *The Housekeeper and the Professor*, 5.
35 Ogawa, *Das Geheimnis der Eulerschen Formel*, 11.
36 Ogawa, *Boshi reai de suanshi*, 8.
37 Ogawa, *Boshi de aiqing suanshi*, 6.
38 Ogawa, *La formule préférée du professeur*, 14.
39 Ogawa, *La formula del professore*, 13.
40 Ogawa, *La formula del professore*, 13.
41 Ogawa, *Hakase no aishita sūshiki*, 8.
42 The Japanese version also could be translated as "He is not senile," but the phrase 惚けているのではありません is somewhat subtler.
43 Ogawa, *Das Geheimnis der Eulerschen Formel*, 11.
44 Ogawa, *Hakase no aishita sūshiki*, 30.
45 Ogawa, *Das Geheimnis der Eulerschen Formel*, 35.
46 Ogawa, *Boshi reai de suanshi*, 29.
47 Ogawa, *The Housekeeper and the Professor*, 22. The French and Italian translations use the word "handicap": Ogawa, *La formule préférée du professeur*, 37; Ogawa, *La formula del professore*, 31. The Japanese term 不自由さ can be translated as "handicap," but it has a wider range of meaning and a softer edge than the English word "handicapped" and its European equivalents, which are more frequently rendered in Japanese as 障害 or しょう害 (disabled).
48 Ogawa, *Hakase no aishita sūshiki*, 64; Ogawa, *Boshi reai de suanshi*, 63; Ogawa, *Boshi de aiqing suanshi*, 53; Ogawa, *La formule préférée du professeur*, 70; Ogawa, *La formula del professore*, 56; Ogawa, *Paksa ga sarang han sushik*, 68.

49 Ogawa, *The Housekeeper and the Professor*, 47; Ogawa, *Das Geheimnis der Eulerschen Formel*, 70–71.
50 Ogawa, *Hakase no aishita sūshiki*, 31.
51 Ogawa, *Hakase no aishita sūshiki*, 64.
52 Ogawa, *Boshi reai de suanshi*, 63; Ogawa, *Boshi de aiqing suanshi*, 54; Ogawa, *The Housekeeper and the Professor*, 47. The Hebrew translation takes this one step further with "those of us who lived in the real/true world": Ogawa, *Matnat ha-misparim*, 53–54. The Hebrew version of *The Equations* is a translation not of the Japanese but of the English version and translates fairly literally the passages examined in this chapter. The one major change is in the title, which the Hebrew translation gives as *Matnat ha-misparim* (Gift of Numbers), in contrast with the English *The Housekeeper and the Professor*. I thank Sunny Yudkoff for this information.
53 Ogawa, *Das Geheimnis der Eulerschen Formel*, 71.
54 Ogawa, *La formula del professore*, 56.
55 Ogawa, *La formule préférée du professeur*, 70.
56 Ogawa, *Paksa ga sarang han sushik*, 68.
57 Ogawa, *Hakase no aishita sūshiki*, 84.
58 Ogawa, *Hakase no aishita sūshiki*, 140–41.
59 Ogawa, *Hakase no aishita sūshiki*, 204.
60 Ogawa, *Hakase no aishita sūshiki*, 245.
61 Ogawa, *Hakase no aishita sūshiki*, 248.
62 Ogawa, *Hakase no aishita sūshiki*, 249.
63 Ogawa, *Hakase no aishita sūshiki*, 254. The book is Paul Hoffman's *The Man Who Loved Only Numbers*, a biography of Erdős, whom the professor somewhat resembles. Erdős earned his doctorate at twenty-one and was known for his itinerant lifestyle, traveling among mathematics conferences and the homes of colleagues around the world; over the course of his life he had hundreds of collaborators. He also established numerous monetary prizes for solutions to challenging mathematical problems. Like Ogawa's professor, Erdős was particularly entranced by prime numbers, which Hoffman describes as his "intimate friends." But unlike the brain-damaged professor, Erdős had such sharp insight into these numbers that "on hearing a new problem about them, he often quickly upstaged those who had spent far more time thinking about it": Hoffman, *The Man Who Loved Only Numbers*, 37–38. The other books in Ogawa's bibliography are a basic introduction to mathematics; a book on Pierre de Fermat's Last Theorem of the seventeenth century; a book on the language of mathematicians; a book on the glory and collapse of mathematical genius; the German writer Hans Magnus Enzensberger's bestselling *Der Zahlenteufel: Ein Kopfkissenbuch für alle, die Angst vor der Mathematik haben* (The Number Devil: A Pillow Book for All Who Are Afraid of Numbers, 1997), which, as its title suggests, is an introductory book on mathematics that follows a young boy who is taught the subject by a devilish creature that visits him in his dreams; and two books on the celebrated Japanese All-Star pitcher Enatsu Yutaka (江夏豊).

64 Born in 1928, John Nash received the Nobel Prize in Economic Sciences in 1994 for his work on game theory. His first symptoms of mental illness appeared in the late 1950s, and he had to be hospitalized briefly several times over the years. He died in a car crash in 2015.

65 Trip Gabriel, "The Day That Went Missing," *New York Times*, July 17, 2016, http://www.nytimes.com/2016/07/17/opinion/sunday/the-day-that-went-missing.html.

BIBLIOGRAPHY

Brock, Charles. *Alice and Oliver*. New York: Random House, 2016.

Brody, Howard. "On Explaining Medicine to Itself." *Atrium* 11 (Winter 2013): 5.

Charon, Rita. *Narrative Medicine: Honoring the Stories of Illness*. New York: Oxford University Press, 2008.

Charon, Rita, and Sayantani DasGupta. "Editors' Preface: Narrative Medicine, or a Sense of Story." *Literature and Medicine* 29, no. 2 (Fall 2011): vii–xiii.

DasGupta, Sayantani. "Narrative Medicine, Narrative Humility: Listening to the Streams of Stories." *Creative Nonfiction* 52 (Summer 2014). https://www.creativenonfiction.org/online-reading/narrative-medicine-narrative-humility.

Downie, Robin. "Medical Humanities: Means, Ends, and Evaluation." In *Medical Humanities*, ed. Martyn Evans and Ilora G. Finlay, 204–16. London: BMJ Books, 2001.

Evans, Martyn, and Ilora G. Finlay. "Introduction." In *Medical Humanities*, ed. Martyn Evans and Ilora G. Finlay, 77–82. London: BMJ Books, 2001.

Frank, Arthur W. "Being a Good Story: The Humanities as Therapeutic Practice." In *Health Humanities Reader*, ed. Therese Jones, 13–25. New Brunswick, NJ: Rutgers University Press, 2014.

Hoffman, Paul. *The Man Who Loved Only Numbers: The Story of Paul Erdős and the Search for Mathematical Truth*. New York: Hyperion, 1998.

Humphreys, Ioan, Roger L. Wood, Ceri J. Phillips, and Steven Macey. "The Costs of Traumatic Brain Injury: A Literature Review." *ClinicoEconomics and Outcomes Research* 5 (June 25, 2013): 281–87.

Hunter, Kathryn. "What We Do: The Humanities and the Interpretation of Medicine." *Theoretical Medicine* 8 (1987): 367–78.

Kaplan, E. Ann. "'Do You Remember Me?' Constructions of Alzheimer's Disease in Literature and Film." In *Health Humanities Reader*, ed. Therese Jones, 295–303. New Brunswick, NJ: Rutgers University Press, 2014.

Kleinman, Arthur. *The Illness Narratives: Suffering, Healing, and the Human Condition*. New York: Basic, 1988.

Mathers, Colin, and Ruth Bonita. "Current Global Health Status." In *Global Public Health: A New Era*, ed. Robert Beaglehole and Ruth Bonita, 23–61. New York: Oxford University Press, 2009.

Nordeen, S. K., L. Lopez Brvo, and T. K. Sundaresan. "Estimated Number of Leprosy Cases in the World." *Bull World Health Organ* 70, no. 1 (1992): 7–10.

Ogawa Yōko. *Boshi de aiqing suanshi*, trans. Li Jianyun. Beijing: Renmin Wenxue Chubanshe, 2005.

———. *Boshi reai de suanshi*, trans. Wang Yunjie. Taipei: Maitian Chuban, 2004.

———. *La formula del professore*, trans. Mimma De Petra. Milan: Il Saggiatore, 2008.

———. *La formule préférée du professeur*, trans. Rose-Marie Makino-Fayoille. Paris: Actes Sud, 2003.

———. *Das Geheimnis der Eulerschen Formel*, trans. Sabine Mangold. Munich: Liebeskind, 2012.

———. *Hakase no aishita sūshiki*. Tokyo: Shinchōsha, 2003.

———. *The Housekeeper and the Professor*, trans. Stephen Snyder. New York: Picador, 2009.

———. *Matnat ha-misparim*. Jerusalem: Schocken Books, 2010.

———. *Paksa ga sarang han sushik*, trans. Kim Nanju. Seoul: Ire, 2004.

Thornber, Karen. "Breaking Discipline, Integrating Literature: Africa-China Relationships Reconsidered." *Comparative Literature Studies* 53, no. 4 (2016): 694–721.

———. "Comparative Literature, World Literature, and Asia." In *Futures of Comparative Literature*, ed. Ursula Heise, with Dudley Andrew, Alexander Beecroft, Jessica Berman, David Damrosch, Guillermina De Ferrari, César Domínguez, Barbara Harlow, and Eric Hayot, 156–61. New York: Routledge, 2016.

———. "Empire of Texts in Motion: Where in the World Is World Literature." In *Contextualizing Japanese Literature in World Literature*, ed. Mitsuyoshi Numano. Tokyo: University of Tokyo Press, forthcoming.

———. "Global World Literature and the Medical Humanities: An Overview," trans. Hua Yuanyuan. *Wenxue lilun* 14 (2016).

———. "The Many Scripts of the Chinese Scriptworld, the Epic of King Gesar, and World Literature." *Journal of World Literature* 1, no. 2 (2016): 211–24.

———. "Mashal Books as Cultural Mediator: Translating East Asian, Middle Eastern, and African Literatures into Urdu in Lahore." In *Customs Officers or Smugglers? Literary Translation and Cultural Mediators in "Peripheral" Cultures*, ed. Reyne Meylaerts and Diana Sanz Roig. Forthcoming.

———. "Neglected Texts, Trajectories, and Communities: Reshaping World Literature and East Asia." *Symposium* 70 (2016): 112–22.

———. "Why (Not) World Literature? Challenges and Opportunities for the Twenty-First Century." *Journal of World Literature* 1, no. 1 (2016): 107–18.

Chapter 8

In But Not of Europe?: The Precarious Rights
of Roma in the European Union

JACQUELINE BHABHA

The presumption of firm placement is inherent in our systems of laws and governance. Indeed, both depend on it. The basic notion is that human well-being and the public good are rooted in an enduring connection between individual identity and a defined place. Being placed somewhere constitutes human beings as full and integrated members of society, and states' ability to govern depends on secure bonds between their territory and the population or citizenry living within it. In short, individuals need to belong somewhere; states need people to fit in somewhere.

The converse is also true. People who are stateless, undocumented, or forcibly displaced (whether international refugees or internally displaced persons) are vulnerable because they lack this constitutive anchoring. The absence of constitutive placement is read as a threat to orderly state governance. We can call this absence "constitutive displacement," to highlight the central impact on belonging and state acceptance that results from a weak or compromised connection between individual identity and place.

Few groups illustrate the pervasive impact of constitutive displacement more clearly than the ten million to twelve million-strong Roma population in Europe. Despite being European residents for at least six centuries, with sizeable communities spread across the continent from east to west and north to south, many lack robust access to citizenship and the rights associated with it. These state-driven deficits are compounded by pervasive stigma and discrimination, often coupled with acts of violence from members of the majority population.

Why do these human rights violations persist in a region with the most highly developed and effective human rights system, a prohibition on discrimination that has been in force for more than half a century, and a rights-based regional citizenship? Does regional citizenship remain a contradiction in terms, given our current resolutely Westphalian dependence on national affiliation and belonging?

Constitutive Placement: The Importance of Enduring National Ties

Legal identity is based on constitutive placement—that is, on the ability to prove a territorial connection that endures through time and place, a citizenship or nationality.[1] Five of the thirty fundamental principles enshrined in the Universal Declaration of Human Rights of 1948, the bedrock international document on which national constitutions worldwide have been modeled and contemporary human rights norms have been erected,[2] insist on the centrality of constitutive placement.[3] Article 15, for example, states: "1. Everyone has the right to a nationality. 2. No one shall be arbitrarily deprived of his nationality nor denied the right to change his nationality." The basic notion here is that human security and the public good depend on legal identity linked to permanent place, that can be proved and that exists from birth to death. Article 29 states: "1. Everyone has duties to the community in which alone the free and full development of his personality is possible." This reflects the enduring Westphalian conceit that a cohesive containment of people within a defined space provides the underpinning for personal success.

But very large numbers of people do not have the luxury of indefinite "free and full development of [their] personality" within a single community. By the summer of 2014, according to the United Nations High Commissioner for Refugees, more than fifty-one million people were displaced from their homes, more than at any other time in recent history since World War II.[4] The luxury of a secure and enduring tie to one place, one community, one bounded territory eludes millions of refugees from Syria, Iraq, Afghanistan, the Central African Republic, and Crimea. It is a challenging aspiration for many Roma Europeans forced to move across borders in search of employment, security, and protection from discrimination. For all of these populations, access to "full and free development of [their] personality" depends on a certain portability of rights de-linked from particular territorial anchoring. Otherwise, as Hannah Arendt complained more than a half-century ago, the right to rights is eviscerated and replaced by a Hobbesian struggle for bare survival. This chapter explores the impact of these principles—we might call them placement principles—in a globalizing world where constitutive displacement is an increasingly pervasive norm. It suggests that the continuing centrality of placement principles has enduring and exclusionary effects on growing sections of the world's population that cannot comply with the idealized norm of constitutive placement. It further argues that the resistance to realization of a more dynamic set of inclusion principles that reflect the complexity of much contemporary boundary drawing, and a more complex or hyphenated conception of citizenship, contradicts the non-discrimination and equality provisions of contemporary constitutional democracies.

The right to a nationality is a cardinal human right that is universally accepted in principle. States are obliged to take whatever steps they can to reduce statelessness, the absence of a nationality, considered not only a personal handicap but a detriment for states. As Arendt noted, everyone has to fit into a system of state structuring or risk dehumanization at their peril.[5] International law concretizes this insight. Consider the common situation in which a child of migrants risks being born stateless, for example, because the country in which he or she is born does not grant nationality on the basis of birthplace (*ius soli*), and because the country of the parents' nationality (or nationalities) does not grant nationality on the basis of descent (*ius sanguinis*). In this case, the very extensively ratified United Nations Convention on the Reduction of Statelessness of 1961 requires states to facilitate acquisition of *their* nationality by the child who otherwise would be stateless. Having a nationality, having constitutive placement, is rightly considered a critical building block for the security and future well-being of the child.

Reality, however, departs radically from this principle. In practice, an estimate reported by the United Nations High Commissioner for Refugees in 2012 shows that there are six million stateless children in the world.[6] In some cases, states fail to enforce their treaty obligations; in others, parents are ignorant of or unable to afford relevant procedures, and in yet others, the complex administrative requirements mediating access to nationality are elusive and require substantiating documentation that is unavailable. The constantly growing population of stateless babies adds to the ten million stateless people documented by the United Nations.[7] Consider the case of the roughly 160,000 stateless Biharis in Bangladesh, former inhabitants of the East Indian state of Bihar, living in destitution in makeshift camps for more than half a century, a tragic leftover of the complex and unresolved history of the British partition of India in 1947 and the creation of Bangladesh out of East Pakistan in 1971. Constitutive displacement describes their condition well. This is not a situation where multiple cultural and social attributes generate an enriching and hybrid reality. Rather, the population is living out a de facto sentence of imprisonment and marginalization, deprived of the bare necessities of life, without access to adequate health care or education. The same can be said of many other de jure (or legally) stateless populations: the Rohingyas in Burma (as a longtime camp resident put it, "We Rohingyas are like birds in a cage. However, caged birds are fed, while we have to struggle alone to feed ourselves"[8]); the Nubians in Kenya; Haitian children born to Haitian parents in the Dominican Republic; and, of course, Palestinians in Israel. For these populations, statelessness—the absence of any nationality—is the legal correlate of radical displacement that occurred generations earlier. It is a legacy that lives on in the reality of political, social, and economic marginalization and entrapment in a space that is not home, despite years of residence. This is also a place where the ability to cross borders and to participate in governance of the political entity where one lives is denied and where borders create imprisonment, not security.

It is not just acquisition of a nationality that is considered critical. Proof of legal identity, as a means of tying a child to a particular place and time of birth, is also considered fundamental as a human right and protective institution. Taking note of the pervasive disappearance, abusive adoption, and child theft perpetrated with impunity on the families of regime opponents during the twentieth-century civil wars in Latin America, the United Nations Convention on the Rights of the Child of 1989 emphasizes the importance of birth registration and of the possession of a legal identity by each child as building blocks of a secure and rights-respecting future life. The reasoning is that children must be able to demonstrate their ties not just to family and community but also to a country, a system of laws and governance, to facilitate their exercise of future rights as autonomous humans and citizens. Implementation of this important principle depends on efficient, accessible, and transparent government administration that is responsive to the needs of remote, illiterate, transient, displaced, and marginalized communities, whose children are at most risk of not having their births registered. Digital technology, open source mapping, and remote access systems are important potential tools to facilitate easy birth registration. In practice, however, in most countries, state registration procedures remain antiquated and sedentary, mired in old technology and rigid bureaucracies, with a resistance to the incorporation of new principles in the system for recording births.

As a result, one-third of the world's children continue to lack birth registration, a proof of legal identity that is a ticket to accessing key citizenship benefits, including state services such as welfare, schooling, and health care.[9] Voting rights, travel documents, and, therefore, mobility may also be prejudiced by the absence of legal identity that often follows the failure to register a child's birth. Populations in which lack of birth registration constitutes a particular risk include those displaced by war; those marginalized by racism, stigma, or other forms of discrimination; and those that are undocumented. In such situations, where fear, inability, or reluctance to engage with the state authorities are widespread, it is particularly urgent that states adopt modern birth registration systems and creative, technologically facilitated, outreach programs. With growing population mobility and transnational ties, and growing numbers of children born to immigrant or noncitizen parents, these measures and the constitutive placement they strengthen, are all the more important, particularly because fewer and fewer countries grant a right to nationality by birthplace alone (the United States is an outlier in this respect), insisting on some form of parental permanence as a necessary precondition.[10]

Beyond National Borders

For a global elite of cosmopolitan migrants, displacement can be a relatively effortless asset, a new currency that enriches one's cultural repertoire, strengthens one's financial bargaining power, and broadens one's lifestyle options. For several decades, corporate executives and their families, successful academics, and entrepreneurial trailblazers have moved across borders without obstacles, often accumulating two or more nationalities for themselves and their children in the process. Many other migrants also benefit from opportunities to cross borders legally, following employment, family, or business ties that generate enhancements to their lives. But for millions, national borders and the dominant Westphalian order trigger powerful negative consequences. Large numbers of disenfranchised migrants fleeing the traumas of civil war and urban violence have been forcibly displaced to squalid internally displaced persons camps in Colombia or Sri Lanka, precarious and overcrowded facilities bordering Syria, or life-threatening Mediterranean boats hoping to reach the shores of Europe. While national borders function as open horizons for some, for millions they operate as challenging fences, evidence of the very partial scope of our postnational modernity.

It was not long ago—as recently as the second half of the twentieth century—that most states considered multiple nationalities undesirable, evidence of split loyalties and the dangerous possibility of treasonous behavior in time of war or other serious threats to the life of a nation. Today, for a mixture of pragmatic and ideological reasons, a growing number of states—from Mexico to India and the United States, eager to keep ties to their diasporic citizens and exercise their virtual presence outside the boundaries of their territory—permit such bifurcated affiliation, an acknowledgment by states that exclusive membership is not a necessary condition of citizenship.

But multiple affiliations are not always considered evidence of strength. What was true of the Jews most evidently in the early and mid-twentieth century remains true today for another heavily stigmatized European group, the Roma. Although European residents for at least six centuries, large numbers of European Roma have partial and compromised access to the fruits of citizenship—both citizenship of the member state in which they reside and European Union citizenship. Their syncretic identity and the cultural heritage associated with it often hinder full enjoyment of the postnational rights European Union citizenship aspires to embody.

Enduring Discrimination—A Constant Theme for Europe's Roma

Historically, the Roma have been the target of extreme discrimination and exclusion in Europe, raising recurring questions about their citizenship. Challenges to the Roma community's legitimacy as a European population date back centuries.[11] Experts agree that the Roma population is descended from discriminated-against Indian groups that first started migrating west from Northern India to escape stigma and exclusion about seven hundred years ago. After periods spent in different parts of the Middle East (where there is still a substantial Roma population), some groups started arriving in what is now the European Union as long ago as the fourteenth century.

The migrants spread all over Europe, adopting some of the mores and religions of the states in which they settled. But they retained a strong tie to their hereditary language, Romani, and to a powerful set of cultural and social traditions centered on fierce family loyalty and a self-protective reluctance to abandon self-employment for paid employment.[12] Stigma and persecution, lack of access to land ownership, and other forms of economic scarcity forced many to migrate again and again, traveling in family groups and mobile homes/caravans to new places, tied closely together as a community by mutual loyalty, conservative social and sexual mores, and linguistic affinity. Over the centuries, Roma populations became firmly settled in many European countries—most notably, in Romania, Bulgaria, Slovakia, the Czech Republic, and other countries in southeastern Europe.

Only small sections of today's Roma community consider themselves travelers or transient, the vast majority aspiring to the sedentary, secure, and predictable lifestyle of their non-Roma counterparts. Nevertheless, in many contexts they continue to be stereotyped as erstwhile Indian "nomads" and therefore quintessential outsiders, in but not of Europe, assumed to have a transient presence and questionable entitlement to the benefits of their European residence. An aspect of this hostile stance from majority populations and governments throughout the twentieth century and up to the present day is that the Roma have been the repeated target of sensationalist criticism and associated dramatized alarm about "the arrival of the wild Gypsies."[13] These stereotypes persist even among relatively well-intentioned constituencies. In the northern Italian city of Torino, for example, which has a progressive local administration and a history of social service engagement with the Roma community, the municipal office responsible for welfare support is called "Ufficio Nomadi."[14] The clientele, however, includes many second- and third-generation native-born Roma who have known no other home outside Italy—anything but nomads. As Jaroka Livia, a Roma-elected representative from Hungary to the European Parliament, stated, "[The Roma] don't want to be nomads. They want dignity. They want opportunity."[15]

Pervasive stigma and hostility toward the Roma community have existed throughout European history. These peaked with the brutal persecution inflicted on large numbers during the Nazi period. According to a report commissioned in 2008 by the Organization for Security and Cooperation in Europe, "Most autochthonous Austrian, German, and Czech Roma were killed in the Holocaust."[16] According to some estimates, up to 1.5 million Roma were killed by the Nazis.[17] Although the Weimar Constitution provided for equal rights for all citizens,[18] the Roma in Germany were subject to progressively discriminatory laws and directives: exclusion from public places (1920), mandatory registration (1925) and identification cards (1927), restrictions on movement and required proof of employment (1929), bans on mixed marriages (1933), revocation of naturalization (1933), forced sterilization (1933), withdrawal of civil liberties (1937), racial evaluation (1938) and internment and deportation to concentration camps (1936 onward).[19]

The Nuremburg Laws were amended to include the Roma and extended throughout incorporated and occupied territories of the Third Reich, yet many European countries had already enacted discriminatory measures targeting the Roma. In 1912, France required "nomads" to register with the authorities when they entered and left the country. In 1927, the former Czechoslovakia's "Law on the Wandering Gypsies" required the Roma to obtain permission to stay overnight in an area.[20] In Hungary, a decree from 1928 prohibited Roma from entering cities, and in 1933, Austrian government officials called for the Roma to be stripped of their civil rights.[21] Following World War II, repressive communist policies of cultural restriction, forcible assimilation, resettlement, and coercive sterilization reflected the ongoing belief that the Roma were not citizens of the countries in which they resided.[22]

Today, the Roma population continues to experience a high degree of racism and discrimination, both institutionally by states and at a quotidian level by large numbers of European citizens. More than sixty years after Europe committed itself to establishing a continent free of discrimination and inhuman or degrading treatment, many Roma experience life as outsiders and outliers to the increasingly integrated and prosperous European population. Still today, small numbers of Roma migrant arrivals can precipitate hysterical headlines about "invasion," triggering official discrimination and brutality rarely inflicted on majority populations. While open borders in the East have facilitated free movement for Roma families seeking to escape endemic unemployment and poverty in postcommunist countries, populist xenophobia in the West, combined with the recent rise of overtly racist right wing parties, have fueled an increase in anti-Roma policies and practices.

In 2011, Italy's Prime Minister Silvio Berlusconi warned of the alleged political threat posed by the Roma, stating, "Milan cannot turn into an Islamic city, a 'gypsyopolis' full of Roma camps besieged by foreigners to whom the left wants to give the right to vote."[23] Pervasive anti-Roma rhetoric has encouraged mob violence and vigilante attacks against Roma individuals and communities, as well as discriminatory measures such as compulsory fingerprinting, mass expulsions, home demolitions, and deportations.[24] The French authorities have also instituted a series of hostile measures, culminating in the brutal destruction of Roma settlements on the outskirts of several French cities and relentless eviction policies that decimate Roma community security. In 2011, French President Nicolas Sarkozy called for the dismantling of "illegal nomad camps," leading to the destruction of 75 percent of Roma camps in France.[25] Roma who left voluntarily were given 300 Euros plus 100 Euros per child by the French government.[26] In 2014, four hundred people were forced out of their settlement in Marseille, which coincided with the beating of a young Roma boy on June 13, 2014.[27] Germany, too, has executed harsh measures against members of its Roma community, compounding popular hostility that generated violent attacks in East Germany in the early years of post-1989 German reunification. In August 1992, an apartment complex in Rostock containing mostly Roma migrants was attacked with stones and firebombs while thousands cheered the attackers on.[28] Settled Roma populations, with children born and schooled in Germany, have been deported to countries that are ill-equipped to accommodate destitute arrivals in a postwar context (such as Kosovo, as per Germany's "Readmission Agreement" with Kosovo). Children and adolescents brought up speaking German and integrated into German schools and inner-city residential neighborhoods have difficulty integrating into Balkan society as do their displaced parents, with consequences that range from children dropping out of school to children taking on increased responsibility in the family due to deteriorating health among their caregivers.[29] Among European Union member states from Western Europe, Sweden and the United Kingdom have also implemented aggressive anti-Roma exclusion and removal policies.[30]

Meanwhile, farther south and east, anti-Roma stigma and discrimination has continued to be evident, both in government pronouncements (Greece and Romania most evidently) and in opposition and civil society groups. It is therefore not surprising that the Roma in Europe are targets of sustained discriminatory behavior, including physical violence. According to an eleven-country survey from 2008 by the European Union Agency for Fundamental Rights—an expert human rights body established by the European Union in 2007—"on average, every second Roma respondent had been discriminated against at least once in the 12 months prior to being surveyed."[31]

This long-standing hostility and exclusionary stance has material correlates. The Roma population continues to experience some of the most difficult and harsh living conditions in evidence in Europe. While the situation varies by country, the general picture is bleak: between one-quarter and two-thirds of Roma live in poverty or extreme poverty, often in segregated, substandard settlements, without access to adequate housing, water, sanitation, and public utilities.[32] Life expectancy is ten years shorter for Roma than for their non-Roma counterparts. A survey of five countries found child mortality rates among the Roma that were two to six times higher than those of the majority population. The Roma also face disproportionately poor health outcomes due to lack of access to preventative care and discrimination when seeking treatment.[33] According to the Pavee Point "All Ireland Traveller Health Study" published in September 2010, a larger percentage of Travellers reported discrimination when getting health care than did Black Americans and Latino Americans living in Ireland (54 percent, versus 17.3 percent and 14 percent, respectively).[34] Travellers have a higher prevalence of chronic diseases than the general population, with the rate of heart attack twice as high.[35] Educational outcomes are similarly poor: just half the Roma students in Europe complete primary education, and fewer than 4 percent complete higher education.[36] In Central Europe and Eastern Europe, where 70 percent of all Roma live, just 20 percent complete primary education.[37] Moving beyond primary school, where state laws mandate attendance (though they do not ensure high-quality education), Roma students are frequently taught in separate classes or schools, and in the Czech Republic, 30 percent are still educated in facilities for the mentally disabled.[38] This contributes to an educational deficit that prevents young Roma jobseekers from developing formal skills and qualifications and obtaining rights-respecting work. Without assets or proof of formal employment, many Roma community members are unable to register their residences and access the social services to which they are entitled.[39]

Many of the social and economic rights violations experienced daily by Europe's Roma population relate directly or indirectly to issues of citizenship and constitutive placement. As Europe moved out of the Cold War and its communist-governed federations (in the former Yugoslavia, Czechoslovakia, and Soviet Union) to an expanded European Union of individual nation-states, citizenship was redefined. In the process, many of the traditional exclusions, papered over under Communism, reappeared, including the sense that Roma minorities were foreigners. Responding to a resurgence of acute racism against them, many Roma communities from Central Europe and southeastern Europe voted with their feet, fleeing discrimination in home countries including the Czech Republic, Poland, Hungary, Slovakia, Serbia, Kosovo, Romania, and Slovenia. But as just noted, their attempts to secure new rights in Western Europe were met with mixed reactions. These are reflected in their complex and compromised legal status.

In some cases, Roma migrants managed to secure refugee status or some form of more limited temporary or subsidiary protection[40]—this was particularly the case during the Balkan conflicts of the early 1990s. In others, their new identity as European Union citizens made exclusion more complicated for member states' governments, although several attempts to discriminate against Roma European Union migrants were defeated only by protracted court proceedings.[41] Even when they secured entry to territories in western Europe, though, Roma Europeans often encountered (and continue to encounter) hostility and outbursts of hysteria and violence. Over the past eight years, the European Court of Human Rights has held on several occasions that European states have violated nondiscrimination provisions in the European Convention. Their findings have included cases concerning illegal expulsion of aliens, racially biased police investigations and abuse, and vigilante "skinhead" anti-Roma violence.[42] Lack of demonstrable residential permanence has led to disqualification from welfare benefits ("the habitual residence" test in Ireland), and from access to public housing, effortless border crossing, and residence within European Union countries. This results in very compromised access to national, regional, let alone international (or global) citizenship.[43]

Conclusion

For a complex set of reasons, the European Roma population continues to instantiate our dependence on constitutive permanence as a precondition of full access to legal personhood. Globalization, the erection of supranational institutions, and powerful international norms notwithstanding, firm national anchoring is still a precondition of the right to have rights. Even long-settled Roma populations have only tenuous access to this because state discrimination and material deprivation continue to obstruct their full entitlement to protection. The absence of identifying documents (particularly birth registration) or qualifying ("habitual") residence, of educational accomplishment, and of residential security leave large numbers of Roma residents excluded from core benefits of European citizenship. As a result, as I have noted, in Italy, long-settled Roma communities are disqualified from public housing; in Ireland, Roma residents are regularly ruled ineligible for state welfare benefits; in France and Germany, Roma families, including many with locally born children, are excluded from the right to remain in their country of residence indefinitely and instead are subject to deportation. Constitutive placement continues to overshadow international rights as an anchor of human well-being and thriving, despite optimistic claims about our postnational era.

NOTES

1 I use these terms interchangeably in this chapter. Historically, "citizenship" has generally denoted the set of rights and duties that bind individuals to a country through domestic legal provisions (its origins dating back to the city as repository of belonging and identity), whereas "nationality" has described the individual's relationship to a particular entity in the international order, a nation: see Bosniak, *The Citizen and the Alien*.
2 For a description of this process of both internationalization and universalization of human rights, see Henkin, *The Age of Rights*.
3 The right to a nationality (Article 15), the right to return to one's own country (Article 13[2]), the right to take part in the government of one's country (Article 21), each person's duty to his or her community "in which alone free and full development of the person is possible" (Article 29[1]), and, finally an acknowledgment that "the will of the people shall be the basis of the authority of government" (Article 21[2]).

4. Bill Chappell, "UN: Number of Displaced People Hits Mark not Seen since World War II," National Public Radio, June 20, 2014, http://www.npr.org/blogs/thetwo-way/2014/06/20/323952215/number-of-displaced-people-hits-a-high-last-seen-in-world-war-ii?wpisrc=nl_wonk.
5. Arendt, *The Human Condition*.
6. United Nations High Commissioner for Refugees, "Under the Radar and Under-Protected: The Urgent Need to Address Stateless Children's Rights," June 2012, http://www.unhcr.org/509a6bb79.html.
7. Goris et al., "Statelessness," 4. See also the UN Refugee Agency, "Figures at a Glance," 19 June 2017, http://www.unhcr.org/en-us/figures-at-a-glance.html.
8. Lewa, "North Arakan," 13.
9. See Bhabha, *Children without a State*.
10. Weil, "Access to Citizenship."
11. Matras, *I Met Lucky People*.
12. See Hancock, *The Pariah Syndrome*; Liégeois, *Roma, Gypsies, Travellers*; Silverman, *Romani Routes*.
13. Hancock, *The Pariah Syndrome*, cited in Cahn and Guild, "Recent Migration of Roma in Europe," 14.
14. An estimated 150,000 Roma live throughout Italy: Office for Democratic Institutions and Human Rights, High Commissioner on National Minorities, *Assessment of the Human Rights Situation of Roma and Sinti in Italy*.
15. Andrew Cohen, "A Deeper, Darker Prejudice," *Ottawa Citizen*, June 14, 2011, http://www2.canada.com/ottawacitizen/news/archives/story.html?id=405f963b-b409-4dd7-b4c4-a531784982e1&p=2.
16. Cahn and Guild, "Recent Migration of Roma in Europe," 35.
17. Exact figures are unavailable, but estimates range from 200,000 to 1.5 million killed, which the Roma call the *Samudaripen* or *Porajmos*: Barany, "Memory and Experience." See also Council of Europe, *Protecting the Rights of Roma*.
18. U.S. Holocaust Memorial Museum, *Sinti and Roma: Victims of the Nazi Era*, http://www.ushmm.org/m/pdfs/20000926-Roma-and-Sinti.pdf.
19. Hancock, *We Are the Romani People*, 37–42. See also U.S. Holocaust Memorial Museum, *Sinti and Roma*, 3–6.
20. Peschanski, "The Gypsies in the Upheaval," 50–55.
21. Lucero and Collum, "The Roma," 98; Hancock, *We Are the Romani People*, 37.
22. Marushiakova and Popov, "State Policies under Communism."
23. "Silvio Berlusconi Attacks Italy's 'Gypsy-Loving' Left-Wing," *The Telegraph*, May 23, 2011, http://www.telegraph.co.uk/news/worldnews/silvio-berlusconi/8531193/Silvio-Berlusconi-attacks-Italys-gypsy-loving-left-wing.html.
24. Human Rights First, *2008 Hate Crime Survey*; Hammarberg, "The Romani Holocaust and Contemporary Challenges"; Chris Bryant, "Deported Roma Return to Poverty," *Financial Times*, September 24, 2010; František Kostlán, "Analysis: Czech Media Baiting Romani Family Attacked by Ultra-Right Arsonists," *Romea*, March 16, 2012.

25 European Roma Rights Centre, "France: Country Profile 2011–2012," April 2013, http://www.errc.org/cms/upload/file/france-country-profile-2011–2012.pdf.
26 BBC, "France Sends Roma Gypsies back to Romania," August 20, 2010, http://www.bbc.com/news/world-europe-11020429.
27 Amnesty International, "France: Forced Evictions Add to Climate of Fear amid Alleged Hate Crimes," June 19, 2014, http://www.fightdiscrimination.eu/discrimination-in-europe/publications/france-forced-evictions-add-climate-fear-amid-alleged-hate-c-0.
28 Charles Hawley and Daryl Lindsey, "Twenty Years after Rostock: Racism and Xenophobia Still Prevalent in Germany," *Spiegel Online*, August 24, 2012, http://www.spiegel.de/international/germany/xenophobia-still-prevalent-in-germany-20-years-after-neo-nazi-attacks-a-851972-druck.html.
29 Knaus and Widmann, "Integration Subject to Conditions." See also Human Rights Watch, *Rights Displaced*.
30 See *Regina v. Immigration Officer at Prague Airport and Another, Ex Parte European Roma Rights Centre and Others*, UKHL 55, Judicial Committee, House of Lords, United Kingdom, December 9, 2004.
31 Andrey Ivanov and Sheena Keller, "The Roma Community in the EU and the work of the FRA: Discrimination of Roma as a Fundamental Rights Issue," ms. on file with the author, 7.
32 United Nations Children's Fund, *Breaking the Cycle of Exclusion*, 20–23, 27; European Union Agency for Fundamental Rights, *Housing Conditions of Roma and Travellers in the European Union*.
33 Council of Europe, *Protecting the Rights of Roma*, 7.
34 *Our Geels*.
35 *Our Geels*.
36 "Half of Roma Children Drop Out of Primary School, UN-backed Report Finds," United Nations News Centre, September 27, 2010, http://www.un.org/apps/news/story.asp?NewsID=36207&Cr=unesco&Cr1; Council of Europe, *Human Rights of Roma and Travellers in Europe*, 118.
37 United Nations Children's Fund, *The Right of Roma Children to Education*, 2, 15–18.
38 Council of Europe, *Human Rights of Roma and Travellers in Europe*, 18, 123.
39 European Union Agency for Fundamental Rights, *The Situation of Roma EU Citizens Moving to and Settling in Other EU Member States*.
40 Some favorable decisions have quashed deportation orders: see, e.g., *D [a Minor] v. Refugee Appeals Tribunal Anor* [2011] IEHC 431 and *K.H. v. Office of Immigration and Nationality* (OIN) 6.K. 34.440/2010/20. Note that the Irish case is an exception to the general policy that European Union citizens may not be granted asylum in other member states on the grounds that they are all "safe countries of origin." Other favorable decisions have reviewed rejection of refugee status by immigration boards or held that deportation would violate international law: see, e.g., *Bors v. Canada (Minister of Citizenship and Immigration)*, 2010 FC 1004; *Mohacsi v. Canada (Minister of Citizenship and Immigration) (T.D.)*, 2003 FCT 429; *Balogh*

v. *Canada (Minister of Citizenship and Immigration)*, 2002 FCT 809; *Case of N.A. v. United Kingdom*, no. 25904/07, ECHR, August 6, 2008; Cour nationale du droit d'asile, November 2, 2011, M.B., no. 10011958.

41 See *Regina v. Immigration Officer.*

42 *Conka v. Belgium*, no. 51564/99, ECHR, February 5, 2002; *Connors v. UK* (2005), 40 EHRR 9; *Hamidovic v. Italy*, no. 31956/05, ECHR, March 4, 2013; *Bekos and Koutropoulos v. Greece*, no. 15250/02, ECHR, December 13, 2005 and *Cobzaru v. Romania*, no. 48254/99, ECHR, July 26, 2007, cited in Cahn and Guild, "Recent Migration of Roma in Europe," 31. See also *Angelova and Iliev v. Bulgaria*, no. 55523/00, ECHR, July 26, 2007; *Nachova and Others v. Bulgaria*, no. 43577/98, ECHR, July 6, 2005; *Stoica v. Romania*, no. 42722/02, ECHR, March 4, 2008; *Beganović v. Croatia*, no. 46423/06, ECHR, 2009; *Vasil Sashov Petrov v. Bulgaria*, no. 63106/00, ECHR, June 10, 2010; *Stefanou v. Greece*, no. 2954/07, ECHR, October 4, 2010; *Carabulea v. Romania*, no. 45661/99, ECHR, October 13, 2010; *Dimitrova and Others v. Bulgaria*, no. 44862/04, ECHR, April 27, 2011; *Šečić v. Croatia*, no. 40116/02, ECHR, May 31, 2007, cited in Cahn and Guild, "Recent Migration of Roma in Europe," 31. See also *Case of Moldovan and Others v. Romania* (no. 2), no. 41138/98 and 64320/01, ECHR, November 30, 2005.

43 Bhabha, "The Politics of Evidence."

BIBLIOGRAPHY

Arendt, Hannah. *The Human Condition*. Chicago: University of Chicago Press, 1958.

Barany, Zoltan D. *Memory and Experience: Anti-Roma Prejudice in Eastern Europe*. Woodrow Wilson International Center for Scholars, Working Paper no. 50, 1998. http://www.wilsoncenter.org/staff/zoltan-barany.

Bhabha, Jacqueline, ed. *Children without a State: A Global Human Rights Challenge*. Cambridge, MA: MIT Press, 2011.

Bhabha, Jacqueline. "The Politics of Evidence: Roma Citizenship Deficits in Europe." In *Citizenship in Question: Evidentiary Birthright and Statelessness*, ed. Benjamin Lawrance and Jacqueline Stevens, 43–59. Durham, NC: Duke University Press, 2017.

Bosniak, Linda. *The Citizen and the Alien: Dilemmas of Contemporary Membership*. Princeton, NJ: Princeton University Press, 2006.

Cahn, Claude, and Elspeth Guild. *Recent Migration of Roma in Europe*, 2nd ed. Strasbourg, France: Organization for Security and Co-operation in Europe, 2010.

Council of Europe. *Human Rights of Roma and Travellers in Europe*. Strasbourg, France: Council of Europe Publishing, 2012. http://www.coe.int/t/commissioner/source/prems/prems79611_GBR_CouvHumanRightsOfRoma_WEB.pdf.

———. *Protecting the Rights of Roma*. Strasbourg, France: Council of Europe, 2011.

European Union Agency for Fundamental Rights. *Housing Conditions of Roma and Travellers in the European Union: Comparative Report*. Luxembourg: Office for Official Publications of the European Communities, 2009. http://fra.europa.eu/sites/default/files/fra_uploads/703-Roma_Housing_Comparative-final_en.pdf.

———. *The Situation of Roma EU Citizens Moving to and Settling in other EU Member States*. Luxembourg: Office for Official Publications of the European Communities, 2009. http://fra.europa.eu/sites/default/files/fra_uploads/705-Roma_Movement_Comparative-final_en.pdf.

Goris, Indira, Julia Harrington, and Sebastian Köhn. "Statelessness: What It Is and Why It Matters." *Forced Migration Review* 32 (2009): 4–6.

Hancock, Ian F. *The Pariah Syndrome: An Account of Gypsy Slavery and Persecution*. Ann Arbor: Karoma, 1987.

Hancock, Ian F. *We Are the Romani People (Ame sam e Rromane džene)*. Hatfield, UK: University of Hertfordshire Press, 2002.

Henkin, Louis. *The Age of Rights*. New York: Columbia University Press, 1990.

Human Rights First. *2008 Hate Crime Survey*. New York: Human Rights First, 2008.

Human Rights Watch. *Rights Displaced: Forced Returns of Roma, Ashkali and Egyptians from Western Europe to Kosovo*. New York: Human Rights Watch, 2010. http://www.hrw.org/sites/default/files/reports/kosovo1010webwcover_1.pdf.

Knaus, Verena, and Peter Widmann. *Integration Subject to Conditions: A Report on the Situation of Kosovan Roma, Ashkali and Egyptian Children in Germany and after Their Repatriation to Kosovo*. Kosovo: UNICEF Kosovo and the German Committee for UNICEF, 2010. http://www.unicef.org/kosovoprogramme/RAEstudy_eng_web.pdf.

Lewa, Chris. "North Arakan: An Open Prison for the Rohingya in Burma." *Forced Migration Review* 32 (April 2009): 11–13.

Liégeois, Jean-Pierre. *Roma, Gypsies, Travellers*, trans. Sinéad ní Shuinéar. Strasbourg, France: Council of Europe, 1994.

Lucero, Florinda, and Jill Collum. "The Roma: During and after Communism." In *Topical Research Digest: Human Rights in Russia and the Former Soviet Republics (Human Rights and Human Welfare)*, 98–106. Denver: Graduate School of International Studies, University of Denver, 2007.

Marushiakova, Elena, and Veselin Popov. "State Policies under Communism." Project Education of Roma Children in Europe, Council of Europe, Strasbourg, France. http://www.coe.int/t/dg4/education/roma/Source/FS/6.1_communism.pdf.

Matras, Yaron. *I Met Lucky People: The Story of the Romani Gypsies*. London: Allen Lane, 2014.

Office for Democratic Institutions and Human Rights, High Commissioner on National Minorities. *Assessment of the Human Rights Situation of Roma and Sinti in Italy*. Warsaw: Organization for Security and Co-operation in Europe, 2009.

Our Geels: All Ireland Traveller Health Study Summary of Findings. Dublin: School of Public Health, Physiotherapy and Population Science, University College Dublin, 2010.

Peschanski, Denis. "The Gypsies in the Upheaval: The Situation in France, 1939–1946." In *Roma and Sinti: Under-Studied Victims of Nazism, Symposium Proceedings*, 49–58. Washington, DC: Center for Advanced Holocaust Studies, U.S. Holocaust Memorial Museum, 2002.

Silverman, Carol. *Romani Routes: Cultural Politics and Balkan Music in Diaspora.* New York: Oxford University Press, 2014.

United Nations Children's Fund. *Breaking the Cycle of Exclusion: Roma Children in South East Europe.* Belgrade, Serbia: UNICEF Serbia, 2007. http://www.unicef.org/ceecis/070305-Subregional_Study_Roma_Children.pdf.

———. *The Right of Roma Children to Education: Position Paper.* Geneva: UNICEF Regional Office for Central and Eastern Europe and the Commonwealth of Independent States, 2011.

Weil, Patrick. "Access to Citizenship: A Comparison of Twenty-Five Nationality Laws." In *Citizenship Today: Global Perspectives and Practices*, ed. T. Alexander Aleinikoff and Douglas Klusmeyer, 17–35. Washington, DC: Carnegie Endowment for International Peace, 2001.

Chapter 9

From World History to World Art:
Reflections on New Geographies of Feminist Art

SHU-MEI SHIH

The pressures of contemporary globalization on scholarship are perhaps most notable in the expansion of scholarship's scope and the new awareness of the variation in scale, which have generated new fields of inquiry. From economics of globalization, we now have transnational studies, which looks at transnational migration as a sociological inquiry and the transnational movement and formation of cultures for humanistic analysis; diaspora studies, which examines dispersions of people across the world; empire studies, which covers large areas of the world's lands and seas over several thousand years; and world history, which looks at the entire world as an integrated and interconnected economic system.

This widespread impulse to account for the world in scholarship is specifically reflected in the emergence of what I call world studies, which attempts to enlarge the scope and scale of scholarship from that of nation or region to the world. World studies are different from transnational studies (which studies how an object of study exceeds the nation-state boundary in its constitution) and globalization studies (which studies how economic globalization has changed human societies). It refers specifically to those subdisciplines in the humanities and the social sciences that carry the word "world" in their names, such as world music, world cinema, world literature, world history, and world art, all of which presume somehow to cover the study of the named scholarly object in the whole world rather than in a slice of the world, such as has been the case in diasporic, international, transnational, and transregional studies.

As a literary and cultural studies scholar, not an art historian, I hope in this chapter to propose a new way of thinking of world art by taking a uniquely modified perspective on world history. The conception of world art offered here aims to help situate the study of Asian and Asian American feminist art in new ways in our increasingly intertwined world and to take seriously the notion of geography (literally, in terms of specific geographical locations such as cities and nations, and metaphorically, in terms of formations of schools or styles or movements of art that are not bound by actual geography). For the former purpose, I offer the conception of world art not as a particular type of art but as a network in which artworks from across the world are enmeshed in complex and power-inflected relations. For the latter purpose, I offer the conception of world art in terms of what I call an artistic arc, connecting as many and as few nodal points of artistic production that make particular sense in the context of world history, without needing to account for the whole world. The relational conception of world art, I contend, allows for minor sites and works of art to serve as nodal points equal to what have been known as major sites and major works, thereby offering a non-centrist (whether Eurocentric or China-centric) model of world art studies.

World History and Relational Comparison

The models of world history with which I am working refer specifically to what came after Immanuel Wallerstein's world systems theory. In very broad terms, world systems theory proposed that the world has become one integrated economic system since the late fifteenth century due to the rise of the West and the spread of global capitalism. Even though Wallerstein's intention is by no means Eurocentric, the implied presumption of European exceptionalism in the narrative of the rise of the West has led many self-styled anti-Eurocentric historians to offer counter-narratives, and "integrative world history" is the term some of these historians have used to mark their difference from Wallerstein.

The two main theses for integrative world historians, simply put, are that the world as we know it has been integrated economically and otherwise for much longer than the modern world system theory proposes and the so-called rise of the West owed much to the more advanced East. For some of these historians, to consider the macro-history of the world is to learn about its interconnectedness since at least the sixth century; what this means is that the ideology of "East is East and West is West" is as fictive as it is false. The historical sociologist Janet L. Abu-Lughod identified the existence of a polycentric world system in the thirteenth century, long before the European-led world system of the sixteenth century suggested by Wallerstein.¹ What is of interest to art historians in Abu-Lughod's discussion of economic circuits in the thirteenth century is that some of the evidence she uses to illustrate the constitution of economic circuits is the circulation of art objects such as Sung celadon ware, Persian turquoise-glazed bowls, and Egyptian furniture with complex inlays of silver and gold.

Andre Gunder Frank's explicitly anti-Eurocentric *ReOrient: Global Economy in the Asian Age* (1998) pays special attention to the structural relations, interconnectedness, and simultaneity in world events and processes during what he calls "the Asian Age," which he dates at AD 1400–1800.² Although in his other works he actually locates, along with Barry K. Gills, the existence of something similar to Wallerstein's world system further back by five thousand years, not five hundred years, his main point in *ReOrient* is to show how Europe "climbed up on the back of Asia, then stood on Asian shoulders."³ John M. Hobson, in the tellingly titled *The Eastern Origins of Western Civilization*, extends these arguments to say that the so-called rise of the West owes crucially to the "resource portfolios" from the Far East and the Middle East, which include technology, institutions, and ideas, such as gunpowder, printing, navigational sciences, the creation of capitalist institutions, advancement in astronomy and mathematics, and the enlightened ideas of rationality.⁴

The historian Micol Seigel sums up succinctly what she considers the major emphasis of this type of world history as "the complex, global network of power-inflected relations that enmesh our world."⁵ To be sure, not all parts of the network are equally affecting or evenly affected by the global system, but all parts of the network are constitutive of the system itself, and there is no hiding from an interconnectedness that is thoroughly infiltrated by the operations of power. This means that histories of empire, conquest, slavery, colonialism, and all forms of domination cannot in any way be disavowed when one does integrative world history; after all, power is a form of relation. To analogize, for the moment, I propose a conception of world art whereby artworks are enmeshed in a "complex, global network of power-inflected relations."

The keyword here is "relation," and I draw partly from the work of the Caribbean thinker Édouard Glissant—specifically, his notion of "Relation," itself inspired by chaos theory, as well as by contemporary conditions of globalization. For Glissant, "Relation" is a way of describing and understanding the globalized world of "infinite interaction of cultures" and an act (as an intransitive verb) that changes all of the elements that come into relation with one another.⁶ Relation is therefore as much a phenomenological description of the world as a movement or a process. As a description, it is akin to the perception of the dynamics of the world in chaos theory; as a movement, it is best exemplified in the worldwide and ceaseless process of creolization. In other words, "Relation" references the state of worldwide entanglements of cultures and peoples, the process of ceaseless creolization as a result of such entanglements, and is something that we enter into and something we can do. It is a description of the dynamics in the world, a way of looking at the world, a way of being—for a person or for an artwork—in the world, and a way to do research as a scholar. This relational way of doing research on world art in the context of world history is what I call *relational comparison*.

In Glissant's thinking, Relation also does not happen in a power vacuum: the Caribbean as a site, like any other where intense cultural entanglements have occurred throughout history, has experienced colonialism, genocide, slavery, and coolie trade. Creolization takes many forms, involves irreconcilable elements, and leads to unpredictable consequences; as a ceaseless process, however, it keeps open the potentiality that something different and new will come out of even violent encounters.

A relational view of world art, then, sees all art of the world to be mutually entangled in uneven terrains of power and to be engaged in the ceaseless process of creolization. In this way, minor sites of art can be brought into relation, and histories of power are not displaced but acknowledged and foregrounded.

Arc versus Totality

A quick survey of world or global art history will help us see why the relational model might work well. *Gardner's Art through the Ages: A Global History*, by Fred S. Kleiner, is a classic textbook in its fourteenth edition.[7] Putatively about the entire world, the book has very little coverage of Asia. In its first chapter, "What Is Art History," Kleiner uses nineteen images to illustrate his sweeping ideas about what the global history of art entails. Only one image shows an Asian artwork, and it is Japanese. Surprisingly, the proportion of Asian art represented in the book is not much better than that in the art catalogue published in 1894 for the World's Fair held in Chicago in 1893. Embossed with an image of Christopher Columbus in gold on the cover, the five-volume catalogue, entitled *The Art of the World, Illustrated in the Paintings, Statuary and Architecture of the World's Columbian Exposition*, included only one work of Asian art, again by a Japanese artist.[8]

Or take a look at two other art history books that share an interesting commonality: *A World View of Art History* (1985), edited by Virgil Bird and others, and *A World History of Art* (2008), by Hugh Honour and John Fleming.[9] In both, all of the non-Western art is identified using geographical markers—for example, Indian, Chinese, Japanese, or Egyptian. But when it comes to Western art, geography suddenly disappears, and the chapter titles are marked by style, school, or periodization, such as "Renaissance Art," "Baroque Art," "Late Eighteenth and Early Nineteenth Century Art," "Post-War to Post-Modern."

An exemplary recent attempt at a non-Eurocentric conception of world art studies is the volume *World Art Studies: Exploring Concepts and Approaches*, edited by Kitty Zijlmans and Wilfried Van Damme and published in Amsterdam in 2008, with essays written by European and American art historians.[10] The new concept of world art studies is said to have been pioneered by John Onians in 1996 and is simply defined as the "global and multidisciplinary examination of the arts."[11] The premise of world art studies is that art is a "panhuman phenomenon" and a "basic feature of our shared humanity."[12] Like the world systems theory of Wallerstein, who was influenced by the systems theory of Niklas Luhmann, Zijlman proposes in the volume to study world art as a system—that is, a world art system. Since society is becoming ever more complex, functional differentiation occurs within the society and there develops a self-organizing set of systems such as economy, law, politics, religion, education, science, media, and art.[13] Each system realizes a kind of "operative closure and self-organization" and is "self-generating or autopoietic."[14] Each system describes itself, refers to itself, and is self-evolving and autonomous, although it interacts with other systems, as well. The art system and the economic system, for instance, intersect in the operation of the art market. Analogically, on the scale of the world, the "development of an evolving functional differentiation of societal systems worldwide" leads to the formation of a global art system or a world art system.[15]

It is obviously productive to consider art to be a panhuman phenomenon to be more inclusive and to consider world art as an integrated and self-generative system to be able to account for its totality. What is glaringly lacking here, however, is the consideration of power relations that inevitably operate in any system, as has been shown in the predominant Eurocentrism of aforementioned art history textbooks. In the specific instance of world art, furthermore, it is helpful for us to recall that, like the terms "world literature" and "world history," the precursor to current conceptualization of world art studies is the nineteenth-century German notion of *Weltkunstgeschichte* (world art history). Ulrich Pfisterer warns us that this concept is in fact not innocent of the German acquisition of colonies in the 1880s—that is, it was an art history correlation to German imperialism, even though it actually included divergent views by different theorists and scholars who ranged from evolutionists, relativists, to nationalists (whom he calls, unambiguously, the racists).

The discussion up to now from world history to world art allows me to formulate a conception of world art in which artworks are enmeshed in a "complex, global network of power-inflected relations." The task of the world art scholar, then, is to excavate and analyze these relations across uneven terrain fractured by the operations of power such as trade, colonialism, conquest, neocolonialism, and global capitalism. Simply put, doing relational studies means setting into motion and bringing into relation terms that traditionally have been pushed apart from one another due to certain interests. I consider the excavation of these relationalities to be the ethical practice of comparison, wherein art from marginalized locations and Western and canonical art can equally be brought to relation. Relational comparison is not a center-periphery model, as the artworks form a network of relations wherever the artworks are created and circulated. Hence, any given work of art can be potentially brought into relation.

But it is, of course, impossible to map all of the layers of interconnections of art the world over. Instead of presuming that this is possible—as the above world/global art history books claimed—I offer here a more modest version of relational method wherein a specific set of relationalities is traced on an arc or a trajectory rather than as a totality. Against the lures of systematization and totalization I propose the notion of the artistic arc as a way to connect artworks, spaces, events, and issues—or nodal points of meaning—across a specific trajectory in world history. So for the subject matter at hand, Asian and Asian American feminist art can be conceived along an arc that constitutes a network of relations in uneven terrains in the context of world history. Asian and Asian American feminist art is not a totality of world art but a discrete trajectory with specific nodal points that we identify and bring into relation through intellectual and affective labor.

Beyond the Binarism of China versus the West

The lesson of anti-Eurocentric world history that I have summarized and drawn from for a theory of world art so far has specific implications for considering contemporary feminist art in Asia and Asian America—namely, in relation to the rise of China. One of the unintended consequences of anti-Eurocentric world history is that in its valorization—indeed, over-valorization—of the civilizational and technological contributions made by Asia, especially China (consider gunpowder, paper, the compass), it has unwittingly served as an apology or justification for the rise of China as a new major power on the world stage. Unwittingly, anti-Eurocentric history has been beneficial for the construction of a new kind of China-centrism.

Chinese intellectuals have been self-consciously utilizing this historiography to make several arguments: (1) China has been an important, if not the most important, contributor to world civilizations; (2) the era of Western hegemony is over and the rise of China is inevitable; and (3) China will be at the center of the new world order. They draw two major supports from this historiography: the existence of the tribute system since time immemorial (see the influence of the work of Takeshi Hamashita in collaboration with people such as Giovanni Arrighi, cited by the world historians mentioned earlier); and the idea that the state form of China exceeds the Westphalian system of sovereign nation-state and it should be considered a civilization-state.[16]

How the new perception of China's importance in world civilizations led to a confident and proud self-perception within China can be found in the reemergence of the discourse of *tianxia* (all under heaven) in China. A decade or so earlier, the notion of all under heaven had been evoked simply as a limited reference to the geographical China itself, as in the following titles: *All under Heaven: A Complete History of China*; *All under Heaven: The Chinese World* (a book of photography); and *Chinese Maps: Images of "All under Heaven."*[17] In all three, the referential limit of the concept of all under heaven is China itself.

The reemergence of the discourse of all under heaven is most powerfully felt within China, and the scholar most responsible for this is Zhao Tingyang, a professor of philosophy at People's University in Beijing who has written numerous books and articles on the topic since the late 1990s, including the widely read *The All-under-Heaven System*, in the series Philosophical Introductions to the World System.[18] Zhao has also been publishing in English, and in 2011 there was a major conference at Stanford University on this concept. In his work, the referential limit is no longer just China or even East Asia but the entire world. Now the concept of all under heaven is part of world political philosophy and concerns the world order from a Chinese civilizational perspective.

Traditionally, the concept was largely cosmological-cum-political, involving the emperor in the center as the son of heaven (*tianzi*; i.e., the emperor) who, with the mandate of heaven (*tianming*), rules over the realm under heaven (*tianxia*). Tianxia as a political cosmology evinces a concentric structure of power, with the son of heaven at the center or apex, emanating its domination over inner subjects, outer subjects, tributary states, and barbarians in all four directions (north, south, east, and west), which belong to outside lands or, more literally, the realm beyond civilization (*huawai zhi di*). The renowned sinologist John K. Fairbank, who wrote about this concept in 1966, translated *tianxia* as "the Chinese world" and explained that it may reach beyond the borders of China, but only in "gradually decreasing efficacy, as parts of a concentric hierarchy."[19] Fairbank noted that, unlike the theoretical equality presumed by the European ideology of nation-states, the Chinese world order "was not organized by a division of territories of sovereigns of equal status but rather by the subordination of all local authorities to the central and awe-inspiring power of the emperor." Its organizing principle is "superordination-subordination."[20]

Within this political structure, all those beyond the center proper constitute barbarian peoples. *Nanman* (southern barbarians; *man* means "barbarous"), *beidi* (northern barbarians; *di* with a beast radical on the left), *dongyi* (eastern barbarians; *yi* means "to eliminate"), and *xirong* (western barbarians; *rong* means "to fight")—all are beastly and wild people who need subjugation and appeasement by the son of heaven, and they all belong to the realm beyond civilization. Only in the twentieth century did these frontier or minority people in China begin to lose these old names, with their references to beastliness: the Beidi, who were also called Huren (barbarians), and the Xiongnu (lit., "fierce slaves") are now called Mongolians. The word *di* also suggests violence, being far away, and exclusion. Today's Uyghurs and Tibetans are the erstwhile western barbarians. In other words, the concept of all under heaven historically has been imbued with the barbarization and primitivism of the other.

The concept undergoes a radical transformation in the work of Zhao, who has made the concept very popular. "All under heaven," Zhao proposes, is "an acceptable empire" form that is also an "ideal" form of empire, a "perfect empire."[21] The term includes three meanings: first, "the whole world under heaven"; second, "the hearts of all people, or the general will of the people"; and third, "a universal system of the world, a utopia of the world-as-one-family."[22] Aspects of such empire can be seen in ancient empires in China, especially the ancient Zhou dynasty, and in the practice of the tribute system, in which tribute was voluntary and reciprocity was the norm.

Under this concept, the whole world will be one world; it will have a world institution with "full popular support," and it will operate with "harmony, communication and cooperation of all nations, guaranteed by a commonly agreed institution."[23] This world institution is different from the United Nations, in which powerful nations tend to impose their values on weaker ones. Furthermore, the United Nations does not have substantial power to govern the world, while the European Union is essentially an economic unit, "company of nation/states."[24] Zhao argues that the system of all under heaven is superior to democracy, because democracy "represents misled minds much more than the independent, the false want much more than true needs, and illusive advantages much more than real goods and virtues."[25] As history has shown, he contends, "the masses always make the wrong choices for themselves through a misled democracy."²⁶

In the preface to the book he published in China in 2005, Zhao notes that the recuperation of this concept is necessary for China. Now as a major economic power, China must also become "a major nation for the production of knowledge."²⁷ It can do so by "creating new ideals of the world and a new world system."²⁸ This is a project of rethinking China so that Chinese knowledge becomes an important basis for the world knowledge system. Since China is a major part of the world, thinking about China must develop into thinking about the world, and thus "the fundamental goal of rethinking China is rethinking the world."²⁹ Here, through a series of rhetorical substitutions, China becomes the world.

The rise of China gives substance and cause to the rise of the discourse of all under heaven, and this discourse in fact justifies the complete denigration of socialist values, even as China presumes to be putatively or still a socialist country. Such socialist values as autonomy of national minorities are tested daily, and the global solidarity of people of color around the world of the 1960s has largely been abandoned by Chinese extractionist policies in Africa and elsewhere. Such is our historical conjuncture where supersize empires of the United States and China vie for power and influence using all means possible.

In Feminist Art Begins Responsibility

Against the lure of the new economy of culture in which Eurocentrism's proposed cure has turned out to be China-centrism, and where artworks bearing the national label "Chinese" acquire unprecedented cultural and economic capital, visual studies scholars and art historians perhaps bear new responsibilities. Responsibility in this context, it seems, means making the effort to cultivate the capacity to respond to changing historical configurations of power and formulate new lines of resistance. For scholars who work on China, this means not being content to benefit from the China-versus-the-West binarism but to critique it, unsettle it, and move beyond it as a matter of ethical practice. Response-ability in this context then requires a new engagement with both old and new forms of otherness, historically but also newly produced by the dominant binarism. This may include such artworks situated on the margins of China and Chineseness, on the margins of the United States and Americanness, and produced from the perspective of the South to the new North that is China.

It is in this context that this chapter now turns to trace an arc of minor and minoritized artists as an illustration for a new conception of world art as a relational network of artists and artworks that intervene in the contemporary conjuncture of world history described earlier. Three artists are particularly significant and represent three sites of contestation against the dominant binarism of China versus the West: Taiwan (at the crossroads of both the American and Chinese empires), Southeast Asia (the perennial South to China's North, despite formerly being European colonies), and Asian America (on the margin of the American empire). I hope to show, with this arc, that relational work opens up new geographies of art, more able to respond to simultaneously consolidating but shifting configurations of power, in representation and in politics.

From Taiwan, the work of Wu Mali is significant for thinking through the issues at hand and specifically for having offered, in advance, a feminist and anticipatory look at the discourse of all under heaven that is now serving as a discursive alibi for a rising China with global ambitions for civilizational supremacy, as discussed earlier. Her installation piece, entitled "Formosa Club" (*Baodao binguan*, 1998), stages the entrance of an interior to space infused with red lights, suggesting a brothel.

The viewer enters a room lit with alluring red lights. On the right is a reception desk where the guests would be checked into the rooms farther inside. Above the counter hangs a plaque that reads "Tianxia Weigong." The first word, *tianxia*, is the same term discussed earlier—all under heaven—and *weigong* can be translated as "for all," "shared by all," or "equally for all." The phrase is from the classic Confucian text *The Book of Rituals* and was later popularized by Dr. Sun Yat-sen, the founding father of the Republic of China, the modern Chinese nation. His calligraphic rendering of the phrase, often carved into wooden plaques like this one, graces many official buildings. The rendering in this installation is also by Dr. Sun, whose aspiration for a world that belongs equally to all is placed, seemingly, in a wrong place: instead of at a government or educational institution, it is here at a "club" (*binguan*), a euphemism for brothel. "Formosa," of course, is the Portuguese term for Taiwan, from Ilha Formosa (the beautiful island), a term supposedly exclaimed in admiration when the Portuguese saw and landed on the island in the mid-sixteenth century.

To understand what this installation piece tries to signify requires some basic historical knowledge of the Cold War and Taiwan's position in that context. Taiwan occupied a significant place in the geographical chain of defenses that the United States controlled in an effort to contain communist China and, later, communist Vietnam. American soldiers and military advisers were stationed in Taiwan, especially during the Vietnam War, when Taiwan was one of the major

FIGURE 9.1: Wu Mali, "Formosa Club—The Magic Power of Taiwan's Fortune," (700 cm × 1,250 cm), 1998. Courtesy of the artist.

recreational destinations for American GIs. The phrase in the plaque, hung at the reception desk in the brothel, thus produces meaning through its intentional misplacedness: the history of American neocolonialism undergirds a sexual economy in which Taiwanese prostitutes vow to serve all under heaven. These prostitutes belong to all and serve all equally. Furthermore, the character *gong* (公) means equality or equally but it is a homonym to another character gong (共) that means "shared," which puns on the idea that prostitutes are public or shared wives. By being everyone's prostitute or wife, then, Taiwanese prostitutes contribute to nothing less than the equality of all under heaven, satirically implying that Taiwan contributes to global security by serving sex to everyone under the sky. While the artwork critiques the sexual economy of American empire in Taiwan, the dramatic contrast between the artist's treatment of the discourse of all under heaven and the contemporary Chinese discourse of civilizational supremacy exposes, with an ironic sleight of hand and in an anticipatory fashion, Chinese imperial intentions that will eventually find unapologetic expressions with the rise of China. Wu's installation piece achieves this double critique, both anticipatorily and retrospectively, at the crossroads of the American and Chinese empires with their at times collaborating and at times dueling intentions and practices.

After a very active period of international exhibition and traveling in the 1990s, Wu has settled back in Taiwan to engage with more community-based art. Her recent artworks range in subject from everyday feminism of ordinary people, as in the project "Empress's New Clothes," for which ordinary housewives are invited to pour their creativity uninhibited into unorthodox fashion designs, dressing themselves however they see fit and wearing their creations out on the streets of Taipei. The result is a stunning outpouring of creativity, long suppressed by everyday chores and duties of housewifery, following age-old injunctions against going beyond prescribed behavior. From such community-oriented work, it would be only a short distance to community work that is concerned about the environment and ecology, as in the multiyear project "Art as Environment: A Cultural Action on Plum Tree Creek, 2010–2012." Art as action was the framework for the series of actions taken when Wu, with the help of volunteers, organized group walks along this waterway in Taiwan to understand the history of the creek and the ecological lives along it as a way to pay homage to her homeland.

As much as her community-oriented work is derived from feminism, it also grows out of the local history of resistance to the exiled Chinese regime of the Nationalist Party that once considered Taiwan merely a temporary station for the recovery of China and hence ignored the ecological consequences of development. It is with the rise of Taiwanese (as opposed to Chinese) consciousness in the 1980s that the Taiwanese eventually learned to assert their erstwhile forbidden love for the land, which was followed by a rise in environmental consciousness in which love has turned into responsibility. The Nationalist Party, of course, has been backed by the U.S. government and in recent years has moved to foster improved relations with China by signing free-trade agreements and opening Taiwan's borders to Chinese tourism and commerce, all the while holding on to the by now unpopular rhetoric of unification with China. Again, Wu engages in a multidirectional critique: ecological activism articulates a resistance against the hegemony of the U.S.-backed and China-favored Nationalist Party and its government and claims ownership of and expresses responsibility toward the environment. The irony and *ressentiment* of "Formosa Club" is now substituted by responsibility toward others (the housewives and others) and toward the environment. She has become an eco-feminist whose work consistently intervenes in the China-U.S. binarism that deprives the local Taiwanese of their agency.

FIGURE 9.2: Wu Mali, "Empress's New Clothes," 2004–2007. Courtesy of Wu Mali.

The Cambodian and French artist Marine Ky has similarly extended feminist work to community and ecological work. Her etchings deploy signs and symbols of traditional Cambodian iconography that reference her early memories, from before she and her family left Cambodia as refugees due to the Khmer Rouge. Her family first escaped to Macau, then France, and then Australia. In her early work, the Cambodia of her memory was negotiated through her lived experience of refugee life, displacement, migration, and minoritization. Images culled from traditional iconography are not typical raw material for postmodernist bricolage; neither are they explicit references to the trauma of the Khmer Rouge. Rather, they are infused with a profound sense of melancholy, unreasonably gentle and subtle, seemingly refusing or unable to address the impossible memory of the genocide. They stand like scars, perhaps signifying fragments of scarred memories, as potential means to access lost memories.

Such an impossibly obscure visual reference, according to the Cambodian American art historian Boreth Ly, is an indirect reaction to the unspeakable trauma experienced under the scopic regime of the Khmer Rouge, which executed violent visual surveillance of the people. The absence of visual representation of the genocide in Cambodian art can be seen as a consequence of the devastation of vision. On one side of this devastation is the liberal blindness of those who escaped to Southern California, where in 1982 about 150 Cambodians were diagnosed with hysterical blindness, a loss of vision due to unspeakable trauma.[30] Perhaps this is the way we can understand Ky's quiet images, but this quietude itself is the most eloquent form of protest.

And the history of the Khmer Rouge is directly related to Cambodia's status as South to China's North. North-South relations existed during communism and even much earlier: the Khmer Rouge's Democratic Kampuchea (1975–1979) was very much a client state of China, which provided military and economic aid, political advisers, and technological transfer, and the Khmer Rouge's practices were partly modeled after Maoist China's Agrarian Revolution.[31] As is known, China-Soviet competition for power and influence in communist Southeast Asia—especially Cambodia and Vietnam—and the American bombing of Cambodia in 1975 provided opportunity for the rise of the Khmer Rouge. Even the fall of the Khmer Rouge was linked to this tripartite competition: it was Soviet-backed Vietnam that invaded Cambodia to force the Khmer Rouge out of power in 1979, and China retaliated by invading Vietnam. Chinese support of the Khmer Rouge is not dissimilar to the conventional American practice of supporting dictatorships; it is almost a form of imperial mimicry. In other words, empires behave in similar ways, whether you are a liberal capitalist one or a communist one. China is now again the most important patron of Cambodia—its largest trading partner and foreign-aid provider—engaging in mining, hydropower, and other development projects while raising concerns over these activities' environmental consequences.

It is, in the context of world history, from the Khmer Rouge's relationship with China to the present day that we can make sense of Ky's turn to environmentally oriented community work after she returned to Cambodia in 2000. Even though Ky can never be fully an insider, Cambodia can no longer be confined to the realm of memory; it has become the site of lived experience. This has started her on a journey, a redefinition, and deeper involvement in the community there. Her work during this period includes community art projects and photography from her tracks around Cambodia. She calls these works "Happy Art Home," implying "Happy at Home." Her installation series "L'épiderme de la Terre" (The Skin of the Earth) uses materials from nature, such as natural dyes from rocks and plants, to explore questions about the impermanence of life; the healing properties of plants; and how one can live a life that embraces human qualities of patience, forgiveness, immanence, introspection, openness, acceptance, responsibility, and gratitude. Again, from patience and forgiveness rise not only acceptance but also responsibility.

The Chinese American artist Patty Chang is situated not on the margins of China but on those of the United States as a so-called ethnic minority. Like Wu and Ky, Chang was known early in her career for explicitly feminist work that combines beauty with terror and explores issues of cultural identity. Dramatically staging the distortions and traumas that women's bodies undergo to abide by social expectations such as cosmetic surgery, she shows how women's bodies have been shaved, "stitched, clamped, hooked, squeezed, and dismantled into femininity."[32] She dramatizes these traumas via a passionate interaction with animate and inanimate objects in such works as "Melons," "Shaved," and "Contortions."

Chang's work took a clearly transnational turn around the start of the twenty-first century. In the video installation piece "Shangri-la" (2005), she explores the mythic construction of Shangri-la in the American imagination and weds her feminist concerns with critiques of American and European Orientalism. Here, the American self functions not as the agent imposing its will and stereotypes on Shangri-la but as a receptacle—mirrors—for what is out there. Built as a sculptural form of a mountain in cellophane and covered in mirrors on three sides, the sculpture, a multifaceted mirrored mountain, was carried on the back of a truck across the land in southwestern China that was supposedly Shangri-la. The sculpture received the fleeting images reflected on its many angled surfaces and could not hold them steady or still or for any duration, because the truck was on the move. She then placed the sculpture in various locations to take in the reflections, always only temporarily, again reflecting but not holding the images and implying that all images are fleeting, and as if there are literally no grounds for inventing stereotypes.

Chang further critiques Western Orientalism in a piece that stages the difficulty of translation, on the one hand, and how mistranslation contributes to and takes away from Orientalist fantasies, on the other. In the two-screen video "Die Ware Liebe" (The Product Love; 2009), several translators are staged, on-screen, to offer oral translations of the German philosopher Walter Benjamin's magazine article about the Chinese American actress Anna May Wong after Benjamin's real-life encounter with, and interview of, Wong in 1928. This video is followed by another, on the opposite screen, in which an actor and actress who are supposed to be Benjamin and Wong enact an awkward sex scene, fully naked. According to the Chinese director of the scene, it exhibits how Benjamin wished to touch the most sensitive part of the Orient, literalized as the erogenous zones of Wong's naked body.

In northwestern China in 2009, Chang shot the video "Minor" (2010) soon after the riots between the Uyghurs and the Han Chinese in Urumchi left

FIGURE 9.3: Patty Chang, "Shangri-la," 40 min., 2005. Courtesy of the artist.

FIGURE 9.4: Walter Benjamin and Anna May Wong in Patty Chang, "Die Ware Liebe" (The Product Love), two-screen digital video installation, 42 min., 2008. Courtesy of the artist.

FIGURE 9.5: Patty Chang, still image from "Minor," 25 min., 2010. Courtesy of the artist.

about two hundred people dead and thousands of people injured. In the video she contemplates the relationships between landscape and movement, Western exploration and the Silk Road, Uyghurs and Han Chinese, communication and conflict, Islam and gender, militarism and cultural repression, and a host of other issues in an understated, open form. Even though Chang does not refer directly to the riots, she stages a performance in which the kind of scarves that would have been worn by Muslim women are stuffed into holes in metal fences erected on a truck and driven around, as if it were a memorial of the dead.

In "Minor" especially, I think, we see her making links between the minoritized American and the minoritized and marginalized Uyghur Chinese who are also Muslims. It is a way to reach out to the other minor and establish a minor-to-minor relationship; hence, the video's title. Just as Americans have a difficult time making sense of 9/11, for which the word "terrorism" only provides limited explanations, so must we also consider the limited representation of the Urumchi riots as terrorism. Chang's reaching out to the Uyghurs, as a minority person in the United States, has profound ethical implications; it is a form of response and an expression of responsibility. If the responsibility to the other is what defines who we are as subjects, even those who are historically considered others (such as minoritized and racialized Americans) must bear this responsibility. Here, of course, the implicit object of critique is China and its increasingly repressive treatment of the Uyghurs and the destruction of their culture.

Chang's critique of the rise of China would become more explicit in "Route 3," a video piece on which she collaborated with the artist David Kelley.

Route 3 is a recently constructed route linking China, Laos, and Thailand, and the main share of the highway is owned by China. The video documents the "spatial, environmental, economic and social impact" of Route 3.[33] The artists express clearly in their statement: "China is the real subject, however, with Route 3 a testament to the way China's economic power translates to political power and regional (not to mention, global) dominance."[34] They do so by zeroing in on Golden Boten City, a Chinese casino town that went through one cycle of boom and bust and is awaiting new development by a Chinese company that has something like extraterritorial rights, both politically and economically. The city is a private concession of a Chinese company, which has jurisdiction over its law, politics, and economy.

In conclusion, from Mali Wu to Marine Ky and Patty Chang, all feminist artists from minor and minoritized subject positions, we see a relational arc of artworks that move from critique to responsibility, situated in and responding to our contemporary moment in world history of competition and collusion among two supersize empires: the United States and China. While world studies tries to map the entire world, the conception of world art offered here, through the notion of the relational arc, is at once modest and limited but takes the responsibility for (and response-ability of) being a world citizen seriously, even as one might be a minority artist or an artist from a minor country. The work of these three artists embodies what could be said to be the feminist ways of being a world citizen, which suggest a new ethics of responsibility. In this way, feminism becomes the medium and is no longer merely the content. In feminism, therefore, begins responsibility.

NOTES

This chapter partly draws from my paper, "Comparison as Relation," in *Comparison: Theories, Approaches, Uses*, ed. Rita Felski and Susan Stanford Friedman (Baltimore: Johns Hopkins University Press, 2013), 79–98. I delivered an earlier version of this paper as the Katz Lecture at the Simpson Center for the Humanities, University of Washington, Seattle. A later version was also presented at the Radcliffe Exploratory Seminar on New Geographies organized by Diana Sorensen. My gratitude to my hosts and audiences in these locations for their input and critique, but all mistakes and failings in this paper are my responsibility.

1. Abu-Lughod, *Before European Hegemony*.
2. Frank, *ReOrient*.
3. Frank and Gills, *The World System*; Frank, *ReOrient*, 5.
4. Hobson, *The Eastern Origins of Western Civilization*.
5. Seigel, "Beyond Compare," 78.
6. Glissant, *Poetics of Relation*, 32, 173.

7 Kleiner, *Gardner's Art through the Ages*.
8 Burnham, *The Art of the World*.
9 Bird et al., *A World View of Art History*; Honour and Fleming, *A World History of Art*.
10 Zijlmans and Van Damme, *World Art Studies*.
11 Zijlmans and Van Damme, *World Art Studies*, 27.
12 Zijlmans and Van Damme, *World Art Studies*, 7–8.
13 Zijlmans and Van Damme, *World Art Studies*, 140–41.
14 Zijlmans and Van Damme, *World Art Studies*, 144.
15 Zijlmans and Van Damme, *World Art Studies*, 143.
16 Arrighi, *Adam Smith in Beijing*; Hamashita, *Trade and Finance in Late Imperial China*.
17 Kruger, *All under Heaven*; Porter and Porter, *All under Heaven*; Smith, *Chinese Maps*.
18 Zhao, *The All-under-Heaven System*.
19 Fairbank, "China's World Order," 8.
20 Fairbank, "China's World Order," 18.
21 Zhao, "Rethinking Empire from a Chinese Concept 'All-under-Heaven,'" 29–30.
22 Zhao, "Rethinking Empire from a Chinese Concept 'All-under-Heaven,'" 30.
23 Zhao, "Rethinking Empire from a Chinese Concept 'All-under-Heaven,'" 30, 36.
24 Zhao, "Rethinking Empire from a Chinese Concept 'All-under-Heaven,'" 38.
25 Zhao, "Rethinking Empire from a Chinese Concept 'All-under-Heaven,'" 32.
26 Zhao, "Rethinking Empire from a Chinese Concept 'All-under-Heaven,'" 32.
27 Zhao, *The All-under-Heaven System*, 2.
28 Zhao, *The All-under-Heaven System*, 3.
29 Zhao, *The All-under-Heaven System*, 16.
30 Ly, "Devastated Vision(s)."
31 See Mertha, *Brothers in Arms*.
32 Oishi, "Interview with Patty Chang."
33 California Institute of the Arts, "Structuring Strategies Presents Patty Chang and David Kelley, Tuesday, October 29, 2013," http://calarts.edu/node/13376.
34 California Institute of the Arts, "Structuring Strategies Presents Patty Chang and David Kelley."

BIBLIOGRAPHY

Abu-Lughod, Janet L. *Before European Hegemony: The World System AD 1250–1350*. Oxford: Oxford University Press, 1991.

Arrighi, Giovanni. *Adam Smith in Beijing: Lineages of the 21st Century*. London, Verso, 2009.

Bird, Virgil H., Katherine B. Crum, Mary Weitzel Gibbons, W. and et al., eds. *A World View of Art History: Selected Readings*. Dubuque, IA: Kendall Hunt, 1985.

Burnham, Daniel Hudson. *The Art of the World, Illustrated in the Paintings, Statuary and Architecture of the World's Columbian Exposition*. New York: Appleton, 1893.

Fairbank, John K. "China's World Order: The Tradition of Chinese Foreign Relations." *Encounter* 27, no. 6 (December 1966): 14–20.

——, ed. *The Chinese World Order: Traditional China's Foreign Relations*. Cambridge, MA: Harvard University Press, 1968.

Frank, Andre Gunder. *ReOrient: Global Economy in the Asian Age*. Berkeley: University of California Press, 1998.

Frank, Andre Gunder, and Barry K. Gills, eds. *The World System: Five Hundred Years or Five Thousand?* London: Routledge, 1994.

Glissant, Édouard. *Poetics of Relation*, trans. Betsy Wing. Ann Arbor: University of Michigan Press, 1997.

Hamashita, Takeshi. *Trade and Finance in Late Imperial China: Maritime Customs and Open Port Market Zones*. Honolulu: University of Hawaii Press, 2014.

Hobson, John M. *The Eastern Origins of Western Civilization*. Cambridge: Cambridge University Press, 2004.

Honour, Hugh, and John Fleming. *A World History of Art*, rev. 7th ed. Laurence King, 2009.

Kleiner, Fred S. *Gardner's Art through the Ages: A Global History*, 14th ed. Boston: Cengage Learning, 2012.

Kruger, Rayne. *All under Heaven: A Complete History of China*. Chichester, U.K.: John Wiley and Sons, 2003.

Ly, Boreth. "Devastated Vision(s): The Khmer Rouge Scopic Regime in Cambodia." *Art Journal* 62, no. 1 (Spring 2003): 66–81.

Mertha, Andrew. *Brothers in Arms: China's Aid to the Khmer Rouge, 1975–1979*. Ithaca, NY: Cornell University Press, 2014.

Oishi, Eve. "Interview with Patty Chang." *Camera Obscura: Feminism, Culture, and Media Studies* 18, no. 3 (2003): 118–29.

Porter, Eliot, and Jonathan Porter. *All under Heaven: The Chinese World*. New York: Pantheon, 1983.

Seigel, Micol. "Beyond Compare: Comparative Method after the Transnational Turn." *Radical History Review* 91 (Winter 2005): 62–90.

Shih, Shu-mei. "Comparison as Relation." In *Comparison: Theories, Approaches, Uses*, ed. Rita Felski and Susan Friedman, 79–98. Baltimore: Johns Hopkins University Press, 2013.

Smith, Richard J. *Chinese Maps: Images of "All under Heaven" (Images of Asia)*. New York: Oxford University Press, 1996.

Zhao, Tingyang. *The All-under-Heaven System (Tianxia Tixi)*. Nanjing: Jiangsu Jiaoyu Chubanshe, 2005.

——. "A Political World Philosophy in Terms of All under Heaven (Tian-xia)." *Diogenes* 221 (2009): 5–18.

——. "Rethinking Empire from a Chinese Concept 'All-under-Heaven' (Tian-xia)." *Social Identities* 12, no. 1 (2006): 29–41.

Zijlmans, Kitty, and Wilfried Van Damme, eds. *World Art Studies: Exploring Concepts and Approaches*. Amsterdam: Valiz, 2008.

PART IV

Crosscurrents and Displacements

· · · · ·

Chapter 10

Technologies of Uncertainty in the
Search for Flight MH370

LINDSAY BREMNER

It is very rare for the southern Indian Ocean to come into view with the intensity that it did during the search for missing Malaysian Airways Flight MH370 in March and April 2014. During that period, major news channels throughout the world carried daily reports of the search under way in a remote part of the ocean, an area that, in the words of Tony Abbott, former prime minister of Australia, is "as close to nowhere as it's possible to be, but closer to Australia than anywhere else."[1] During the search, media channels showed a great deal of footage of the sea and people scanning it, simulations of ocean eddies and ships scurrying across it, data visualizations of possible flight paths and ocean depths, and daily statistics of ships and aircraft searching for the plane—how far they went each day, where they searched, and whose they were. Little-known terms that communications companies used in the search—"Aircraft Communications Addressing and Reporting System (ACARS)," "Inmarsat," "pings," "towed pinger locators," and "Bluefin 21s"—became household words. Measurements, statistics, and simulations served in lieu of evidence and as the basis of authoritative pronouncements with political affect. At the same time, satellite systems, technology, and science itself were shown to be full of delays, glitches, error, and uncertainty. In short, the ongoing search for the missing airplane opened apertures into aerial and oceanic space, encountered as dynamic materialities, information environments, scopic media, sociopolitical fields, and bodily sensoria, and charged them with uncertainty. In this chapter, I will reflect on these uncertainties, the technology that produced them, and how they were engineered as regimes of truth to authenticate authority during the initial search for the missing plane in March and April 2014. I will do so by examining the tenuous clues of MH370 after it disappeared from radar screens—seven satellite pings, hundreds of pieces of floating debris, and six underwater sonic recordings, as what the marine anthropologist Stefan Helmreich calls "theory machines"—things with which to think about the atmosphere and the ocean and generate insights about their entanglements in human affairs.[2]

A Brief Chronology of the Disappearance of MH370

- On Saturday, March 8, 2014, at 00:41 Malaysian time, Malaysian Airlines Boeing 777-200 Flight MH370 departed from Kuala Lumpur International Airport bound for Beijing, where it was due to arrive at 06:30 on March 9, 2014, with 227 passengers and twelve crew on board.
- At 00:42, the aircraft was cleared to climb to eighteen thousand feet (and subsequently to thirty-five thousand feet) and issued a direct track by the Kuala Lumpur Air Traffic Control Centre (KLATCC) to the Igari way point (N6°56.87′, E103°34.63′).
- At 01:07, the aircraft's ACARS data transmission link, which transmits signals about speed, altitude, position, and fuel level every thirty minutes, sent its routine signal.
- At 01:19, the KLATCC instructed the aircraft to contact the Ho Chi Minh Air Traffic Control Centre (HCMATCC) as it was passing out of Malaysian airspace and into Vietnamese airspace. MH370 acknowledged with "Good Night Malaysian 370."
- Two minutes later, at 01:21, the aircraft was observed on the KLATCC radar screens as it passed over the Igari way point.
- At 01:22 MH370's ACARS transponder ceased operating.
- At 01:35 (in data revealed three days later), Thai military radar showed the aircraft climbing to forty-five thousand feet and turning sharply to the west. It then fell to twenty-three thousand feet and climbed again to thirty-five thousand feet. Its radar signal was infrequent and did not include a flight number.
- At 01:37, the aircraft's expected thirty-minute ACARS update was not sent. A minute later, the HCMATCC asked the KLATCC about MH370's whereabouts. The KLATCC made inquiries to the Malaysian Air Services Operations Centre, Singapore Air Traffic Control, Hong Kong Air Traffic Control, and Phnom Penh Air Traffic Control to establish

the jet's location. No contact had been established with any of these air traffic control centers.
- At 01:45, the aircraft is thought to have dropped to five thousand feet in what is known as "terrain masking" to avoid radar detection. This belief is based on reports from a Malaysian villager of having seen bright lights and heard loud aircraft noises.
- At 02:15, what is thought to be the aircraft showed up on Malaysian military radar, wildly off course over the Strait of Malacca.
- At 05:30, a search-and-rescue (SAR) operation was activated by the Kuala Lumpur Rescue Coordination Center.
- At 08:11, an Inmarsat satellite 22,245 miles above the Earth's surface recorded a faint signal from the aircraft. This is its last known contact.

After MH370 went missing, the search for it initially took place in the South China Sea, south of Vietnam's Cà Mau Peninsula, the direction the aircraft would have been heading if it had stuck to its course. When Thai military radar data was released on March 11, the search moved to the Strait of Malacca and, on March 14, after Inmarsat satellite data and calculations were released, to the southern Indian Ocean. On March 24, Malaysia's Prime Minister Najib Razak announced that "beyond reasonable doubt" the aircraft had crashed in the southern Indian Ocean, with no survivors.[3] To date, no shred of evidence to support this has been found.[4]

However, while MH370 has remained invisible, a great deal else has been brought to light.

Seven Satellite Pings

The Aircraft Communications Addressing and Reporting System is a digital data-link system for transmission of messages between aircraft and ground stations via radio or satellite that began replacing voice communication on commercial airplanes in 1978.[5] The ACARS equipment on an aircraft is linked to that on the ground via a data-link service. Flight MH370 was fitted with an ACARS system called Classic Aero, and its data-link service provider was company Inmarsat, based in the United Kingdom.[6] Classic Aero is turned on and off manually via a switch on the ceiling of the cockpit or behind the throttles between the pilot and co-pilot, but it also has a second terminal that operates independently and cannot be switched off while the aircraft still has power.[7] After MH370's ACARS data transmission link ceased operating or was shut down, this terminal continued to respond automatically to seven hourly "pings" from Inmarsat-3 F1, a geostationary satellite that hovers 22,245 miles above the equator over the Indian Ocean, with a footprint that covers Africa and much of Asia and Australia.[8] The last ping from MH370 was received by Inmarsat's satellite ground station in Perth, Australia, at 08:19 on March 9, 2014.

"Ping" is a common term in IT networking vocabulary. It refers to the utility used to test the reachability of a host on an Internet Protocol (IP) network and to measure the round-trip time of the signal. Similar to a local area network (LAN), a satellite sends a signal about once an hour to a receiver on an aircraft, which sends back a response signal, or handshake, thus signaling that it is still on the network.[9] One source has likened this to a global game of Marco Polo played over 22,245 miles of outer space.[10] It is a legacy of an analogue version of sending greetings across distance, the hands-across-the-sea postcards used to carry messages between individuals in Britain and its colonies in the early twentieth century.[11] These postcards, replaced after World War I by the telegraph and the telephone, then by the Internet and satellites, were signals of emotion across dividing space, feeding into and alleviating anxiety associated with distance and uncertain communication.

The little batch of seven pings or handshakes between MH370 and Inmarsat-3 F1 is, as yet, the only confirmed evidence of the plane's existence after it disappeared from radar screens on March 8, 2014.[12] Located "deep inside the architecture of the system,"[13] pings do not specify a plane's location or the direction it is heading, but they provide two kinds of data that narrow down the possibilities of where an aircraft may be. The first is the time it takes for the ping to travel between satellite and aircraft, from which the distance between the two can be calculated; the second is the radio frequency at which the response is received by the satellite (the pitch of its voice), from which can be calculated whether the aircraft was moving toward or away from the satellite when it was transmitted (the so-called Doppler effect, which we commonly experience as the sound of a train approaching and leaving a platform).[14] Inmarsat engineers took the data provided by the seven pings from Flight MH370 and modeled possible flight paths to fit them.[15] Malaysian authorities released distance data on March 15 in the form of the now famous two arcs graph, derived in part from the distance of the last ping received by the Inmarsat satellite. They later released data about ping frequencies in the form of graphs for hypothetical flight paths along the northern and southern arcs.[16] These show the frequency shifts or offsets—that is, the differences between the normal pitch of the ping's frequency and the one actually received by the satellite. When the plane was moving away from the satellite, the radio signal was stretched out, so the frequency decreased, and vice versa. The graphs show the shifts that could be expected for two hypothetical flight paths—one northbound and one southbound—with the measured values closely matching the southbound path.[17] This graph is the basis on which engineers and officials have been so confident that the plane went south. This probability graph has since been challenged as other investigators have subjected the data to different analytical techniques,[18] and even the southern arc trajectory has been contested.[19] Inmarsat engineers themselves adjusted their initial calculations after changing their assumptions about how fast the plane was moving and further refinement of the data has recently shifted the long-term search site farther south again.[20]

If one examines the ping data and their ongoing interpretation by investigators, it becomes apparent that the judgments made about them were "intricate, inductive arguments."[21] They were models, not verifiable truths, on the basis of which decisions were made about how to act in the world. Models cannot be verified; they can only be validated—that is, shown to have internal consistency. At best, they can be confirmed if their results agree with observation, but they can never be proved correct.[22] The ping data were subjected to mathematical and computational techniques for drawing information out of them to model likely flight paths and predict where the plane went down, against which the data were then matched. This involved a raft of assumptions, parameterizations, judgments, and approximations; theories about airplane speed and height, satellite position and movement, and atmospheric conditions; and so on, all of which produced different results. For example, initial results released by Inmarsat showed that the faster it was assumed the plane was moving, the more sharply its path arced away from the satellite. As a result, the Australian Transportation Safety Bureau announced that the next phase of the search for the missing airplane would focus on a new "hot spot" hundreds of miles south of the first suspected crash site.[23] This was not based on new data but on further analysis of the existing data. "There was a very complex analysis and there were several different ways of looking at it. Specialists have used several different methodologies and bringing all of that work together to get a consensus view is what we're finalizing at the moment," Mark Dolan, chief commissioner of the Australian Transport Safety Bureau (ATSB) said on June 20, 2014.[24] Modeling, then, is always an "inexact science."[25]

Even most data themselves depend on modeling and are inherently uncertain.[26] Joseph Dumit reminds us that in all communication systems, every transponding event, such as a satellite ping, is cause for existential doubt. Each interface a ping passes through generates a new ping; the interface does not just pass along the ping it received. Pings are like whispered messages in a game of broken telephone. Participants (interfaces) can never be certain about what they have heard; they compile data from fuzzy audio sensoria and make judgments about them before relaying them. "Each interface, gap and infinitesimal delay," Dumit tells us, "poses the question of truth."[27] How much more so in the case of remote sensing systems, where interfaces are required to aggregate uncertain signals transmitted across vast distances through changing atmospheric conditions distorted by Doppler and other effects and to sort and rank them for truth before emitting them again. They are, says Dumit, "structurally and logically paranoid," wired with uncertainty, anxiety, and neurosis.[28]

The Inmarsat data, once released, coursed through the media as maps, charts, diagrams, and pronouncements and was mobilized in the service of sociopolitical priorities and agendas.[29] The official map shared by Malaysian authorities with the families of the victims and the public on March 15 and sent around the world on a Reuters Twitter feed showed a series of concentric circles radiating out from the Inmarsat-3 F1 satellite.[30] On one of them, two arcs are outlined in red, indicating the "last known possible position" of MH370 based on "satellite data."[31] Stamped with the seal of authority, this map ascribed to the data a regime of truth, anchoring analyses of the ping data with scientific and graphic certainty. Meanwhile, Inmarsat engineers began further modeling of the pings coming from the plane, and comparing them with other MH777 flights on the network, to work out whether a northern or a southern path was most likely. At the same time, independent analysts used Systems Tool Kit (STK), an analytical engine for simulating and visualizing complex aerospace, to chart and make calculations about flight scenarios and test Inmarsat's analysis and shared findings on blogs and e-mail chains.[32] The pattern finally built by Inmarsat and corroborated by other data analysts ruled out the northern corridor and was sent to the Malaysian authorities on March 23. Inmarsat's spokesman, Chris McLaughlin, said, "What we discovered was a correlation with the southerly route and not with the northern route after the final turn that the aircraft made, so we could be as close to certain as anybody could be in that situation that it went south."[33] On March 24, 2014, Prime Minister Razak announced that, "beyond reasonable doubt," the airplane had crashed in the southern Indian Ocean and was lost with no survivors, attributing agency to the Inmarsat data: "It is with deep sadness and regret that I must inform you that, according to this new data, flight MH370 ended in the southern Indian Ocean."[34]

Families of the victims received the announcement with anguish, anger, and mistrust. Deep skepticism prevailed over how the Malaysian authorities had handled the investigation. They were accused of delays and of failing to share information because they did not want to admit weaknesses in their radar and satellite capabilities.[35] Prime Minister Razak denied this, saying that the country "shared information in real time with authorities who have the necessary experience to interpret the data."[36] The Chinese government begged to differ, asking Malaysia to provide "more detailed information in its possession, including third-party information, in a timely, accurate and comprehensive manner."[37]

While the arguments went on, British and U.S. intelligence agencies were gathering military and civilian satellite images to analyze them for possible debris in the southern Indian Ocean. By March 14, the United States had dispatched a Poseidon P8 submarine and the USS *Kid* into the southern Indian Ocean. On March 18, rescue teams announced that they had narrowed the search for the airplane to a location 1,500 miles southwest of Perth, in Western Australia, where sightings of debris had been made.

Hundreds of Pieces of Floating Debris

The search for the missing airplane had been directed to a vast, unbounded, deep, cold, turbulent stretch of ocean subject to some of the most dynamic weather conditions on the planet. It is swept by unrelenting westerly winds driving cold fronts ahead of them.[38] In addition, during the search for MH370, a typhoon swirled across the sea, canceling search operations for two days. The waves in this part of the ocean are monstrous, dwarfing the ships sent out to search it; the ocean is whipped up into storms by the bands of low-pressure sweeping eastward across it. Powerful undercurrents run along its surface slopes: the Antarctic Circumpolar Current transports 4.9 billion cubic feet of water per second eastward around the southern part of the planet virtually unobstructed,[39] and the Indian Ocean Gyre swirls counterclockwise up the western coast of Australia. Molded by little-known trenches and mountains on the seafloor, these currents connect deep, cold, abyssal waters with the surface and, influenced by differences in speed, temperature, salinity, and pressure, they collide, swirling, eddying, and transmitting energy in complicated, turbulent, and nonlinear ways. The crash site was located in the boundary between these two currents, in a "sea of uncertainty,"[40] where eddies are about sixty miles wide and debris can travel up to thirty miles a day. Oceanographic and meteorological experts expressed doubts about finding any plane debris at all, because even if it was spotted, it could have drifted hundreds of miles before it could be verified.[41]

Data about oceans, including their flow patterns, are gathered today from a host of observation platforms—satellites, floats, drifting buoys, data collection systems on commercial ships, scientific research vessels, and moorings in the open sea—and coordinated by the permanent Global Ocean Observing

System (GOOS), established in 1991 by the United Nations.[42] Three satellites are particularly important to this work: Jason-2, Cryosat-2, and SARAL.[43] Jason-2, launched in 2008, is a collaboration of the French National Center for Space Studies (CNES), the European Organization for the Exploitation of Meteorological Satellites (EUMETSAT), and the U.S. National Aeronautics and Space Administration (NASA) and National Oceanic and Atmospheric Administration (NOAA).[44] Cryosat-2 is a research satellite launched in April 2010 by the European Union Space Agency.[45] And SARAL, launched in 2013, is part of a technological collaboration between the Indian Space Station and CNES.[46] These satellites carry high-precision Poseidon-2 altimeters that can map ocean-surface topography accurately within a tolerance of two inches.[47] Complementing these satellite missions is a collaborative partnership among more than thirty countries to produce real-time data about the world's oceans, underpinned by a protocol of global data sharing called the Argo Program. It has deployed a fleet of approximately 3,600 drifting floats in the ocean worldwide since 2000.[48] Argo floats are extraordinary sensing instruments stationed at a depth of three thousand feet beneath the ocean surface (the so-called parking depth), from where they transmit regular data regarding their drift. They are programmed to change their buoyancy every ten days by changing their density, dive to a depth of six thousand feet, and ascend to the sea surface, measuring conductivity, temperature profiles, and pressure as they do so.[49] These data are then transmitted to shore via satellites and distributed by the World Meteorological Organization, adding to the data about sea level, speed, direction, ocean currents, and heat stored in the oceans provided by Jason satellite missions.[50]

In the search for MH370, Australia's national science agency, the Commonwealth Scientific and Industrial Research Organization (CSIRO), used GOOS data; data from Australia's Integrated Marine Observation System (IMOS),[51] a national array of observing equipment (satellites, floats, moorings, radars, robotic gliders, etc. that monitor the ocean around Australia); and data from self-locating data marker buoys dropped into the ocean in support of the search to run drift models to produce a possible debris field. This involved backtracking items spotted on the ocean's surface by satellite to their possible origin and forward tracking items from where they were spotted to where they could have drifted to direct planes and boats to search areas.[52]

Looking for plane debris in the ocean mobilized this vast assemblage of hardware and software in what Karin Knorr Cetina calls a "scopic system"[53]—a system of screen-based technologies that make distant and invisible phenomena accessible and unfold remote spaces and information worlds.[54] In the first instance, this meant looking at the ocean's surface from outer space. On March 11,

2014, China's Meteorological Administration requested activation of the International Charter for Space and Major Disasters to gain access to satellite imagery to assist in the search.[55] The fifteen national and international organizations that are signatories to the charter were required to supply space-based remote-sensing data free of charge in support of the search effort.[56] The commercial U.S. satellite operator Digital Globe took the opportunity to expand its Tomnod crowdsourcing platform to engage the public in the hunt for the missing plane.[57] It tasked its satellites (including the sub-meter-resolution satellites WorldView-1, WorldView-2, and GeoEye-1) to capture images of potential search areas and uploaded the imagery to the Tomnod site. Alerted on Facebook when new imagery was available, amateur data analysts were able to view it and tag potential signs of wreckage by dropping a pin onto a satellite map. About thirty viewers were tasked with scanning the same image, and a CrowdRank algorithm was used to identify overlaps in tagged locations before they were investigated by Digital Globe analysts.[58]

On March 16, 2014, Digital Globe sent satellite images of two large objects captured floating in the Indian Ocean 1,500 miles southwest of Perth to the Australian Maritime Safety Authority.[59] By now, Australia was coordinating the search operation because it fell within its Search and Rescue Region (SARR), as defined by the International Maritime Organization's International Convention on Maritime Search and Rescue.[60] Australia has the largest SARR in the world. It covers 12 percent of the earth's surface,[61] stretching from the middle of the Indian Ocean in the west, incorporating Tasmania in the east, more or less following its Exclusive Economic Zone boundary in the north (though significantly excluding Christmas Island but including the Cocos Islands), and extending southward to the South Pole.

The images of the two Digital Globe objects—one as large as seventy-two feet long—were assessed as credible by the Australian Geospatial-Intelligence Organization. A Norwegian car carrier, the *Hoegh St. Petersburg*, traveling from Madagascar to Melbourne was diverted to look for them.

On March 18, the Chinese news agency Xinhau published images of two objects—one measuring sixty-five feet by forty feet, and the other seventy-two feet across—spotted close to the Digital Globe sightings by one of its satellites. China sent nine vessels to verify the sightings, including its largest rescue ship, *Haixun 01*, and the icebreaker *Xuelong*.[62] An Australian Hercules aircraft was deployed to drop data marker buoys to gather data on water movement. On March 21, Parakou Shipping's bulk carrier *Greenery Sea* was diverted on a voyage from Cape Town to Adelaide, and Australia deployed the support vessel *HMAS Success* to the search area. There were other vessels 460 miles to the north of the site, including the Turkish-owned tanker *Value*, which left Sydney for West Africa on March 9; *Besiktas*, a Turkish-owned bulk carrier carrying coal from Hay Point to Fos in France; and the British-owned nuclear fuel carrier *Pacific Grebe*. All were diverted to verify the sightings.

A third set of satellite data, released on March 23 by French satellite sources, indicated a possible debris field of 122 objects of varying sizes, some measuring up to seventy feet long, in the ocean 1,600 miles southwest of Perth. Malaysia's acting Transport Minister Hishammuddin Hussein confidently said the find was "the most credible lead we have" and "consistent with a plane having struck the sea nearby."[63] On March 24, more than three hundred new objects, ranging from six feet to forty-five feet in length, were spotted by Thailand's Earth Observation Satellite (Thaichote) about 1,700 miles from Perth, 125 miles outside the international search area. According to a report from Tokyo, a Japanese satellite also spotted about ten objects possibly related to the missing airplane, the biggest of which measured twenty-five feet by twelve feet.[64]

With this mounting evidence of possible plane debris, Australia's Prime Minister Tony Abbott announced on March 30, 2014, that responsibility for coordinating and communicating the search operation would be transferred from the Australian Maritime Safety Authority to a specially created Joint Agency Coordination Centre (JACC),[65] set up in terms of Section 2.2 of the International Convention on Maritime Search and Rescue, possibly, it is alleged, due to sensitivities about classified surveillance data on border protection activities in its northern waters being leaked.[66] The JACC set up at Pearce Air Force Base, twenty miles north of Perth, and began coordinating daily search operations, initially for plane debris on the surface, followed by an underwater search, continuing throughout April 2014. Over this period, nineteen military aircraft, ten civilian aircraft, fourteen ships, and two submarines representing eight countries (Australia, China, Japan, Malaysia, New Zealand, South Korea, the United Kingdom, and the United States) are known to have participated in the operation.[67]

Each morning, the JACC issued a media release about the search to be conducted that day, the number of aircraft and ships to be involved, the size of the search area, and the weather conditions at sea. This included maps prepared by the Australian Maritime Safety Authority of the SARR, showing the position of key search vessels, search areas planned for the day, the search vessels' distance from shore, and the growing gray stain of areas of the ocean previously searched. These media releases were the official basis of global reporting on the search operation, and the maps were reproduced in the media around the world. Aircraft searching for debris flew from Pearce Air Force Base on ten-hour missions each day: three hours heading out to sea, three to four hours searching (depending on weather conditions), and three hours heading back to base. Searches were divided into legs, straight lines of flying lasting for thirty to forty minutes, clearly visible on the maps of areas searched released by the JACC.[68] At this point, the vast scopic system of satellites, ships, floats, drifting buoys, imaging techniques, and so on, activated by the search came down to the human eye and a particular way of looking. Each plane carried five observers, one resting while two peered through the airplane's windows in each direction. Most of the people doing this were drawn from the more than two hundred Australian State Emergency Service volunteers from Western Australia, New South Wales, and Victoria who signed up for it.[69] Searching required saccading, a particular way of looking that involved moving the head up and down in a fixed position to scan foreground, middle ground, and background with pinpoint accuracy while talking to keep the concentration going. Once a piece of potential debris was spotted, ships in the vicinity were alerted, and divers were sent to investigate it further.[70]

On April 6, the Australian Defence Force released a video of a group of divers investigating a piece of ocean debris.[71] A diver surfaces from the water with a small item held between thumb and forefinger. He swims to the side of a dinghy, where he hands it to a member of the Australian Navy. This person takes the item between thumb and forefinger of both hands, inspects it briefly, then tosses it contemptuously into the bottom of the dinghy. There is something enormously incongruous, funny even, about a search for a missing airplane that began in outer space, mobilized vast scopic systems, and was modeled and simulated by countless agencies and thousands of computer screens coming down to this minute, intimate conclusion—a second or two of a tiny piece of marine trash, held between eye and thumb and forefinger, casually inspected before being tossed aside. Sightings of objects became more sporadic, and none were linked to the disappeared plane. They turned out to be abandoned fishing equipment, the carcass of a dead whale, and other pieces of marine trash.[72]

What MH370's disappearance had made visible was the sheer volume of trash in the ocean. For a long time, there was a general understanding that it was acceptable to dispose of trash in international waters, unless it was chemical waste. Some of this was deposited via rivers; other was the result of natural disasters or accidents at sea. In turbulent weather, cargo is swept overboard, and it is cheaper to allow a certain amount of loss from container ships than to make them absolutely stormproof.[73] Other trash is simply dumped by cruise and cargo ships. To counter this, the United Nations Convention on the Law of the Sea encouraged nations to take "all measures necessary to prevent, reduce, and control pollution of the marine environment from any source,"[74] and in 2012, the International Maritime Organization adopted measures to prohibit the disposal of plastic anywhere in the world.[75] Despite this, the amount of plastic in the ocean has mounted; estimates vary from 5.25 trillion particles weighing half a million tons, according to a report released by the Five Gyres Institute, to 200 million tons, based on belief that 2.5 percent of the world's plastic ends up in the ocean, by the oceanographer Charles Moore of Algalita Marine Research Institute.[76] Most of this is pushed around by currents and global winds, ending up in five gyres—the North Atlantic, South Atlantic, North Pacific, South Pacific, and Indian Ocean gyres, the last of which flows just west of the search area for MH370.[77] A baseline study of the accumulation of Indian Ocean debris observed that, while plastics were insignificant and virtually unreported forty years ago, accumulation levels were high in 2004, even on remote mid-ocean islands.[78]

This swirling plastic soup means that the world's oceans have, to all intents and purposes, been urbanized. The proposal by Michel Serres that "appropriation takes place through dirt,"[79] that humans appropriate the physical world through soiling it, can now be applied to the world's oceans. "At the limits of growth," he says, "pollution is the sign of the world's appropriation by the species."[80] Plastic and other forms of industrial waste, products of social production and consumption, have taken possession of the ocean's complex fluid systems and plumbed its depths. Trash has incorporated the ocean into everyday life and spatially expanded human influence and territory unevenly, but without limits. It has rendered the vision of the sea as empty, without law and beyond human culture, underpinning European colonial and modern geopolitical and cultural projects, obsolete.[81]

Six Underwater Sonic Recordings

As the surface water search for debris went on, the underwater search for the airplane's black boxes began. This brought the oceanic volume and floor into view for the first time. The search had been narrowed to an area of ninety thousand square miles of ocean.[82] The region was rugged and craggy, incorporating scraps of continental crust left behind when India broke off from Australia relatively recently in geological history, about 120 million years ago. Some of its peaks were less than six hundred feet below the surface, but it was also suspected of having deep troughs exceeding twenty-three thousand feet (4.3 miles).[83] A U.S. NOAA map of this oceanic region, reproduced by *BBC News: Science and Technology* in April 2014, represents this ocean floor as a multicolored image crisscrossed by black lines of various thicknesses.[84] The colors on the map indicate the depth of the ocean floor (deep to shallow—blue, turquoise, yellow, red). These colors are visual interpretations of satellite radar bathymetry of the ocean's surface topography. The ocean's surface follows gravity; it is pushed up over underwater ridges and slumps down into underwater troughs. From surface readings of these height variations by satellite altimeters, the ocean floor topography is inferred. This produces "fuzzy maps" with an accuracy of only 12.5 miles.[85] The thin black lines crisscrossing the map indicate lines of echo soundings from ships fitted with low-tech sounding equipment that provides direct though unreliable measurement of ocean depths, and the thick lines indicate tracks surveyed by vessels equipped with modern swath-mapping echo sounders (such as that of the Bluefin-21 remote underwater vehicle used in the search for MH370) that map a swathe under the path of a ship using sonic waves, giving accurate soundings to about 2 percent.[86] In terms of the images of the sea floor, the lines are errors, indexically recording the routes of the vessels that produced the soundings.[87] Because ocean depth cannot be directly observed, visualizing it relies on sensing and recording reflected or emitted energy and then processing, analyzing, and interpreting these data.[88] Maps of the sea floor are not so much images as simulations of mathematical data culled from an assemblage of satellites, altimeters, electromagnetic waves, ships, echo sounding equipment, ultrasound waves, computer interfaces, and data visualization software. In viewing them, we do not see the ocean; we only interact with data. Like the aerial ping maps discussed earlier, these are "question(s) thrown across space in the form of energy, and response(s) bounced back, transformed into answer(s) through processes of analysis and visualization."[89] This sensorium transforms the "opaque ocean . . . into a technically and scientifically *sound* oceanic volume."[90]

All commercial airplanes are required to carry underwater locator beacons, otherwise known as "pingers," to locate their black boxes should they crash into water. The pingers emit ultrasonic signals, or pings, at a frequency of 37.5 kHz (the human ear hears sounds up to about 2 kHz) about once a second for approximately thirty days after an aircraft goes missing, until their batteries die.[91] The race to find MH370's black boxes began on day twenty-nine after the aircraft went missing. Three types of devices were used to search for them. The Australian naval vessel *Ocean Shield* towed a three-foot-wide, seventy pound underwater trailed pinger locator (TPL-25) built and operated by U.S. company Phoenix International, on loan from the U.S. Navy. We saw a great deal of TPL-25 in the media; it looked like a yellow stingray and was equipped with a sensor that could recognize flight recorders' signals up to eighteen thousand feet below the ocean's surface while towed at speeds of up to three knots. At this speed, and because turning around was a long process because of the huge lengths of cable involved, it was able to scan only an area of nine square miles a day in seven- to eight-hour stretches. The Chinese patrol ship *Haixun 01* used handheld devices lowered over the side of small open boats with inflatable rubber sides, and Royal Australian Aircraft dropped sonobuoy listening devices—small, sonar portable units—into the ocean.[92] In addition, the British naval vessel HMS *Echo* and the Trafalgar-class nuclear-powered attack submarine HMS *Tireless* were deployed to the southern Indian Ocean two weeks after the first release of images of suspected wreckage. This was significant, because HMS *Tireless* possesses advanced sensor platforms, possibly even the 2076 sonar system, one of the United Kingdom's most advanced, classified programs that complements "integrated active-passive detection capabilities," with sophisticated imaging processes, enabling naval scientists to "see what they hear."[93]

Soundwaves move through water more than four times faster than they do through air. However, this movement is affected by the temperature, pressure, and salinity of ocean layers, which have the effect of warping them, sometimes through ninety degrees.[94] The ocean has three layers. The top layer is about 330 feet deep, through which sunlight can penetrate and where asphytoplankton, the organisms essential to all marine life, live. The bottom layer, referred to as the deep ocean, averages about two miles deep and collects the rich, nutrient-filled sediment of decayed plant and animal matter. Between the two is a middle, or barrier, layer, also known as the thermocline, which is 1,600–3,300 feet deep. The ocean's temperature and density change very quickly in this layer.[95] Soundwaves can take squiggly paths through the thermocline, bouncing back and forth and getting caught up in sound channels that carry them sideways for long distances. The retired French naval officer Paul-Henry Nargeolet, who led the searches for the *Titanic* and Air France Flight 447, said that, because of this, he did not put much faith in acoustic findings and would not believe the plane's whereabouts had been located until wreckage was seen.[96]

On April 5, news that a pinger detector aboard the *Haixun 01* had detected an ultrasonic pulse emerged via Xinhua. This caused considerable consternation at the JACC, as the news was released before the coordination team had verified the signals. The pulse had a frequency of 37.5 kHz, which Dukane Seacom, the manufacturer of the black box beacons, confirmed was the standard frequency emitted by its pingers. It was detected for ninety seconds within the eighty-five thousand square mile search zone, where the ocean was estimated to be about 13,500 feet deep. The *Haixun 01* had picked up a fleeting signal one nautical mile away twenty-four hours earlier. A day later, the towed pinger locator dropped from the Australian vessel *Ocean Shield* about three hundred nautical miles away from the Chinese ship detected a signal on the northern edge of a small oceanic plateau called the Wallaby or Zenith Plateau. *Ocean Shield* went back over the same area and, in all, picked up signals on four separate occasions, one holding for five minutes and thirty-two seconds and another for seven minutes.[97]

The Australian Defence Force released two short videos of the pings picked up by TPL-25 on April 6.[98] In the first, the yellow towed pinger locator is lowered into the water from the deck of *Ocean Shield*. The video then cuts to an operator in front of a computer screen, the bottom half of which is covered with flickering horizontal yellow lines on a dark background and the upper half with a corresponding vertical graph; the visual display is accompanied by an acoustic hum. The video then cuts to full-screen, where we learn that this is a screen shot of data visualized by Spectrumlab V2.79b11, freely downloadable spectrum analysis software. It displays the frequency of signals being picked up on the horizontal axis and amplitude on the vertical axis as a color spectrum. The towed pinger locator appears as a red dot moving slowly across the lower part of the screen, where a point is marked and labeled as 33.20271 kHz, -66.98 db. Slowly, a distinctive acoustic beat emerges from the low-level humming noise at approximately one-second intervals, corresponding with a spike on the vertical axis of the graph at the top of the screen. The display then changes to a three-dimensional sweep across a topography of soundwaves visualized as a colorful undulating surface, the distinctive signal puncturing upwards into the red color spectrum at regular intervals. The second video repeats similar footage.[99] This imaging of the acoustic signal was an enormously powerful one. The signal was made available to experience through scopic media as rhythmic waveforms resembling those of heartbeats as displayed by electrocardiographic machines. The missing airplane was made situationally present through what looked and sounded like tenuous, fragile, yet still living heartbeats.

This anthropometric association made the revelation on May 30, 2014—after the fruitless underwater scan for the missing airplane in the area the pings had been detected—that these signals were not from the aircraft's black boxes after all doubly hard to bear. The pinger sounds, it was suggested, could have come from the search boat, the ping detector itself, or from other sources, such as tagged sea creatures.[100] Flight MH370's pulses also could have been drowned out by many other sounds in an increasingly urbanizing marine environment of shipping traffic, oil and gas exploration and production, recreational activity, and so on, which scientists refer to as "ocean smog."[101] The ocean, they say, is "full of pings."[102] Not only had the ocean been shown as capable of lying and the instruments used to listen to it proved faulty and prone to error, but the screen-based media that filtered and translated their data also had been shown to be cruelly deceptive. The effect was not a reduction of uncertainty in the face of disaster but its magnification, increasing feelings of anger and helplessness in families of the crash victims and affirming, more generally, the "dangerous threshold of existence" in a contemporary world that is increasingly dependent on such remote sensing technology."[103]

However, at the time, scientists and political authorities viewed the ping data as incontestable evidence of the airplane's whereabouts. "There is no other noise like this," said the oceanographer Chari Pattiaratchi. "I have absolute confidence that the airplane will be found."[104] On an official visit to China five days later, Prime Minister Abbott said he was confident that the position of the black box flight recorder was known to within kilometers.[105] On April 14, the *Ocean Shield* began scanning the ocean floor for the airplane within an eight-mile radius of the strongest pings, while the surface hunt for debris continued. Another instrument on loan from the U.S. Navy was deployed for this task: Phoenix International's Autonomous Underwater Bluefin-21 vehicle *Artemis*, a sixteen-foot-long, 1,600 pound, yellow ROV (remotely operated underwater vehicle). The depth at which it could operate was upgraded from 4,500 feet to 13,500 feet only in July 2013, so this was likely one of its first deployments at this depth.[106] *Artemis* works by sweeping sonar pulses underneath its chassis in two arcs, producing acoustic reflections of objects on the seabed, while also collecting high-resolution black-and-white imagery at up to three frames per second.[107] Hopes of finding the plane were pinned on this single piece of equipment diving to unprecedented depths. After some initial programming glitches, it was deployed on eighteen twenty-four-hour missions, taking four hours to dive and resurface, sixteen hours to scan, and four hours to download the recorded data each time.[108] Significantly, none of these data have ever been released publicly. In their absence, some extraordinary and somewhat comical depictions of the oceanic volume appeared in the media in attempts to visualize the ocean's depth and make it more humanly comprehensible.

The *Washington Post Online* published a scroll-down visualization of ocean depth titled "The Depth of the Problem."[109] At the top are vector shapes of a Boeing 777-200 and the Australian Navy's *Ocean Shield*, with their dimensions annotated (two hundred feet wide for the airplane, 347 feet long and a draft of twenty-two feet for the vessel). Beneath this, a number of buildings are overlaid, floating upside down, with their heights annotated: the Washington Monument (−555 feet), the Empire State Building (−1,250 feet) and, currently the world's tallest building, the Burj Khalifa (−2,717 feet). As one scrolls down, one passes lines annotated with water depth and pressure, and the color of the ocean gets gradually darker. After the Burj Khalifa, sea creatures, underwater submersibles, and previous disasters are used to give a sense of scale: the test depth of the America Seawolf-class submarine (−1,690 feet); the maximum known depth at which giant squid swim (−2,600 feet); the maximum depth sperm whales are known to dive (−3,280 feet); the depth at which the tower pinger locater detected ping signals (−4,600 feet); the depth the pinger locater would probably have to reach to hear a pinger on the ocean floor, depending on oceanic conditions (−6,000 feet); the maximum known depth reached by Cuvier's beaked whale (−9,816 feet); the depth at which the wreck of the *Titanic* was found (−12,500 feet); the depth at which flight data recorders from Air France Flight 447 were found (−13,100 feet); the depth *Alvin*, the first deep-sea submersible able to carry passengers, dove (−14,763 feet); the depth at which the signal from MH370 was thought to have been detected (−15,000 feet).

This graphic is interesting for a number of reasons. Firstly, it is a patchwork of data drawn from multiple sources—the Australian Maritime Authority, Hydro International magazine, NOAA Fisheries, BBC.co.uk, and Plosone.org. It reveals its own institutional address, the *Washington Post*, through the selection of objects it uses to scale the ocean. These lay claim to the ocean as a cultural artifact by comparing it with objects whose dimensions are likely to be familiar to a U.S. audience. A similar graphic on the United Kingdom's *Guardian* website lays claim to the ocean through a different set of cultural coordinates that would be more familiar to a British and European audience: the wreck of the Russian submarine *Kursk* (−354 feet); an inverted London Shard (−1,004 feet) and New York's One World Trade Center (−1,776 feet); the depth light can penetrate the ocean (−3,280 feet); the average depth of the Mediterranean (−4,900 feet); and the deepest living octopus (−13,000 feet).[110] Making the ocean comprehensible in this way uses familiarity to appropriate and colonize it: it is represented as a U.S. ocean or a U.K. ocean by way of the things that inhabit it in media space.

The second interesting thing about these graphics is that they incorporate an eclectic mix of land-based and sea-based icons: buildings, mountains (in other examples), bits of technology, sea creatures, and times; past disasters at sea, current events, and straightforward empirical measurements; ocean depth and pressure. Sense is made of the ocean by portraying it as a hybrid, unreal, ungrounded diagram, in which multiple places and times overlap and multiple representations conjoin. These diagrams are not so much diagrams of the ocean as diagrams of ways to navigate the assemblage of technology and institutions through which ocean space is made visible today. To quote Stephan Helmreich in his discussion of Google Ocean, they are diagrams of "the ways that many of us image now, layering icons, indexes, and symbols on top of a world of previous infrastructures, transparent and opaque, taken for granted, and found as well as forgotten."[111] But this eclectic collection of icons and measurements really make relative sense only of one another; they render the entity they are supposed to give scale to even more vast and incomprehensible. Beyond a certain depth, there are no measures left, and uncertainty prevails; the depth a pinger locator would probably have to reach, the depth the signal was thought to have been detected, and so on, are the only clues we are given. The ocean ultimately exceeds attempts to scale it against things or events whose dimensions are known or open to human imagination.

These diagrams reduce the oceanic volume to a two-dimensional vertical gradient of turquoise color overlaid with a rhetorically selected collection of textual information and icons. In many ways, they resemble medieval nautical charts, such as the Catalan Atlas (1375) or the Cantabrian sailor and cartographer Juan de la Cosa's Mappa Mundi (1500), which depicted the ocean as a two-dimensional surface crossed by rhumb lines and illustrated with astronomical, astrological, and religious references and images from travel literature. The "Depth of the Problem" diagram, like the nautical charts, evacuates the ocean's material substance—fluidity, turbulence, temperature gradients, salinity, chemistry. The viewer of the diagram animates it by scrolling up and down at will. The ocean's lack of weight, substance, or fluidity allows a sense of mastery over ocean depth, if only of its representation.

A third graphic, posted on the *Mail Online* website on April 11, 2014, places a rudimentary and scale-less "Depth of the Problem" diagram alongside a map of the eastern Indian Ocean and Western Australia.[112] On the map, one can faintly read the seventh ping arc and the outline of the areas of ocean being searched for MH370. The map is boldly overlaid with a graphic of the parties engaged in the search; countries are named and represented by their flags, and their fleets of aircraft and vessels are numbered and represented by color-coded icons. These elements are not drawn to scale and are laid in tabular form over the ocean. This miniaturizes the ocean, reducing it to an immaterial game board in a strategy game called "Search and Rescue," with the airplanes and ships as the pieces pitted against the uncertainty of the ocean's depth. The graphic also reveals the relative size and strength of each country's stake in the game. China, represented with red icons, has eight ships and two aircraft; Australia, in blue, has five ships and seven aircraft; New Zealand, also in blue, has one aircraft; South Korea, in white, has two aircraft; Japan, also in white, has two aircraft; the United Kingdom, in pink, has one ship and one submarine; the United States, in pale blue, has one ship and two aircraft; and Malaysia, in bright pink, has one ship and two aircraft. This is not only a diagram of ocean depth versus operational strength; it is a diagram of the competitive geopolitics of the search-and-rescue operation.

International search-and-rescue operations, while important in themselves, serve a number of other geopolitical and scientific objectives, both directly and indirectly, and expose geopolitical fault lines. For Australia, the search for MH370 served as a way to increase national pride, testing its military and scientific capabilities, building fraternal relations, and establishing itself as a regional power. "While search and rescue operations are important in themselves, they also serve an important political purpose; they build patterns of peaceful interaction between countries with limited experience of each other, and so help generate strategic trust," states a post on an Australian Strategic Policy Institute blog.[113] However, while the search for MH370 produced unprecedented military cooperation among traditionally antagonistic countries, trust went only so far. Early in the search, when Thailand admitted it had surveillance information it did not initially share, it was clear that Southeast Asian countries were not coordinating as well as they might.[114] The International Maritime Organization's SAR Convention requires that parties allow other countries to enter their territorial waters, meaning that among the Association of South East Asian Nations (ASEAN), only Indonesia, Singapore, and Vietnam are signatories of the convention, as long-standing antagonisms overrule SAR.[115] However, these regional tensions were overridden during the search for MH370 by competition between the U.S., its allies, and China. When the search shifted from the South China Sea to the Indian Ocean, China accused the U.S. of withholding intelligence about the disappearance of the airplane[116] and during the Indian Ocean search, it acted independently of its obligation to cooperate through the JACC on a number of occasions.[117] For instance, its announcement in *Xinhau* that it had detected black box signals was made before the information was analyzed by the JACC, and was followed a day later by the detection of signals by the U.S. towed pinger locator on the Australian vessel, later shown to be false. Countries involved also took the opportunities the search offered to find out about each other's military assets and capabilities. A Reuters report suggests that the Chinese "no doubt" used the opportunity to spy on the U.S. Poseidon submarine and that its sophisticated remote sensing capabilities were a prime target for Chinese intelligence.[118] The same applied in reverse, born out in a conversation I had on June 27, 2014, with Ian Lyn, Deputy Director of the Royal Navy's National Maritime Information Centre,[119] who stated that the opportunity offered by the MH370 search to "see the opposition's kit" at close range in a non-adversarial situation was unprecedented. The search was not only about finding the airplane; it was about minimizing exposure to present and potential future adversaries.[120]

At the end of April 2014, President Barack Obama became the first U.S. president to visit Malaysia in fifty years. His Deputy National Security Advisor

Ben Rhodes stated, "Malaysia is a growing partner of the United States, which seeks to deepen that relationship."[121] Obama made frequent reference to the U.S.'s contribution to the search operation during his visit. A month later, Malaysian Prime Minister Najib Razak paid a six-day visit to China to celebrate forty years of diplomatic ties.[122] He acknowledged that the disappearance of the airplane had "tested the friendship between the two countries" and that he was "grateful for the support of the Chinese government, which has spared no expense in the search effort."[123] The missing airplane had exposed not only the vulnerabilities, but also the strategic importance of Malaysia in the region.[124]

At the end of April 2014, the search-and-rescue operation was called off. Malaysia named an international investigation team to review and reevaluate the satellite data,[125] and parties met in Canberra, Australia, to plan the next phase of the search.[126] On May 2, Malaysian Airlines issued a press release and a preliminary report on the flight's disappearance, including a cargo manifest, seating plan, and maps generated from the Inmarsat data.[127] With this in the public domain, fresh rounds of conspiracy and speculation about causes of the aircraft's disappearance and what had happened circulated. In Canberra later that month, the ATSB announced that sixty thousand square miles of seabed would be subject to a full bathymetric survey using multi-beam echo sounders to help refine the search area.[128] The Chinese naval vessel *Zhu Kezhen* started on the project and was later joined by the Dutch-owned *Fugro Equator*. By mid-June 2014, a consensus had been reached among the members of the international investigation team on new interpretations of the satellite data, and on June 26, 2014, the ATSB released a sixty-four-page report on the future of the search operation.[129] The report summarized the search to date, explained the revised satellite data analysis, and concluded, "Based on all the above, it seems reasonable to propose a search width of 50 NM (20 NM to the left of the arc and 30 NM to the right of the arc),"[130] the arc referring to the arc of the seventh and final satellite ping identified by Inmarsat. The following phase of the search was to be a commercially contracted deep sea search expected to begin in August 2014, after the mapping was complete, and expected to take up to twelve months.[131]

Conclusion

After Malaysian Airlines Flight MH370 disappeared on March 8, 2014, its ongoing invisibility made new encounters with aerial and oceanic space possible. The search made remote spaces (aerial space and the high seas of the southern Indian Ocean) and invisible information worlds (the multiple sensing platforms and devices that blanket them to survey, observe, and monitor them and the objects in them, and the screen-based technologies that simulate and project them) situationally present via the global media, the Internet, blogs, social media, reports and official statements, videos, diagrams, and images. Air and ocean were made present through this vast scopic system, transformed from air, waves, and currents into what Charles Heller and Lorenzo Pezzani call "a vast and extended sensorium, a sort of digital archive that can be interrogated and cross-examined as a witness."[132]

As we have seen, however, the ocean was not a very reliable witness, and the very instruments and techniques used to probe, monitor, and digitize it were easily outwitted by its materiality—its fluidity, turbulence, crushing water pressure, and impenetrable depths and seawater's capacity to "suck up" the electromagnetic radiation on which most modern communication technology relies.[133] The ocean was revealed to be a "more-than-human space," requiring that its materiality be taken into account when examining social processes that occur on and under its surface.[134]

At the same time, air and ocean were encountered as urbanized spaces, incorporated into global processes of industrial production and consumption as workplaces, laboratories, communication fields, sewage farms, and landfills. Air and ocean today are forms of urban infrastructure, recognized not only as the engines that drive the way the world works, but also as elements humans are irreversibly altering.[135] Serres argues that the increasing volume of industrial waste produced by humans appropriates physical space in ways that are similar to bodily excretions (sweat, blood, urine) and is today "engulfing the planet."[136] The millions of sightings of ocean trash that were made during the search for MH370 revealed that it is no longer possible to view the ocean as outside culture; it has been urbanized through waste. It was Michael Hardt and Antonio Negri who first made the observation that "there is no more outside." Although "we continue to have forests and crickets and thunderstorms in our world," they told us (and the ocean is still made up of winds and waves and currents), "we have no nature in the sense that these forces and phenomena are no longer understood as outside, that is, they are not seen as original and independent of the artifice of the civil order. In a postmodern world all phenomena and forces are artificial, or as some might say, part of history."[137] As such, air and ocean are striated by juridical protocols that attempt to draw lines across them and allocate sovereignty over them in various ways. Of these, the most significant during the search for MH370 were: the International Charter for Space and Major Disasters, which required that satellite data be released free of charge in support of the search effort; the International Convention on Maritime Search and Rescue, which determined that Australia coordinate the search effort in the southern Indian Ocean because it fell within its SARR; and the Montreal Convention for the Unification of Certain Rules for International Carriage by Air, which governed compensation for the victims of the aircraft's disappearance. These disaster-related protocols overlaid other legislative regimes, such as the Chicago Convention on International Civil Aviation of 1944, which governs sovereignty over airspace, and the United Nations Convention on the Law of the Sea of 1982, which codifies the legal jurisdictions of maritime territory. These overlapping protocols produce what Heller and Pezzani call a "patchy legal space constituted by overlapping and often conflicting fragments" that calls into question the territorial biases of geopolitics.[138]

The air and the ocean cannot be enclosed or known in the same way that land-based territories can: "The ocean is not a world of stable places that are impacted by moving forces. Rather, in the ocean, moving matter constitutes places, and these places are specifically mobile."[139] This is beautifully illustrated in an animation released by Australia's CSIRO during the search for MH370, which shows how ocean currents would have distributed debris in the southern Indian Ocean between March and December 2009.[140] The simulation shows an area of the ocean off the western coast of Australia between latitudes 24° and 47° South, with the ocean's temperature as a color gradient, from blue (6° C) in the south to red (27° C) in the north. Two strands of debris in the form of black particles are released into this swirling mass of color from the bottom left-hand corner. They are caught up in eddies and swirls and pushed in complex, nonlinear ways northeastward, dispersing laterally as they move. Ultimately they are caught in a temperature gradient at around 30° South and spun around in swirling eddies while being dispersed into a vast debris field. Finding an airplane or its fragments within this dynamic and constantly moving physicality will continue to stretch the technology used to engage it, challenge the notion of place as static and stable, and alert us to the material realities of the oceanic world in new ways.

NOTES

1 Adam Withnall, "Missing Malaysian Flight MH370: Satellite Images Show 122 Objects in Indian Ocean 'Debris Field,'" *Independent News*, March 26, 2014, http://www.independent.co.uk/news/world/asia/missing-malaysia-flight-mh370-french-satellite-images-show-possible-debris-field-of-122-objects-in-search-area-9216139.html.
2 Helmreich, "Nature/Culture/Seawater," 132.
3 "Flight MH370 'Crashed in South Indian Ocean'—Malaysia P[rime] M[inister]," *BBC News: Asia*, March 24, 2014, http://www.bbc.co.uk/news/world-asia-26716572.
4 The initial search operation for the missing plane discussed in this paper ended at the end of April 2014. In May that year, the Australian JACC announced that the search operation would be moving to a new phase: reinterpretation of the flight data, plane

speed, and altitude had identified a new zone of highest priority along the so-called seventh arc, a line analysis suggested the jet had to have crossed as it made its final connection with ground systems. This was an arc 46,332 square miles in extent, south of the initial search area, 1,100 miles west of Perth. Two ships, the Chinese survey vessel *Zhu Kezhen* and the Australian-contracted and Dutch-owned *Fugro Equator* were commissioned to produce detailed bathymetric maps of this area before the search recommenced. By October 2014, the survey was complete, and four ships—the *Fugro Discovery*, *Fugro Equator*, GO *Phoenix* (hired by Malaysia) and Chinese vessel *Dong Hai Jiu 101*—began scanning the ocean floor. Two years later, in July 2016, this multimillion-dollar search had yielded no evidence of MH370. In July 2015, however, a flaperon had washed ashore on Réunion Island, close to Madagascar in the Western Indian Ocean. Analysis of ocean currents suggested that it could have drifted to the island from the Southern Indian Ocean and belong to MH370: Sara Nelson, "MH370: Malaysia Airlines Boeing 777 'Very Likely' to Be Found by July," *Huffington Post*, March 7, 2016, http://www.huffingtonpost.co.uk/2016/03/07/mh370-malaysia-airlines-boeing-777-very-likely-found-july_n_9397778.html?utm_hp_ref=malaysia-airlines. In April 2016, the ATSB confirmed that two debris pieces—a segment of Boeing 777 engine cowling and an interior panel from the main cabin, found on the beaches in Mossel Bay, South Africa, and Rodrigues Island in Mauritius—were "almost certainly" from the missing plane. The agency also said two items found on the beach in Mozambique, on December 27, 2015, and February 27, 2016, provided "almost irrefutable evidence" that they were from the missing plane. Despite these pronouncements, none of this debris has been irrefutably confirmed as evidence of the fate or whereabouts of the missing aircraft: see Suman Varandani, "Flight MH370 Search Update: New Debris Pieces Found in Mauritius and Mozambique to Be Tested in Australia," *International Business Times*, May 26, 2016, http://www.ibtimes.com/flight-mh370-search-update-new-debris-pieces-found-mauritius-mozambique-be-tested-2374333. In January 2017, the JACC finally called off the search for MH370.

5 "Aircraft Communications Addressing and Reporting System," Wikipedia, http://en.wikipedia.org/wiki/Aircraft_Communications_Addressing_and_Reporting_System.

6 Nils Pratley, "Inmarsat Has Been Recognised Globally, but Now It Has the City's Attention," *Guardian Business*, March 27, 2014, http://www.theguardian.com/business/2014/mar/27/inmarsat-recognised-globally-city-attention-satellite-company. Until MH370, Inmarsat was a relatively low profile U.K. satellite communications company. It was created in 1979 as the International Maritime Satellite Organization, a not-for-profit venture created by the International Maritime Organization to enable ships to stay in contact with shore and call for help; emergency distress calls are still routed as priority for free. The company was privatized in 1999, bought by private equity houses Apax and Permira in 2003, then floated in London two years later, trebling in value in the next half-decade. It was briefly a member of the FTSE 100 before a fall in the share price in 2010 and 2011. Now the share price has almost regained its old levels, rising by 9 percent as a result of Inmarsat's contribution to the MH370 search.

7. Gordon Rayner and Nick Collins, "MH370: Britain Finds Itself at Centre of Blame Game over Crucial Delays," *Telegraph World Asia*, March 24, 2014, http://www.telegraph.co.uk/news/worldnews/asia/malaysia/10720009/MH370-Britain-finds-itself-at-centre-of-blame-game-over-crucial-delays.html.
8. Duncan Steel, "The Locations of Inmarsat-3F1 When Pinging MH370," March 24, 2014, http://www.duncansteel.com/the-locations-of-inmarsat-3f1-when-pinging-mh370. A geostationary satellite is one that moves around the Earth at the Earth's own angular velocity and thus appears not to move. Because it was launched in 1996 and has deteriorated, however, Inmarsat-3 F1 is no longer absolutely geostationary but moves from a height of 35,793.3–35,806.2 kilometers from the Earth's surface and from 1.539N to 1.539S and 64.471E to 64.594 E. Taking into account these slight movements in relation to the Earth adjusted analysts' predictions of where the plane had come down. The location of Inmarsat-3 F1 can be seen in real time at http://www.n2yo.com/satellite/?s=23839.
9. David Cenciotti, "What Sitcom, ACARS and Pings Tell Us about the Missing Malaysia Airlines MH370," *The Aviationist*, March 16, 2014, http://theaviationist.com/2014/03/16/satcom-acars-explained.
10. Ari N. Schulman, "Why the Official Explanation of MH370's Demise Doesn't Hold Up," *Atlantic Technology*, May 8, 2014, http://www.theatlantic.com/technology/archive/2014/05/why-the-official-explanation-of-mh370s-demise-doesnt-hold-up/361826.
11. Coxhead, "A Link to Bind Where Circumstances Part." The phrase "Hands across the Sea" was used in Britain and the United States in the 1890s to signify friendship between the two countries, a policy of promoting closer international cooperation, diplomatic alliance, and military assistance. From the early twentieth century onward, it became associated with personal friendship.
12. Schulman, "Why the Official Explanation of MH370's Demise Doesn't Hold Up."
13. Alan Schuster Bruce, "Where Is Flight MH370?" *BBC Two Horizon*, June 17, 2014, accessed December 2014 (no longer available), http://www.bbc.co.uk/programmes/b047czkj.
14. Schulman, "Why the Official Explanation of MH370's Demise Doesn't Hold Up."
15. "Britain Finds Itself at Centre of Blame Game over Crucial Delays," *The Telegraph*, April 18, 2014, http://www.telegraph.co.uk/news/worldnews/asia/malaysia/10720009/MH370-Britain-finds-itself-at-centre-of-blame-game-over-crucial-delays.html.
16. Duncan Steel, "The Inmarsat-3F1 Doppler Data Do not Exclude a Northerly Flight Path for MH370," April 2, 2014, http://www.duncansteel.com/archives/507.
17. Schulman, "Why the Official Explanation of MH370's Demise Doesn't Hold Up."
18. Schulman, "Why the Official Explanation of MH370's Demise Doesn't Hold Up"; Andrew Marszal, "MH370 Search Area 'to Shift Gain' amid New Doubts over Speed and Altitude," *The Telegraph*, June 9, 2014, http://www.telegraph.co.uk/news/worldnews/asia/malaysia/10887283/MH370-search-area-to-shift-again-amid-new-doubts-over-speed-and-altitude.html.
19. Steel, "The Inmarsat-3F1 Doppler Data Do not Exclude a Northerly Flight Path for MH370."

20 "Flight MH370: 'Objects Spotted' in New Search Area," *BBC News: Asia*, March 28, 2014, http://www.bbc.co.uk/news/world-asia-26786549; Associated Press, "MH370: Plane Search to Move South, Australia Announces," *The Guardian*, June 20, 2014, http://www.theguardian.com/world/2014/jun/20/mh370-plane-search-to-move-south-australia-announces; Australian Transport Safety Bureau, *MH370*.
21 Edwards, "Global Climate Science, Uncertainty and Politics," 446.
22 Edwards, "Global Science, Uncertainty and Politics," 446.
23 Jonathan Amos, "Malaysian MH370: Inmarsat Confident on Crash 'Hotspot,'" *BBC News: Science and Environment*, June 17, 2014, http://www.bbc.co.uk/news/science-environment-27870467.
24 Associated Press, "MH370."
25 Edwards, "Global Science, Uncertainty and Politics," 446; Rayner and Collins, "MH370."
26 Edwards, "Global Science, Uncertainty and Politics," 439.
27 Dumit, "Neuroexistentialism," 184.
28 Dumit, "Neuroexistentialism," 185.
29 Helmreich, "Nature/Culture/Seawater," 138.
30 "Two Red Arcs Pinned up in Media Centre Describe Possible Position of #MH370," Reuters Aerospace News, Twitter post, March 15, 2014, https://twitter.com/ReutersAero/status/444870615330078720.
31 "Two Red Arcs Pinned up in Media Centre Describe Possible Position of #MH370."
32 Steel, "The Inmarsat-3F1 Doppler Data Do not Exclude a Northerly Flight Path for MH370."
33 "Britain Finds Itself at Centre of Blame Game over Crucial Delays."
34 "Malaysia Plane: Families Told Missing Flight Lost," *BBC News: Asia*, March 24, 2014, http://www.bbc.co.uk/news/world-asia-26718462.
35 Trefor Moss, "Lack of Radar Reveals Asian Defense Flaw," *Wall Street Journal*, March 17, 2014, http://online.wsj.com/news/articles/SB40001424052702303563304579445202957835142.
36 Andy Pasztor, Jon Ostrower, and James Hookway, "Critical Data Was Delayed in Search," *Wall Street Journal*, March 20, 2014, http://online.wsj.com/news/articles/SB20001424052702304026304579449680167673144.
37 Pasztor et al., "Critical Data was Delayed in Search."
38 The "roaring forties," "furious fifties," and "shrieking sixties" correspond to the lines of latitude they blow across.
39 John Roach, "Ocean 'Conveyor Belt' Sustains Sea Life, Study Says," *National Geographic News*, June 15, 2004, http://news.nationalgeographic.com/news/2004/06/0615_040614_SouthernOcean.html. The world's next most powerful current, the Gulf Stream, transports 1.4 billion cubic feet per second.
40 Jonathan Amos, "Malaysian Airlines MH370: Searching in an Ocean of Uncertainty," *BBC News: Science and Technology*, April 9, 2014, http://www.bbc.co.uk/news/science-environment-26956798.

41 Paul Farrell, "Flight MH370: Indian Ocean Objects Might Have Drifted Hundreds of Miles," *The Guardian*, March 1, 2014, http://www.theguardian.com/world/2014/mar/21/flight-mh370-indian-ocean-objects.
42 Global Ocean Observing System, http://www.ioc-goos.org.
43 Kirsten Lea, "What's Our Role in the Search for Missing Flight MH370?" *News@CSIRO*, March 28, 2014, http://csironewsblog.com/2014/03/28/whats-our-role-in-the-search-for-missing-flight-mh370.
44 NASA Jet Propulsion Laboratory, "OSTM/Jason-2 Fact Sheet," http://sealevel.jpl.nasa.gov/missions/ostmjason2/jason2factsheet.
45 European Space Agency, "ESA's Ice Mission," http://www.esa.int/Our_Activities/Observing_the_Earth/The_Living_Planet_Programme/Earth_Explorers/CryoSat-2/ESA_s_ice_mission. Cryosat-2 is used largely to monitor changes in the thickness of ice in polar regions.
46 Centre National d'Études Spatiales, "SARAL/Altika," December 13, 2013, http://smsc.cnes.fr/SARAL/; Indian Space Research Organisation, "Earth Observation Satellites," http://www.isro.org/spacecraft/earth-observation-satellites.
47 Lea, "What's Our Role in the Search for Missing Flight MH370?"
48 The program was named after the mythical Greek ship *Argo* to emphasize its complementary relationship with Jason satellites and Poseidon altimeters.
49 Argo, "How Argo Floats Work," http://www.argo.ucsd.edu/How_Argo_floats.html. To do this, mineral oil is forced into a rubber bladder at the bottom end of a float's pressure case. As the bladder expands, the float becomes less dense than seawater and rises to the surface. Upon finishing its tasks at the surface, the float withdraws the oil and descends again.
50 Wikipedia, "Argo (Oceanography)," http://en.wikipedia.org/wiki/Argo_(oceanography). The third chapter of the Intergovernmental Panel on Climate Change's Fifth Assessment Report of September 2013 was written on the basis of Argo data.
51 Lea, "What's Our Role in the Search for Missing Flight MH370?" IMOS is a collaboration of ten national Australian research institutions that delivers the IMOS Ocean Portal, providing open access to Australian marine and climate data. See Integrated Marine Observing System, http://imos.aodn.org.au/imos123.
52 Lea, "What's Our Role in the Search for Missing Flight MH370?"
53 Cetina, "From Pipes to Scopes"; Cetina, "The Synthetic Situation"; Heller and Pezzani, "Liquid Traces," 667.
54 Michael Martinez, "Timeline: Leads in the Hunt for Malaysia Airlines Flight 370 Weave Drama," CNN, April 7, 2014, http://edition.cnn.com/2014/04/05/us/malaysia-airlines-search-chronology/index.html?iid=article_sidebar.
55 International Charter for Space and Major Disasters, 2000, http://www.disasterscharter.org/home.
56 Amy Svitak, "DigitalGlobe Supplies Images to MH370 Search," *Aviation Week*, March 20, 2014, http://aviationweek.com/space/digitalglobe-supplies-images-mh370-search.
57 "Missing Airplane: Malaysian Airlines MH370," *Tomnod*, March 18, 2014, http://www.tomnod.com/nod/challenge/malaysiaairsar2014. Germany's commercial

remote-sensing services provider BlackBridge offered a similar crowdsourcing capability, with images from its satellites loaded onto a MapBox platform: see https://www.mapbox.com/labs/blackbridge/flight-mh370/#4/-25.44/105.73.

58　David Lee, "Malaysia Missing Plane: Armchair Aeroplane Hunters Head Online," BBC News: Technology, March 18, 2014, http://www.bbc.co.uk/news/technology-25051663; Svitak, "DigitalGlobe Supplies Images to MH370 Search."

59　Svitak, "DigitalGlobe Supplies Images to MH370 Search." It was not revealed whether Tomnod played a role in identifying the data sent by DigitalGlobe to the Australian authorities. What was released was that before its use in the MH370 search, Tomnod had ten thousand users. After the flight went missing, 3.6 million participants visited the platform, generating more than 385 million map views and tagging 4.7 million objects.

60　International Maritime Organization, "International Convention on Maritime Search and Rescue (SAR)," 2014, http://www.imo.org/About/Conventions/ListOfConventions/Pages/International-Convention-on-Maritime-Search-and-Rescue-(SAR).aspx.

61　Anthony Bergin and Daniel Grant, "Search and Rescue: A Growing Responsibility," *The Strategist*, Australian Strategic Policy Institute blog, June 24, 2014, http://www.aspistrategist.org.au/search-and-rescue-a-growing-responsibility.

62　Kate Hodal, "Flight MH370: China Sends Ships to Verify Debris," *The Guardian*, March 22, 2014, http://www.theguardian.com/world/2014/mar/22/mh370-china-sends-ships-verify-debris-sighting.

63　Withnall, "Missing Malaysian Flight MH370."

64　"Malaysian Plane Search: Thai, Japan Satellites Detect over 300 Objects in Indian Ocean," *Zee News*, March 28, 2014, http://zeenews.india.com/news/world/malaysian-plane-search-thai-japan-satellites-detect-over-300-objects-in-indian-ocean_920705.html.

65　Hon. Tony Abbott MP, Prime Minister of Australia, "Air Chief Marshall Angus Houston to Lead Joint Agency Coordination Centre," March 30, 2014, http://www.pm.gov.au/media/2014-03-30/air-chief-marshal-angus-houston-lead-joint-agency-coordination-centre.

66　Sam Bateman and Anthony Bergin, "Nations Scared to Drop Their Guard," *Australian Financial Review*, April 9, 2014, https://www.aspi.org.au/publications/opinion-pieces/nations-scared-to-drop-their-guard/Nations-scared-to-drop-their-guard.pdf. Section 4.1.1 of the Annex to the Convention requires that coordinating parties be given access to any information that may provide assistance in a search-and-rescue operation; in the MH370 search, this included classified surveillance data.

67　Kashmira Gander and Kathy Marks, "Missing Malaysia Airlines Flight MH370: Air Search Called Off as New Area of Focus on Ocean Floor Announced," *The Independent*, April 28, 2014, http://www.independent.co.uk/news/world/australasia/malaysia-airlines-flight-mh370-new-search-area-announced-9294890.html.

68　Joint Agency Coordination Centre, http://www.jacc.gov.au.

69 Paul Farrell, "SES Volunteers the Eagle Eyes of the MH370 Search," *The Guardian*, April 19, 2014, http://www.theguardian.com/world/2014/apr/19/ses-volunteers-eagle-eyes-mh370-search.

70 Farrell, "SES Volunteers the Eagle Eyes of the MH370 Search."

71 Australian Government, Department of Defence, *OP Southern Indian Ocean—ADV Ocean Shield—Divers checking debris*, DDM Video V20140204, April 6, 2014. This video is no longer available on the Australian Defence Force website, http://video.defence.gov.au.

72 "Flight MH370: Chinese and Australian Ships Draw Blank," *BBC News: Asia*, March 29, 2014, http://www.bbc.co.uk/news/world-asia-26797866.

73 Andre Mayer, "Malaysian Airlines Flight MH370 Search Shows Extent of Ocean Trash," *CBC News: Technology and Science*, April 1, 2014, http://www.cbc.ca/news/technology/malaysia-airlines-flight-mh370-search-shows-extent-of-ocean-trash-1.2594539. The World Shipping Council estimates that about 350 containers are lost each year, but in reality the number is probably far higher.

74 *United Nations Convention on the Law of the Sea of 10 December 1982*, Part 12, Article 194.1, http://www.un.org/depts/los/convention_agreements/convention_overview_convention.htm.

75 International Maritime Organization, *International Convention for the Prevention of Pollution from Ships (MARPOL, adopted 1973)*, Annex V: "Prevention of Pollution by Garbage from Ships (Entered into Force 31 December 1988)," http://www.imo.org/About/Conventions/ListOfConventions/Pages/International-Convention-for-the-Prevention-of-Pollution-from-Ships-%28MARPOL%29.aspx.

76 Mayer, "Malaysian Airlines Flight MH370 Search Shows Extent of Ocean Trash."

77 Monterey Bay Aquarium Research Institute, "MBARI Research Shows Where Trash Accumulates in the Deep Sea," June 5, 2013, http://www.mbari.org/news/news_releases/2013/deep-debris/deep-debris-release.html; Schlining et al., "Debris in the Deep." This study by the Monterey Bay Aquarium Research Institute (MBARI) was based on eighteen thousand hours of underwater video over twenty-two years. It located and classified more than 1,500 observations of deep sea debris in the Pacific Ocean up to four thousand meters deep. About 30 percent of these were plastic objects, more than 50 percent of those plastic bags. Other debris included aluminum cans, shipping containers, rope, fishing equipment, glass bottles, and paper and cloth items.

78 David K. A. Barnes, "Natural and Plastic Flotsam Stranding in the Indian Ocean," in *The Effects of Human Transport on Ecosystems: Cars and Planes, Boats and Trains*, ed. John Davenport and Julia L. Davenport (Dublin: Royal Irish Academy, 2004), 193–205.

79 Serres, *Malfeasance*, 3.

80 Serres, *Malfeasance*, 53.

81 Helmreich, "Nature/Culture/Seawater."

82 Gwyn Topham, "MH370: Time Running Out in Search for Malaysian Airlines Plane's Black Box," *The Guardian*, April 5, 2014, http://www.theguardian.com/world/2014/apr/04/mh370-time-running-out-search-malaysian-airlines-planes-black-box.

83 Amos, "Malaysian Airlines MH370."
84 Amos, "Malaysian Airlines MH370."
85 Amos, "Malaysian Airlines MH370." Most contemporary maps of the seafloor, including those on Google Ocean, are generated in this way.
86 Amos, "Malaysian Airlines MH370."
87 Helmreich, "From Spaceship Earth to Google Ocean."
88 Bassett, "Remote Sensing," 200.
89 Bassett, "Remote Sensing."
90 Höhler, "Depth Records and Ocean Volumes," 119; Helmreich, "From Spaceship Earth to Google Ocean," 1226.
91 Holly Yan and Mike M. Ahlers, "Tick, Tock: What Happens after the Malaysian Plane's Pingers Die?" CNN International, April 5, 2014, http://edition.cnn.com/2014/04/04/world/asia/malaysia-plane-after-the-pinger-dies.
92 "Missing MH370: Facing 'the Underwater Alps,'" *Sky News*, April 7, 2014, http://news.sky.com/story/1238464/missing-mh370-facing-the-underwater-alps.
93 Tom Rogan, "Secrecy below the Surface—Western Intelligence and the MH370 'Ping,'" *The Telegraph*, April 8, 2014, http://blogs.telegraph.co.uk/news/tomrogan/100266812/secrecy-below-the-surface-western-intelligence-and-the-mh370-ping.
94 Ben Brumfield, "Listen for a Ping, and the Water May Play Tricks on You," CNN, April 13, 2014, http://edition.cnn.com/2014/04/11/tech/innovation/mh-370-underwater-sound/index.html?iid=article_sidebar.
95 National Geographic, "Ocean Conveyor Belt," http://education.nationalgeographic.co.uk/education/encyclopedia/ocean-conveyor-belt/?ar_a=1.
96 Brumfield, "Listen for a Ping."
97 Michael Safi and Tania Branigan, "MH370: Search for Missing Airlines Spurred on by Possible Black Box 'Pings,'" *The Guardian*, April 6, 2014, http://www.theguardian.com/world/2014/apr/06/mh370-search-continues-after-black-box-ping-claim; "Missing Malaysia Airlines Plane: Fresh Signals in MH370 Search," *BBC News: Asia*, April 9, 2014, http://www.bbc.co.uk/news/world-asia-26950414.
98 Australian Government, Department of Defence, *OP Southern Indian Ocean—ADV Ocean Shield—Waveforms of Possible Black Box Signal*, DDM video V20140203, April 6, 2014. This video is no longer available on the Australian Defence Force website, http://video.defence.gov.au.
99 Australian Government, Department of Defence, *OP Southern Indian Ocean—Second Ping Waveform*, DDM video V20140224. This video is no longer available on the Australian Defence Force website, http://video.defence.gov.au.
100 "MH370 Searchers 'Confident' despite Ping Error," *Sky News World*, May 30, 2014, http://news.sky.com/story/1271977/mh370-searchers-confident-despite-ping-error; Chris Richards, "MH370: Black Box 'Pings' May Actually Have Come from Satellite Tracking Devices Tagged to Marine Animals," *Daily Record*, May 8, 2014, http://www.dailyrecord.co.uk/news/uk-world-news/mh370-black-box-pings-actually-3511000. For some time, pingers with frequencies of 30 to 50 kHz have been used to track deep ocean animals or as fishing net protectors.

101 Brumfield, "Listen for a Ping."
102 Richards, "MH370."
103 Evans and Reid, *Resilient Life*, 13.
104 "Malaysia Airlines Flight MH370 Will Be Found, Expert Says," *CBC News: Technology and Science*, April 19, 2014, http://www.cbc.ca/news/technology/malaysia-airlines-flight-mh370-will-be-found-expert-says-1.2615099.
105 Tania Branigan, "MH370: Australia 'Very Confident' Pings are from Black Box, Says Prime Minister," *The Guardian*, April 11, 2014, http://www.theguardian.com/world/2014/apr/11/mh370-australia-very-confident-pings-are-from-black-box-says-prime-minister.
106 Phoenix International, Underwater Solutions Worldwide, "Phoenix AUV Now Capable of Diving to 4,500 Meters," July 9, 2013, http://www.phnx-international.com/news/Phoenix_4500%20meter_AUV_Upgrade.pdf. Designed and manufactured by Bluefin Robotics, the Bluefin-21 is typically used by the oil and gas industry to conduct deep-water oilfield surveys.
107 "Phoenix AUV Now Capable of Diving to 4,500 Meters." Specifications given for the vehicle are as follows: "The Phoenix AUV is equipped with field-swappable acoustic and optical payloads. The acoustic payload section can concurrently operate a Reson 7125 multibeam (400 kHz), Edgetech 2200-M side scan sonar (120/410 kHz), and Edgetech DW2-16 sub-bottom profiler (2–16 kHz) on twenty-hour dives at speeds up to 3.5 knots. The optical payload section can collect high resolution black and white imagery up to three frames per second using a Prosilica GE1900 camera system with 1920 [by] 1080 pixel resolution."
108 "Missing Flight MH370: Robotic Sub First Mission Cut Short," *BBC News: Asia*, April 15, 2014, http://www.bbc.co.uk/news/world-asia-27030741.
109 Richard Johnson and Ben Chartoff, "The Depth of the Problem," *Washington Post: World*, http://apps.washingtonpost.com/g/page/world/the-depth-of-the-problem/931.
110 Branigan, "MH370."
111 Helmreich, "From Spaceship Earth to Google Ocean," 1236.
112 Ted Thornhill and Sophie Jane Evans, "The Race to Find MH370: Eight Countries Using 17 Vessels and 19 Aircraft in the Hunt for Missing Plane's Black Box Lying 15,000 Feet at the Bottom of the Indian Ocean," *Daily Mail Online*, April 11, 2014, http://www.dailymail.co.uk/news/article-2602631/The-race-MH370-Eight-countries-using-17-vessels-19-aircraft-hunt-missing-planes-black-box-lying-15-000ft-bottom-Indian-Ocean.html.
113 Bergin and Grant, "Search and Rescue."
114 Bateman and Bergin. "Nations Scared to Drop Their Guard."
115 See, for the history of ASEAN search and rescue cooperation, Carl Thayer, "Flight MH370 Shows Limits of ASEAN's Maritime Cooperation," *The Diplomat*, March 18, 2014, http://thediplomat.com/2014/03/flight-mh370-shows-limits-of-aseans-maritime-cooperation.
116 Thayer, "Flight MH370 Shows Limits of ASEAN's Maritime Cooperation."
117 Bateman and Bergin, "Nations Scared to Drop Their Guard."

118　Matt Siegel and Jane Wardell, "At Edge of Malaysian Airlines Search, Questions of Security and Diplomacy," Reuters U.S. Edition, March 28, 2014, http://www.reuters.com/article/2014/03/28/us-malaysia-airlines-security-idUSBREA2R0TH20140328.
119　This conversation took place at an ESRC-sponsored Ideaslab on Maritime Security at Cardiff University, June 26–27, 2014, http://piracy-studies.org.
120　Rogan, "Secrecy below the Surface."
121　Kevin Liptak and Faith Karimi, "MH370: Obama Visits Malaysia as Questions Loom over Missing Jetliner," CNN, April 27, 2014, http://edition.cnn.com/2014/04/26/world/asia/malaysia-airlines-plane.
122　Tho Xin Yi, "Najib Begins Six-Day Visit to China," *Star Online*, May 27, 2014, http://www.thestar.com.my/News/Nation/2014/05/27/Najib-begins-China-visit.
123　Agence France-Presse, "Chinese Ship in Latest Glitch in MH370 Search Mission," *NDTV*, May 31, 2014, http://www.ndtv.com/article/world/chinese-ship-in-latest-glitch-in-mh370-search-mission-533823.
124　"The Geopolitics of MH370," *The Economist*, May 10, 2014, http://www.economist.com/news/asia/21601902-having-bashed-malaysia-over-missing-flight-china-now-making-up-geopolitics-mh370.
125　This team included representatives from the U.S. National Transport Safety Board, the United Kingdom's Air Accidents Investigation Branch, China's Aircraft Accident Investigation Department, France's Land Transport Accident Investigation Bureau, Australia's Transport Safety Bureau, Boeing, Inmarsat, and representatives from Singapore and Indonesia.
126　"Missing Flight MH370: Search 'Could Take a Year,'" *BBC News: Asia*, May 2, 2014, http://www.bbc.co.uk/news/world-asia-27250078.
127　"Media Statement and Information on Flight MH370," Malaysia Airlines, March 9, 2015, http://www.malaysiaairlines.com/my/en/site/mh370.html.
128　Smith and Marks, "Seafloor in the Malaysia Airlines Flight MH370 Search Area." The only available surveys of this part of the ocean had been made by two Russian vessels during the International Indian Ocean Oceanographic Expedition (1959–65), using dead reckoning.
129　Australian Transport Safety Bureau, *MH370*.
130　Australian Transport Safety Bureau, *MH370*, 35.
131　It has taken far longer than this. By the end of July 2016, almost two years later, this multimillion-dollar search (estimated at $135 million) had scanned 40,540 square miles of ocean floor two thousand feet to four miles deep but yielded no concrete clues of MH370, despite numerous sightings of ocean floor debris, which was attributed to previously uncharted shipwrecks. At a meeting on July 22, 2016, the three countries still involved in the search—Australia, China, and Malaysia—agreed that when the vessels had finished sweeping the designated area, they would call off the search.
132　Heller and Pezzani, "Liquid Traces," 674.

133 Charlie Campbell, "The Reason We Can't Find MH370 is That We're Basically Blind," *Time*, April 18, 2014, http://time.com/67705/mh370-ocean-oceanography-sonar-exploration.
134 Peters, "Taking More-than-Human Geographies to Sea," 177.
135 Earle, "Foreword"; James West, "One Reason It May Be Harder to Find Flight 370: We Messed Up the Currents," *Mother Jones: Environment*, March 21, 2014, http://www.motherjones.com/environment/2014/03/climate-change-malaysia-airlines-370-search.
136 Serres, *Malfeasance*, 35.
137 Hardt and Negri, *Empire*, 186–87.
138 Heller and Pezzani, "Liquid Traces," 663.
139 Steinberg, "Free Sea," 272.
140 Carol Saab, "What's Our Role in the Search for Missing Flight MH370?" *News@CSIRO*, March 28, 2014, http://csironewsblog.com/2014/03/28/whats-our-role-in-the-search-for-missing-flight-mh370.

BIBLIOGRAPHY

Australian Transport Safety Bureau. *MH370—Definition of Underwater Search Areas, ATSB Transport Safety Report, External Aviation Investigation AE-2014-054*. Canberra: Commonwealth of Australia, 014. http://www.atsb.gov.au/media/5243942/ae-2014-054_mh370_-_definition_of_underwater_search_areas_18aug2014.pdf

Barnes, David K. A. "Natural and Plastic Flotsam Stranding in the Indian Ocean." In *The Effects of Human Transport on Ecosystems: Cars and Planes, Boats and Trains*, ed. John Davenport and Julia L. Davenport, 193–205. Dublin: Royal Irish Academy, 2004.

Bassett, Caroline. "Remote Sensing." In *Sensorium: Embodied Experience, Technology, and Contemporary Art*, ed. Caroline A. Jones, 238–40. Cambridge: MIT Press, 2006.

Cetina, Karin Knorr. "From Pipes to Scopes: The Flow Architecture of Financial Markets." *Distinktion* 4, no. 2 (2003): 7–23.

———. "The Synthetic Situation: Interactionism for a Global World." *Symbolic Interaction* 32, no. 1 (2009): 61–87.

Coxhead, Gabriel. "A Link to Bind Where Circumstances Part." *Cabinet* 36 (Winter 2009–10): 103–7.

Dumit, Joseph. "Neuroexistentialism." In *Sensorium: Embodied Experience, Technology, and Contemporary Art*, ed. Caroline A. Jones, 182–89. Cambridge, MA: MIT Press, 2006.

Earle, Sylvia A. "Foreword." In Helen M. Rozwadowski, *Fathoming the Ocean*, viii–xiii. Cambridge, MA: Harvard University Press, 2005.

Edwards, Paul. "Global Climate Science, Uncertainty and Politics: Data-laden Models, Model-filtered Data." *Science as Culture* 8, no. 4 (1999): 437–72.

Evans, Brad, and Julian Reid. *Resilient Life: The Art of Living Dangerously*. London: Polity, 2014.

Hardt, Michael and Antonio Negri. *Empire*. Cambridge, MA: Harvard University Press, 2000.

Heller, Charles and Lorenzo Pezzani. "Liquid Traces: Investigating the Deaths of Migrants at the EU's Maritime Frontier." In *Forensis: The Architecture of Public Truth*, ed. Forensic Architecture, 657–84. Berlin: Sternberg, 2014.

Helmreich, Stefan. "From Spaceship Earth to Google Ocean: Planetary Icons, Indexes, and Infrastructures." *Social Research* 78, no. 4 (Winter 2011): 1211–42.

———. "Nature/Culture/Seawater." *American Anthropologist* 113, no. 1 (2011): 132–44.

Höhler, Sabine. "Depth Records and Ocean Volumes: Ocean Profiling by Sounding Technology, 1850–1930." *History and Technology* 18, no. 2 (2002): 119–54.

Peters, Kimberley. "Taking More-than-Human Geographies to Sea: Ocean Natures and Offshore Radio Piracy." In *Water Worlds: Human Geographies of the Ocean*, ed. Jon Anderson and Kimberley Peters, 177–91. Farnsworth, UK: Ashgate, 2014.

Schlining, Kyra, Susan von Thun, Linda Kuhnz, and Brian Schlining et al. "Debris in the Deep: Using a 22-Year Video Annotation Database to Survey Marine Litter in Monterey Canyon, Central California, USA." *Deep-Sea Research Part I: Oceanographic Research Papers* 79 (2013): 96–105.

Serres, Michel. *Malfeasance: Appropriation through Pollution*, trans. Anne-Marie Feenberg. Stanford, CA: Stanford University Press, 2011.

Smith, Walter H. F. and Karen M. Marks. "Seafloor in the Malaysia Airlines Flight MH370 Search Area." *Eos, Transactions, American Geophysical Union* 95, no. 21 (May 27, 2014): 173–80.

Steinberg, Philip E. "Free Sea." In *Spatiality, Sovereignty and Carl Schmitt*, ed. Stephen Legg, 268–75. London: Routledge, 2011.

Contributors

HOMI K. BHABHA is the Anne F. Rothenberg Professor of the Humanities, Director of the Mahindra Humanities Center, and Senior Advisor to the President and Provost at Harvard University. In 2012 he was conferred the Government of India's Padma Bhushan Presidential Award in the field of literature and education, and received the Humboldt Research Prize in 2015. He is the author of numerous works exploring postcolonial theory, cultural change and power, contemporary art, and cosmopolitanism, including *Nation and Narration,* and *The Location of Culture*, which was reprinted as a Routledge Classic in 2004. His next book will be published by the University of Chicago Press.

JACQUELINE BHABHA is Professor of the Practice of Health and Human Rights at the Harvard T. H. Chan School of Public Health. She is also the Jeremiah Smith Jr. Lecturer in Law at Harvard Law School and the Director of Research at the Harvard FXB Center for Health and Human Rights. Before joining the faculty at Harvard, Bhabha worked as a human rights lawyer in London and founded and directed the Human Rights Program at the University of Chicago.

LINDSAY BREMNER is currently Director of Architectural Research at the University of Westminster in London. Her work positions architectural thought in wider material and sociopolitical fields. This has included the projects *Folded Ocean*, which investigated the spatial transformation of the Indian Ocean world, and *Geoarchitecture*, an exploration into intersections among architecture, geology, and politics. She currently holds European Research Council grant no. 679873 for *Monsoon Assemblages*, a project researching monsoonal conditions in three South Asian cities (www.monass.org).

FINBARR BARRY FLOOD is William R. Kenan Jr. Professor of the Humanities at the Institute of Fine Arts and Department of Art History, New York University. Recent publications include articles on marble, mosques, and modernism; iconoclasm and the Islamic State (Daesh); the ingestion of images and words; Islamic figurative art; and the Danish cartoon controversy. His books include *The Great Mosque of Damascus: Studies on the Makings of an Umayyad Visual Culture* (2000) and *Objects of Translation: Material Culture and Medieval "Hindu-Muslim" Encounter* (2009).

ROSARIO HUBERT is Assistant Professor of Language and Culture Studies at Trinity College, Hartford, CT. Her book project *Disorientations: Writing China in Latin America* discusses the epistemological and disciplinary problems of writing across cultural boundaries and proposes a novel entryway into the study of East Asia and Latin America. Her research has been funded by the National Endowment for the Humanities, the American Council of Learned Societies, and the David Rockefeller Center for Latin American Studies.

ALINA PAYNE is the Paul E. Geier Director of Villa I Tatti, the Harvard University Center for Italian Renaissance Studies, and Alexander P. Misheff Professor of History of Art and Architecture at Harvard University. In 2006 she was awarded the Max Planck and Alexander von Humboldt Prize in the Humanities (2006–12). She is the author of, among others, *The Architectural Treatise in the Italian Renaissance* (1999), *The Telescope and the Compass. Teofilo Gallaccini and the Dialogue between Architecture and Science in the Age of Galileo* (2012), *From Ornament to Object. Genealogies of Architectural Modernism* (2012) and *L'Architecture parmi les arts. Matérialité, transferts et travail artistique dans l'Italie de la Renaissance* (2016) and editor of *Dalmatia and the Mediterranean. Portable Archaeology and the Poetics of Influence* (2014) and *Vision and Its Instruments. Art, Science and Technology in Early Modern Europe* (2015).

Ethnomusicologist KAY KAUFMAN SHELEMAY is G. Gordon Watts Professor of Music and of African and African American Studies at Harvard University. A member of the American Academy of Arts and Sciences, the American Academy for Jewish Research, the American Philosophical Society, and the Ethiopian Academy of Sciences, Shelemay is the author of numerous books, editions, and articles. She is currently completing a book about musicians who have migrated from the Horn of Africa to the United States, based in part on a collection she established at the U.S. Library of Congress as Chair for Modern Culture at the John W. Kluge Center during 2007–2008.

SHU-MEI SHIH is Professor of Comparative Literature, Asian Languages and Cultures, and Asian American Studies at the University of California, Los Angeles (UCLA). During 2013–15, when her chapter in this volume was drafted, she was on leave from UCLA and held the Hon-yin and Suet-fong Chan Professorship of Chinese at the University of Hong Kong. Her monographs and edited volumes include *Minor Transnationalim* (2005), *Visuality and Identity: Sinophone Articulations across the Pacific* (2007), *Creolization of Theory* (2011), and *Sinophone Studies: A Critical Reader* (2013).

DIANA SORENSEN is James F. Rothenberg Professor of Romance Languages and Literatures and of Comparative Literature at Harvard University. She was previously Dean of Arts and Humanities in the Faculty of Arts and Sciences. She is a specialist in nineteenth- and twentieth-century Latin American literature and in comparative literature, with additional expertise in cultural theory and gender theory. She is the author of books that include *The Reader and the Text: Interpretative Strategies for Latin American Literatures* (1986), *Facundo and the Construction of Argentine Culture* (1996), and *A Turbulent Decade Remembered: Cultural Scenes from the Latin American Sixties* (2007).

KAREN THORNBER is Professor of Comparative Literature and of East Asian Languages and Civilizations at Harvard University, where she is also Victor and William Fung Director of the Harvard University Asia Center, Chair of the Harvard University Council on Asian Studies, and Director of the Harvard Global Institute Environmental Humanities Initiative. Her major publications include *Empire of Texts in Motion: Chinese, Korean, and Taiwanese Transculturations of Japanese Literature* (2009) and *Ecoambiguity: Environmental Crises and East Asian Literatures* (2012).

XIAOFEI TIAN is Professor of Chinese Literature at Harvard University. She is the author of several books, including *Tao Yuanming and Manuscript Culture: The Record of a Dusty Table* (2005) and *Visionary Journeys: Travel Writings from Early Medieval and Nineteenth-Century China* (2011).

Index

aesthetics, 114–15, 133, 136–39, 151, 156–57
agency, 9, 11, 20, 24, 40, 58, 96, 151, 212, 228; personal, 49, 57, 152
aniconism, 20, 26, 110, 115–17, 119, 122, 133; Islamic, 116, 121–22, 134–35; Jewish, 125; ornament, 114, 131, 133, 140n5; Protestant, 119–20, 122. *See also* iconoclasm
anthropology, 43, 97; museums of, 98
architecture, 4, 7, 45n16, 94–96, 98–99, 103–4, 105n8, 111, 137; history of, 25–26, 96, 105, 152; Islamic, 138; materials of, 94–95; textiles and, 7, 95, 99, 104. *See also Kleinarchitektur*; portability
Astatke, Mulatu, 22, 51–52, 58, 63n19

belonging, 2, 3, 4, 18, 24–25, 185–86
Benjamin, Walter, 1, 6–7, 11, 93, 96, 215
Berenson, Bernard, 99, 151, 153; as connoisseur, 27, 152, 155–56; and Isabella Stewart Gardner, 152–53, 157–58; writings, 156–58
border, 2, 11, 15, 18–19, 24, 26, 97, 101, 104, 120, 232; country, 3–4, 70, 76, 207, 212; crossing, 16, 47, 186, 188–89, 194; national, 37, 189; open, 192; studies, 18
boundaries, 11, 18, 21, 28, 44, 52, 58, 62n15, 70, 101, 104, 120, 189, 229, 231; crossing, 26, 42, 47; national, 26, 47, 105, 201; political, 69, 80, 82, 125; remapping, 122–23, 129, 187; role of, 17
Braudel, Fernand, 19, 101
Buddhism, 43, 70–73; women in, 72

cartography, 14, 23, 26, 41, 123, 240; imaged, 16, 52, 93
Carvalho, Bernardo, 37, 42–44
circulation, 7–9, 13, 24, 92, 153; of art, 27–28, 103, 116, 152, 159, 203; of ideas, 11, 25, 129; of goods; 40, 44n16, 97, 151; of music, 47–48, 51–52, 58
cities, 2–3, 18, 49, 111, 138, 191–92, 202
citizenship, 4, 18, 21, 186–87, 190, 194–95; access to, 185, 188; rights of, 25, 185
colonialism, 36, 41, 203–4, 206, 211
consumption, 137, 153, 234, 243
convergence, 8–11, 14, 18, 41, 118
cosmopolitan, 15, 18, 25, 35, 152, 154, 189

Deleuze, Gilles, 21; and Félix Guattari, 13, 59–60
diaspora, 4, 19, 24, 49, 52–53, 56–57, 61; communities, 50, 52; Ethiopian, 48, 50–51, 53–54, 59, 62nn17–18; studies, 201
Dirlik, Arif, 14, 17, 36
displacement, 3, 5, 8, 17, 19, 21, 37, 49, 61, 97, 123, 188–89, 213; constitutive, 4, 185, 187; narratives, 25, 93

empire, 16, 22, 36, 45n17, 70, 73, 103, 123, 125, 135, 163, 203, 208–12, 214; Age of, 23; Chinese, 68–69, 77, 80, 208, 211–12, 218; studies, 201
emplacement, 18, 24–25, 27
Ethio-jazz, 6, 21, 52, 63n21
ethnography, 39, 43, 47, 69
ethnomusicology, 47. *See also* musicology
European Union, 4, 190, 193–94, 208, 230
exile, 5, 21–22, 48–49, 57, 104
exoticism, 37, 39–41, 43–44

Faxian, 22, 73; *A Record of the Buddhist Kingdoms*, 68–70, 74–76, 78, 80–83; travels, 69, 74, 77, 79–81
Frank, Andre Gunder, 19, 203
Freyre, Gilberto, 23, 37, 39–44
frontier, 2, 26, 100, 103, 115, 151, 208

Gardner, Isabella Stewart. *See* Berenson, Bernard
geographic imaginary, 2, 15, 17–18, 48–52, 61n3, 115–16, 136, 163
geography, 17–18, 52, 76, 82, 93, 104, 152, 179n13, 202, 205; cultural, 16, 69, 82, 96, 105n11; political, 69, 82, 122
globalization, 2, 15–16, 19, 195, 201, 203; era of, 24
Global South, 14, 19, 36–37
global studies, 5, 16
Grand Tour, 153–54
Greenblatt, Stephen, 2, 19
Guattari, Félix. *See* Deleuze, Gilles

health care, 24, 166, 178n10, 188, 193; providers, 165
hemispheric studies, 15–17
homeland, 2–7, 22, 50–53, 55–57, 61, 82, 92, 155, 212; imaginary, 49; loss of, 48–49
homeless, 2, 77
humanities, 9–10, 201; health, 6, 24, 165, 178n10, 179n12; value of, 9

human rights, 193–94; studies, 4; Universal Declaration of, 4, 186; violations of, 179n13, 186

iconoclasm, 26, 114–16, 118–19, 122, 125, 128–29, 133, 136. *See also* aniconism
identity, 1, 9, 13, 17–18, 28, 37, 40, 42–44, 58, 68, 82, 115, 119, 129, 134, 190, 215; ethnic, 62n15; legal, 4, 24, 186, 188, 194; national, 22, 96; religious, 81, 136; self-, 77, 185
immigration, 23, 37–38
imperialism, 43, 205
indigenous, 16, 36, 60, 102, 125
interdisciplinary, 4, 8, 20, 41, 151

Kleinarchitektur, 95, 103

Latour, Bruno, 9–10, 98
Lisboa, Henrique Carlos Ribeiro, 23, 37–40, 43–44
local, 2, 7–8, 14–16, 19, 21, 23, 28, 43, 47, 80, 83, 97, 151–52

mapping, 5, 14, 18, 22, 51–52, 61n5, 129, 188, 235, 242; models for, 13, 15, 17, 20; remapping, 115–16, 122–23; textual, 69, 93
maritime, 16, 19, 40, 244; networks, 101–3; studies, 18, 27
material culture, 25, 27, 70, 151
materiality, 83, 129, 135, 138, 153, 243; theorization of, 137
media, 11, 21, 50, 205, 223, 228, 232, 235, 237–38, 243
mediation, 10, 40, 44, 48, 51, 58, 60, 82, 103, 114, 122, 137, 187; process of, 9, 17
migrants, 2–3, 16, 105, 187, 189–90, 192, 194; movement of, 104
migration, 2–3, 16–17, 21, 25, 59, 201, 213; forced, 48, 50; voluntary, 50
mobility, 1–5, 8, 10–11, 13–14, 17–18, 21–22, 27, 42–43, 51, 68, 70–71, 73, 98, 105, 135, 151, 153, 157, 165, 167, 188–89;

consequences of, 24, 26, 99; musical, 47, 53; pedagogy of, 1–2, 19
modernity, 41, 64n28, 116–17, 135–36, 138–39, 189; critics of, 14
monk, 71, 73; Buddhist, 22, 43, 68–72, 74, 77, 80
mosque, 94, 103, 112, 114–15, 123, 129, 131, 133, 136, 138; Friday Mosque of Damascus, 26, 104, 114, 139. *See also* whitewash
museum, 1, 26, 93–94, 96–98, 156, 158–59
musicology, 6, 21, 47, 152. *See also* ethnomusicology

nationalism, 47, 96, 139
nation-state, 1–2, 13, 15, 36, 152, 201, 207–8
networks, 5, 8–9, 21, 25–26, 50, 94, 98, 101, 104, 151, 157, 163, 202, 210, 228; financial, 19, 73, 79; global, 2, 16, 203, 206
nostalgia, 6, 22, 53, 56–59. *See also* "Tizita"

Ogawa Yōko, 164; *The Equations the Professor Loved*, 165–67, 172, 175–76; translations of, 167–71, 173–74, 177

patrimoine, 26, 96–97
periphery, 18, 22–23, 74, 76, 100, 206
pilgrimage, 19, 73, 95, 120, 153
portability, 4, 9, 25, 91, 96–97, 100, 105, 153, 186; of architecture, 94; of art, 7, 94, 98–99, 104
postcolonial, 14, 39

racism, 36, 189, 192, 194
refugee, 18, 24, 49, 185–86, 194, 213
relational, 13–14, 16, 19, 23, 97, 116, 202, 218; networks, 5, 210; study, 23, 206; worldview, 21, 28, 48, 203–4
relationality, 4, 19–20, 23, 159, 163, 206
relocation, 6–7, 95, 156
representation, 3, 10, 15, 36–37, 39, 41–42, 76, 117, 121, 128, 152, 210, 213, 217, 239–40; of Islam, 115–16, 119, 122–23, 129; spaces of, 8, 20

Said, Edward, 2–3, 48; *Orientalism*, 37, 48
scale, 3, 8–10, 13, 15, 36, 69–70, 201, 205, 239–40
sovereignty, 3, 7, 243–44
space, 102, 5, 7, 9, 11, 13–14, 16–19, 21, 26, 37, 47, 52, 61, 69, 77, 95, 123, 129, 133, 165, 174, 186, 188, 206, 210, 223, 226, 235, 239, 242–43; sacred, 111–12, 114–16, 134, 136–38; and time, 8, 20, 49, 56, 60, 83, 93–94, 97, 125, 156–57
statelessness, 187–88

"Tizita," 22, 52, 58; examples of, 53–55, 59–60; meaning of, 53, 55–57; mode, 53, 60, 63n21, 64n31
trade, 2, 70, 73, 93, 119, 206, 212; slave, 16, 37, 204
trajectories, 8, 11, 14, 20, 23, 28, 60, 94, 163
transatlantic, 157; studies, 15–16
translation, 7, 9, 11, 19, 24, 37, 43, 54–55, 69–71, 80–81, 104, 165, 167–71, 173–74, 177, 215; cultural, 4, 6, 10
travel, 19, 39–40, 49–50, 60, 71–72, 75, 80–82, 96, 119, 156, 165, 188, 226, 229; music, 52, 63n22; writing, 22–23, 36–37, 42, 68–69, 73–74, 76, 83, 101, 240

vernacular, 14–15, 24, 40, 96, 138

Wallerstein, Immanuel, 19, 202–3, 205
wealth, 73, 153–55
Westphalian, 4, 24, 186, 189, 207
whitewash, 110, 133, 136–37; implications of, 26, 138, 144n73; of mosques, 26, 110–12, 114–15, 136, 138–39, 140nn4–5; Protestant, 114–15, 123, 129, 133, 136–37
world literature, 6–7, 14, 24, 37, 96, 165, 179nn12–13, 201, 205
world studies, 201, 205, 218